TRANSACTIONS
of the
AMERICAN PHILOSOPHICAL SOCIETY
Held at Philadelphis
For Promoting Useful Knowledge
Volume 93, Part 5

ISAIAH BERLIN'S
COUNTER-ENLIGHTENMENT

Edited by
Joseph Mali and Robert Wokler

American Philosophical Society
Philadelphia • 2003

Copyright © 2003 by the American Philosophical Society for its *Transactions* series. All rights reserved.

ISBN: 0-87169-935-4
US ISSN: 0065-9746

Library of Congress Cataloging-in-Publication Data
Isaiah Berlin's Counter-Enlightenment/edited by Joseph Mali and Robert Wokler.
    p. cm. – (Transactions of the American Philosophical Society; v. 93, pt. 5)
Includes bibliographical references and index.
ISBN 0-87169-935-4 (pbk.)
1. Berlin, Isaiah, Sir. 2. Philosophy. I. Mali, Joseph. II. Wokler, Robert, III. Series.
B1618.B454I84 2003
192–dc21

2003056005

Contents

The Editors	Preface	vii
Chapter 1 Mark Lilla	What Is Counter-Enlightenment?	1
Chapter 2 Robert Wokler	Isaiah Berlin's Enlightenment and Counter-Enlightenment	13
Chapter 3 Roger Hausheer	Enlightening the Enlightenment	33
Chapter 4 Joseph Mali	Berlin, Vico, and the Principles of Humanity	51
Chapter 5 John Robertson	The Case for the Enlightenment: A Comparative Approach	73
Chapter 6 Darrin M. McMahon	The Real Counter-Enlightenment: The Case of France	91
Chapter 7 Frederick Beiser	Berlin and the German Counter-Enlightenment	105
Chapter 8 Graeme Garrard	Isaiah Berlin's Joseph de Maistre	117
Chapter 9 Lionel Gossman	Benjamin Constant on Liberty and Love	133

Chapter 10

John E. Toews Berlin's Marx: Enlightenment, Counter- 163
Enlightenment, and the Historical
Construction of Cultural Identities

Chapter 11

Michael Confino Isaiah Berlin, Alexander Herzen, and 177
Russia's Elusive Counter-Enlightenment

Index of Names 193

List of contributors

Frederick Beiser is Professor of Philosophy at Syracuse University. His publications include *The Fate of Reason: German Philosophy from Kant to Fichte* (Harvard, 1987), *Enlightenment, Revolution, and Romanticism: The Genesis of Modern German Political Thought, 1790–1800,* (Harvard, 1992), *German Idealism: The Struggle against Subjectivism, 1781–1801* (Harvard, 2002), and *The Romantic Imperative* (Harvard, forthcoming). He is currently writing a book on the philosophy of Friedrich Schiller.

Michael Confino is Professor of History emeritus at Tel Aviv University. He is the author of *Daughter of a Revolutionary: Natalie Herzen and the Bakunin-Nechaev Circle* (London, 1974), *Société et mentalités collectives en Russie sous l'Ancien Régime* (Paris, 1991), *Anarchistes en exil. Lettres de Pierre Kropotkine à Marie Goldsmith, 1897–1917* (Paris, 1995), and numerous articles on intellectuals and intellectual traditions in Russia in the eighteenth and nineteenth centuries.

Graeme Garrard is Lecturer in Political Philosophy and European Thought at Cardiff University. He is the author of *Rousseau's Counter-Enlightenment: A Republican Critique of the Philosophes* (New York, 2003), and the forthcoming *Counter-Enlightenments: From the Mid-Eighteenth Century to the Present* (London, 2004).

Lionel Gossman is the M. Taylor Pine Professor of Romance Languages and Literatures emeritus at Princeton University. He has written extensively on French literature and literary theory, as well as on historiography. His most recent books are *Between Literature and History* (Harvard, 1990) and *Basel in the Age of Burckhardt* (Chicago, 2000).

Roger Hausheer is an Honorary Senior Research Fellow of Bradford University. His publications include essays on Fichte and Schelling and, with Henry Hardy, editions of Berlin's *Against the Current* and *The Proper Study of Mankind*. He is currently working on an intellectual biography of Isaiah Berlin.

Mark Lilla is Professor in the Committee on Social Thought at the University of Chicago. He is the author of *G.B. Vico: The Making of an Anti-Modern* (Harvard, 1993) and *The Reckless Mind: Intellectuals in Politics* (New York, 2001), and co-editor of *The Legacy of Isaiah Berlin* (New York, 2001).

Darrin M. McMahon is the Ben Weider Associate Professor of History at Florida State University. He is the author of *Enemies of the Enlightenment: The French Counter-Enlightenment and the Making of Modernity* (Oxford, 2001), and the forthcoming *Happiness: A History* (New York, 2004).

Joseph Mali teaches history at Tel Aviv University. His publications include *The Rehabilitation of Myth: Vico's New Science* (Cambridge, 1992) and *Mythistory: The Making of a Modern Historiography* (Chicago, 2003).

John Robertson teaches Modern History at St Hugh's College, Oxford. He has published on the Enlightenment in Scotland and in Naples, and on the Anglo-Scottish Union of 1707. He is currently completing a comparative study: *The Case for the Enlightenment: Scotland and Naples 1680–1760*.

John E. Toews is Professor of History and Director of the Program in the Comparative History of Ideas at the University of Washington. He is the author of *Hegelianism: The Path toward Dialectical Humanism, 1805–1841* (Cambridge, 1981) and *Becoming Historical: Cultural Reformation and Public Memory in Early Nineteenth-Century Berlin* (Cambridge, 2004), and has written numerous articles on the history of psychoanalysis, contemporary historiography and historical theory.

Robert Wokler is currently at the Whitney Humanities Center at Yale University and was formerly Reader in the History of Political Thought at the University of Manchester. His publications include *Rousseau on Society, Politics, Music and Language* (New York, 1987) and *Rousseau* (Oxford, 1995), as well as joint editions of *Diderot's Political Writings* (Cambridge, 1992), *Inventing Human Science* (Berkeley, 1995), *The Enlightenment and Modernity* (New York, 2000), and the forthcoming *Cambridge History of Eighteenth-Century Political Thought*.

Editors' Preface

When asked about the origins of the term "Counter-Enlightenment" Isaiah Berlin once replied that he did not know who invented the concept. "Could it be myself?" he wondered playfully. "I should be somewhat surprised. Perhaps I did. I really have no idea."[1] As the essays in this collection make plain, Berlin invented neither the word, which in German seems to be of late nineteenth-century vintage and in English appeared in print fifteen years before he came to employ it, nor the concept, which can be traced within the age of Enlightenment itself to debates about its own achievements and failures. More than any other figure since the eighteenth century, however, Berlin appropriated the term "Counter-Enlightenment," made it the heart of his own political thought, and imbued his interpretations of particular thinkers with its meanings and significance.

His diverse treatments of writers at the margins of the Enlightenment, who themselves reflected upon what they took to be its central currents, were at once historical and philosophical. By way of elucidating eighteenth- and nineteenth-century doctrines which challenged the fallacies and confronted the implications of an overarching faith in the unity of all sciences, Berlin sought to show that our patterns of culture, manufactured by ourselves—if not exactly as we choose—must be explained differently from the ways in which we seek to fathom laws of nature. In the writings of Vico, Herder, and Hamann, he uncovered philosophies of history encapsulated in language, laws, and mythology that were especially sensitive, moreover, to the aesthetic dimensions of human activity. In the works of these and other luminaries of the Counter-Enlightenment he identified notions of understanding human actions which prized empathy or "reconstructive imagination" on the part of the observer as necessary means for grasping from within the motivations of their agents. According to Berlin, inasmuch as the thinkers of the Counter-Enlightenment sought to reassert the singularity and validity of the human sciences as against the concepts and categories of the natural sciences, they anticipated the hermeneutic revolution of nineteenth-century philosophers and sociologists.

Although he elaborated the fundamental assumptions of his theory of the human sciences in some of his early philosophical essays and in his more historical essays of the early 1950s, it was only in the late 1970s, following the publication of his essay on "The Counter-Enlightenment" for Scribner's *Dictionary of the History of Ideas*, and especially with the appearance of his study of Vico and Herder, that his ideas on this subject came to attract widespread public attention. Berlin had by then secured his reputation on other foundations, above all as the leading modern advocate of liberalism in the tradition of Benjamin Constant and

John Stuart Mill, articulated most clearly in 1958 in "Two Concepts of Liberty," his celebrated inaugural lecture as Oxford's Chichele Professor of Social and Political Theory. With the diffusion of his writings on Counter-Enlightenment thinkers, he came to win a host of unexpected friends from other quarters in the humanities and social sciences. For by the 1970s, opposition to the allegedly uniformitarian strictures of the Enlightenment was rampant throughout universities in Europe and America, in Europe mainly on account of the rise to public prominence of postmodernist philosophers following the Prague Spring of 1968 and the events in France in May of the same year, in America principally through the advent of feminism and multiculturalism. Without aiming to address these audiences, Berlin, already in his late sixties, was to find that his writings on Counter-Enlightenment thinkers had a positive resonance in an epoch within which difference had come to be celebrated and the pretensions of universalism deplored. Just as the rise of Fascism and Communism in the 1930s had, according to some commentators, unmasked the illusions of another epoch whose totalitarian politics could be traced to ideals of scientific progress and wholesale social change, Eastern and Western philosophies of globalization in the 1970s were once again put to the test and found wanting. On the other hand, Berlin's historical investigations of the origins of modern anti-rationalism, conservatism, and nationalism incited hostile reactions from many liberal thinkers, who seemed to find in his sympathetic recapitulation of the methodological innovations of the opponents of the Enlightenment an apparent rehabilitation of their ideology.

Berlin's skeptical realism and apparent attachment to thinkers who swam against the currents of their own times accorded well with readers who had come to mistrust the great metanarratives of modernity and to believe that both Eastern and Western utopian schemes of social regeneration had proven a sham. Pluralism cast in the image of Counter-Enlightenment philosophy came to be judged by a new generation of readers as more appealing than liberalism, whose anti-totalitarian principles seemed too much tainted by the ethics of a now-defunct Cold War. More forcefully than any American critic of liberal universalism, perhaps even more incisively than French deconstructivists or the critical theorists of the Frankfurt School who commonly attacked the alleged tyrannies of Enlightenment thought, Berlin brought Baltic and Danubian perspectives to bear upon his assessments of past thinkers. While turning his attention to the populist myths by which the members of diverse communities identified both themselves and strangers, this most peripatetic scholar, at home in three continents, seemed to share virtually none of his subjects' illusions. A polyglot who was by origin foreign to the academic and intellectual circles over which he came to preside in England, he remained a firm Zionist and yet the most cosmopolitan nationalist of the twentieth century, himself a perfect personification of his own pluralist philosophy.

In his studies of Counter-Enlightenment thinkers, no less than in his writings on liberty, Berlin was also the bearer of an Oxford tradition of textual interpretation different from that which came to prevail in Cambridge and methodologically distinct as well from the approaches to political philosophy which, again in the 1970s, came to ascendancy, first at Harvard and thereafter throughout virtually the whole of the English-speaking world. Berlin was only the second holder of Oxford's Chichele Chair, all of whose incumbents except the first, G.D.H. Cole, have been foreigners, whereas all the holders of the Cambridge Chair of Political Science since its establishment in 1927 have been English. At least until the mid-1980s, political thought in Oxford was taught differently from the ways in which it is now studied in both Cambridge and Harvard, the syllabus at Oxford having been cast in the image of "Greats", that is, the school of *Literæ humaniores*, which had long concentrated on classics in conjunction with modern philosophy and which, after 1920, had come to figure in the new school of "Modern Greats" or Politics, Philosophy and Economics. In Cambridge, largely because political science was taught in the Faculty of History, revisions of the syllabus were associated with refinements of the discipline of history itself, such that, after the mid-1960s in particular, contextualism in various forms came to supplant all other approaches. But in Oxford, in the tradition of "Greats" developed at the height of Britain's age of imperialism to foster a spirit of public office and service, there had been scant interest in pursuing a strictly demarcated historical approach, irrelevant to contemporary political issues.

Berlin's treatment of Counter-Enlightenment luminaries was unencumbered by doubts about the abiding pertinence of their philosophies. His scholarship was both wide and deep, while his command of languages, his literary sensibilities, and his philosophical acumen enabled him to penetrate the meaning of arguments which readers wedded only to contextualism might not always be able to grasp. But he had few anxieties about identifying the profundities of Vico, Herder, or Hamann as anticipations of later developments in the history of European thought and judged that the purported division of labor between philosophers and historians in their interpretations of political ideas was obscure. In the Oxford tradition of "Greats" and "Modern Greats" his approach to texts, somewhat similar to that which informed the "Great Books" syllabus launched in the 1930s at the University of Chicago, was specially suited to a political theorist with broad interests in international affairs who was both trained in and drawn to the study of classics and also warmed to seminally significant writers who had been outsiders in their own world, all the more perceptive in their readings of its principles, he believed, on account of their estrangement.

It has sometimes been argued that Berlin's pluralism and liberalism were, or even had to be, fundamentally in conflict. While he occasionally allowed that his views of these two concepts might be inconsistent, his whole career, and particularly his writings on the Counter-Enlightenment, nonetheless appear to bring them together. Philosophical pluralism, or the celebration of variety, multiplicity, and difference, figures prominently in the philosophies of most of the thinkers of the Counter-Enlightenment whom he discusses, including Hamann's, whose theological objections to Enlightenment ideals Berlin did not share himself, and even de Maistre's, whose misanthropic perceptions of human nature he deemed at once captivating and alarming. Pluralism, as Berlin understood it, also lay at the heart of modern liberalism, not only in its commitment to toleration and respect for ethnic and other minorities, but above all in its opposition to dogmatic faith and all uniformitarian doctrines, whether religious or secular. Like other liberal philosophers, Berlin, when commenting on Counter-Enlightenment figures, sided mainly with the foxes who know many things rather than the hedgehogs who know just one.

Berlin's Russian and, above all, his Jewish origins and interests, raise issues of particular significance which bear upon his treatment of the Enlightenment and the Counter-Enlightenment. While he had no patience for theocratic justifications of a Jewish state, his sympathy for Moses Hess, Chaim Weizmann, and other proponents of Jewish nationalism form a part—perhaps the deepest part with respect to his own personal convictions—of his attachment to the Counter-Enlightenment and his mistrust of homogenous cosmopolitanism and similarly Procrustean strains of the Enlightenment. Such beliefs did not exclude but on the contrary, he claimed, required equal respect for the aspirations of other cultures and peoples, including the Palestinians. In virtually his last remarks, Berlin expressed the wish that a Palestinian state might be established alongside Israel, and he imagined that the prospects of mutual respect among disparate peoples might be enhanced, or at least would not be jeopardized, in a world of multiple nationalities, out of which trust and cross-border exchanges could perhaps slowly be generated.

But with respect to his own presence in England and America, where his exuberant humanity was judged irresistible at least by legions of admirers who might have supposed that his knighthood had been gained for services to conversation, he seemed an altogether welcome foreigner, an illustrious exile and refugee from barbarism such as had spawned the European Enlightenment itself around the end of the seventeenth century, first in Holland and then England. However reticent he appeared in public about the pressing crises of the day, no major political thinker of the twentieth century who resided in England was more conspicuously contemporary, international, undogmatic, and unparochial in his treatment of philosophical issues. He was convinced that the eighteenth-century battles of the Enlightenment and the Counter-Enlightenment between the *philosophes* and their critics were still prevalent today and that historians of ideas could help to illuminate both their meaning and significance.

Since modern liberalism is itself in many respects a child of the Enlightenment, Berlin's perspectives on these subjects give rise to questions about the connection between the Enlightenment and the Counter-Enlightenment, as he envisaged these two intellectual movements. This volume addresses such questions. Was pluralism an invention of the Counter-Enlightenment or can notable strains of it be identified within mainstream eighteenth-century philosophy as well? If the latter is the case, just how are the Enlightenment and the Counter-Enlightenment to be properly distinguished? These themes are addressed in the first essay by Mark Lilla, who suggests that the clash between the Enlightenment and the Counter-Enlightenment revolves essentially around divergent philosophies of history and perceptions of modernity. Another question pertains to Berlin's apparent attachment to the Counter-Enlightenment: Was that attachment purely methodological or also, however inadvertently, ideological? This question is addressed in the second essay by Robert Wokler, who contends that throughout his career Berlin remained fundamentally a figure of the Enlightenment—a Westernizer rather than Slavophile—in his campaigns against obscurantism and intolerance, and in the third essay by Roger Hausheer, who argues that Berlin was sufficiently impressed by German and other critics of eighteenth-century philosophy to have tempered his essentially Enlightenment outlook under their influence. In the fourth essay, Joseph Mali shows how Berlin found in Vico's theory of the mythopoeic construction of social reality new principles of moral and cultural evaluation that enabled him to counter the positivistic ideology and methodology prevalent in the humanities and social sciences since the Enlightenment.

In the fifth and sixth essays John Robertson and Darrin McMahon, respectively, set out to define the true Enlightenment and the real Counter-Enlightenment in appropriate national contexts, Robertson with reference to common assumptions and interests shared by Scottish and Neapolitan thinkers of the eighteenth century, and McMahon with reference to French commentators' claims that the doctrines of the *philosophes* had come to undermine the political foundations of civil society and the state. In the seventh essay, Frederick Beiser shows that Hamann's, Herder's, and Jacobi's denunciations of the tyranny of reason in the age of *Aufklärung* evolved from their perceptions of its association with political absolutism, while in the eighth chapter Graeme Garrard explains how, even in de Maistre's philosophy of anti-liberalism which Berlin deplored, he identified violent principles of psychological realism that he considered more profound than the unwarranted optimism of the Enlightenment. In the ninth essay, Lionel Gossman examines the political philosophy of Benjamin Constant in the light of the Romantic belief that vital human energies had been anesthetized by civilized life and with respect to his conceptions of ancient and modern liberty, which were to influence Berlin's ideas profoundly. In the tenth essay, John Toews examines themes in Berlin's own intellectual biography that were launched in the 1930s by his study of Karl Marx, including, with reference to Marx's Hegelian inheritance, anticipations of the Counter-Enlightenment as he would later portray it. In the eleventh essay, Michael Confino argues that even though there might never have been a "Russian Enlightenment" in the common historical meaning of the term, there was a Russian Counter-Enlightenment that arose and developed as a reaction to the Western European movement of Enlightenment.

Most of the essays in this volume were prepared for the International Seminar in Memory of Sir Isaiah Berlin, held at the School of History in Tel Aviv University during the academic year 1999–2000. The seminar was generously funded by the Yad Hanadiv Foundation in Jerusalem. We are grateful to the seminar's convenor, Professor Shulamit Volkov, for her firm judgment and encouragement in the preparation of this selection of essays for publication. We also wish to thank Hanita Atias-Wenkert for her meticulous attention to all practical matters at every stage of the project, and to express our gratitude to Mary McDonald for closely supervising its production and publication by the American Philosophical Society.

1 Ramin Jahanbegloo, *Conversations with Isaiah Berlin* (London: Peter Halban, 1992), pp. 69–70.

1 What Is Counter-Enlightenment?

Mark Lilla

I.

The critique of the modern age is as old as the age itself. Ever since men began seeking distinction by virtue of their modernity they have also been plagued by doubt about its ultimate worth. Like brothers squabbling over an inheritance, two related but nonetheless antagonistic figures have been present throughout the history of modern thought. Whenever Jacob has asserted his birthright to curiosity or autonomy, Esau has challenged it as vain or dehumanizing. The legitimacy of their claims and counter-claims is difficult to judge, however. Deciding for either brother would mean accepting their shared assumption that the modern age represents a fundamental transformation of human experience. And this assumption (about which we must come to a summary judgment) is certainly open to question. But even if we do question it, the persistence of this fraternal quarrel over the worth of modernity gives us good reason to not dismiss it out of hand. I will argue that there are grounds to suppose that the quarrel springs out of deeper tensions within the Western tradition and is only superficially about the modern age. If this is so, or even possible, then the quarrel deserves to be taken seriously even by those unconvinced by the claims of either brother.

The assumption that our age represents a "new order of things" is a historical assumption. If we take it to be correct, then our judgment of the age will depend on how we judge its history. And since this history is in constant motion, the critics of modernity can at best reach only provisional judgments about it, and even these will depend on *fortuna*—on the military exploits of a Corsican general, the aim of an assassin, the eureka of a scientist, or the disappearance of a wall. A historical critique of the age will also be prone to overestimate the significance of the present moment, if only to escape the nagging sense of insignificance which historical consciousness brings with it. Myopia creates the illusion that the "now" is the moment of ultimate crisis, and pride adds the conviction that the mystery of "age" has been revealed to us through it. If we consider the critique of modernity in the historical light which it so assuredly casts on others, we discover that two moments of presumed crisis have decisively shaped modernity's own philosophical judgment.

The first, and more significant crisis, was the French Revolution. Well before the Revolution, the critique of modernity was conceived by Vico, Hamann, and Herder, and received its classic formulation from Rousseau. Whatever these thinkers found to object to in modern thought and modern society, however, they did not focus their discontent on a passing historical moment. Vico's *New Science* and Rousseau's two *Discourses* sketch the history of the human race in allegorical terms, showing the dangers facing all refined societies—and not just modern ones—that turn their backs on traditional authority (in Vico's case) or on nature (in Rousseau's). The one instance when a historical event did become the subject of philosophical dispute was the Lisbon Earthquake of 1755, which gave sudden, morbid actuality to the question of theodicy. Yet even here the debate about the meaning of a historical event did not descend into a polemic about philosophy's responsibility for it. God was on trial for the earthquake, not the philosophers. But the Revolution, along with the Terror and conquests that followed, changed all that. For the first time, philosophy was put in the dock for having caused a transformation in history, and the earlier, mainly moral, objections raised against the ideas of Descartes and Bacon, Galileo and Newton, Voltaire and the Encyclopedists, Lessing and Kant, now gave way to a historical critique of the world they allegedly had created.

A second transformation in the critique of modernity took place within living memory, in the period bounded by the two World Wars. It is commonly asserted that the second, more radical critique that developed at this time was initiated and given its definitive formulation by Nietzsche. Philosophically this may be so, but it should be borne in mind that Nietzsche only became central to German thought in the midst and aftermath of the Great War, not before, and that his works were embraced almost simultaneously with those of Kierkegaard, which had just been translated. This seemingly trivial fact is actually quite important for understanding the subsequent development of the critique of modernity, which has always been an unstable mix of Nietzschean hardness and Kierkegaardian softness.

This new critique of the modern age was unquestionably more extreme than the one developed in the wake of the French Revolution. It accepted the assertion that early modern philosophy was responsible for the errant course of modern history, but it rejected romantic appeals to nature, feeling, or tradition. The new critique saw Romanticism as part of the modern problem, as an unhealthy outgrowth of the Enlightenment's own errant humanism. The new critique took its proponents in very different philosophical directions, so different that today it takes effort to see their common point of departure. The radiating paths marked out in the postwar years by Martin Heidegger, Carl Schmitt, Karl Barth, and Walter Benjamin—to take four prominent examples—were destined not to cross. Yet they all set out by assuming that the modern age had entered a decisive historical crisis whose original source was philosophical. They all conceived modernity as a "project" whose fruits could now be seen in the development of mass society, uncontrolled technological advance, mechanized killing, the trivialization of religion and art, and the flattening of human aspiration. In short, modern humanism had brought about the dehumanization of man. And when Europe and then the world were plunged into a second, more destructive war, that brought with it new, unimagined forms of erasing human life, the radical critique of modernity appeared to receive immediate, if unwelcome, confirmation.

It is difficult to overestimate the degree to which the experience of Europe's latest Thirty Year War has marked Western political philosophy ever since. The critique of modernity had begun as a purely philosophical dispute about the nature of the human good and the conditions under which it could be achieved. After the French Revolution it became a debate about a singular break in history and the effects flowing from it. The radical critique of modernity, which was forged in the crucible of two world wars, then drew the apocalyptic conclusion that the moment of ultimate crisis anticipated by modern thought had arrived, and that this crisis was the only conscionable object of philosophical reflection. Conditions in the West changed dramatically after the wars, but they continued to be conceived in terms of the radical critique. Hot wars were followed by a cold peace, dull consumer societies succeeded those riven by class conflicts, ancient racial hatreds dissolved before a flaccid toleration—and these too were heaped like coals upon the head of modernity, which now was made to answer a contradictory set of charges. Every significant German thinker of the inter-war period took the crisis of modernity for granted; and since we have not managed to advance beyond those thinkers in this respect, the presuppositions of the radical critique remain the presuppositions of much political philosophy today.

I began by stating that the critique of modernity is based on assumptions about history, and therefore is highly susceptible to changes in opinion about the historical moment. Only with distance do we begin to gain perspective on these opinions and learn to distinguish what may be true within them. Our distance from the passions of the French Revolution, for instance, has finally given us the perspective necessary to distinguish the philosophically enduring works of Tocqueville from the superficial polemics of Bonald, Lamennais, or Donoso Cortes. Gaining perspective on the radical critique of modernity is more difficult because the events which shaped it are fresh memories for so many. Yet perspective must be sought if our judgment of the critique is not to remain one opinion among others.

Two paths are open to those who genuinely wish to take seriously the critique of modernity today. One is to seek historical perspective on its historical claim that we live in a moment of decisive crisis and that the experiences of our century, and the so-called "lessons" to be drawn from them, provide a measure by which modern philosophy is to be judged. Such experiences certainly have thrown an extreme light on modern life and thought; of that there is no doubt. But extreme light sometimes distorts our vision rather than sharpening it. Some critics of modernity, following Hobbes, give the opposite impression by asserting that "the extreme case is the common one" or that "the exception" proves the rule. But we are permitted to wonder whether this is so, and to ask whether the intensity of this century's experiences has not caused us to overestimate their novelty, and thus to miscontrue their significance.

This sort of historical questioning would engage the radical critique of modernity on its own terrain. Another sort of questioning, which we will only begin here, would examine the philosophical presuppositions of any critique rather than examine this or that account of modern history. Such an undertaking would have to pay particular attention to assumptions about relations between ideas and events within history, and about whether anything can be philosophically deduced from such relations. We cannot aspire to novelty in taking up these questions, since they have been with us ever since Hegel and perhaps before. But they deserve to be considered again, especially today, when the philosophical critique of modernity gives every appearance of decaying into journalistic chatter about the postmodern age. Those who have not seriously reflected upon the presuppositions packed into the simple phrase "the modern age" can hardly be expected to advance beyond it. In returning to those presuppositions we hope to take the critique of modernity seriously, perhaps more seriously than it takes itself, at least today. We do so with the suspicion that it has something to teach us, if not about the course of modern history, then about something beyond history.

II.

The critique of modernity is undertaken by modern thinkers. These are thinkers who are in the modern age, but claim not to be of it. Their very existence would therefore seem to contradict the claim many of them make, that modernity is a historical bloc, with a single meaning or tendency. The critique of modernity itself shows that the modern age is divided, at least intellectually, over its own legitimacy and worth. But what are we to call thinkers in these two camps, since they are both "modern," historically speaking? One suggestion—it is the suggestion of Isaiah Berlin, and it is a good one—is that we employ the terms "Enlightenment" and "Counter-Enlightenment," since the issue dividing them really concerns the development of early-modern philosophy through the eighteenth century. I will adopt this suggestion, but with the following proviso. I will not employ the terms polemically to distinguish those I consider enlightened from the unenlightened; nor will I employ them in a narrow historical sense to group thinkers into discrete periods, such as the "age of Enlightenment" or "Romanticism." In using these terms I will adopt the meaning given them by the Counter-Enlightenment itself. To the Counter-Enlightenment belongs any thinker over the past three centuries who has claimed that the cause of the crisis of the age is to be found in the development of modern philosophy. To the Enlightenment belongs any thinker in this same period who has been made to answer for this crisis.

The critique of modernity is, therefore, the province of the Counter-Enlightenment, which first brought the Enlightenment to court and empowered world history to act as presiding judge. Many charges have been leveled against the defendant over the past two centuries, but these can be reduced to two. The first is that the Enlightenment was a self-conscious "project" conceived to transform human existence; the second is that, alas, it succeeded. Let us take up these charges in turn.

The notion that the Enlightenment was a self-conscious project, designed in the works of a few early thinkers and then carried out, more or less consciously, by others who followed, is a commonplace of the Counter-Enlightenment. It is the source of that tireless search—sometimes serious, sometime cavalier—for *the* pivotal point in the history of modern ideas where the fundamental error was first made. Some have thought to find it in the works of Descartes or Bacon, others in Galileo or Newton, still others in Hobbes or Machiavelli. The problem we face in judging this charge is not that projects cannot be derived from these works, read in a certain, sometimes strained, light. It is that such projects, if they existed, were utterly incompatible with each other. If we are to accept at face value the textual evidence gathered by the Counter-Enlightenment, we can only conclude that there was no single modern "project," but rather many contradictory ones. If we define each of these so-called projects as a thesis or antithesis, we see that they fall into a series of antinomies.

The first antinomy concerns the relation between reason and morality. The thesis: that the Enlightenment project was based on a new, aggressive form of reason that severed the bonds of natural human feeling, turned men into machines, and extinguished their moral instincts. The antithesis: that the Enlightenment actually sought to constrict reason's horizon, making modern reason the servant of the passions, corrupting morality by giving free rein to the will.

The second antinomy concerns the relation between reason and the sacred. The thesis: that by rationalizing the world the Enlightenment simultaneously "disenchanted" the world, foreclosing genuine human experiences of religion, art, or nature. The antithesis: the Enlightenment is itself a secularized form of religion, a new gnostic heresy that sacralizes human creativity in politics and art.

The third antinomy concerns the relation between reason and political authority. The thesis: that the Enlightenment wished to depoliticize and thus neutralize social relations, securing peace by distracting individuals with the vegetable and animal satisfactions of private life. The antithesis: that the Enlightenment was a polemical movement that politicized every aspect of human interaction, giving rise to new forms of intolerance, utopianism, and absolutism.

The existence of these antinomies poses a difficulty for any global judgment of Counter-Enlightenment claims. Certain critics of modernity accept only one or several of the theses, others only the antitheses. Some, the most challenging thinkers, accept them all, and we will turn our attention to them presently. But first we must pose a somewhat naive question about the unspoken presupposition underlying them. And that is, can the Enlightenment be conceived of as a "project" at all?

Let us take, for example, the most widely repeated charge that the Enlightenment was a rationalizing project. It is asserted that the thinkers of the Enlightenment applied a narrow rule of reason to all human experience, which rendered them by turns cold, inflexible, intolerant, utopian, blind to differences, and potentially authoritarian. Descartes and Bacon are often named as parties in this case for having inspired the fantastic works of Holbach, Helvétius, and La Mettrie, if not the mad dreams of Bentham, Saint-Simon, Fourier, even Sade. For the sake of argument, let us accept this questionable line of interpretation. The fact remains that the mainstream of the European Enlightenment and its greatest thinkers remained utterly untouched by this so-called rationalism, and indeed were among its first critics. Locke, Smith, Hume, Hutcheson, and Shaftsbury in England; Montesquieu, Voltaire, d'Alembert, and Diderot in France; Lessing, Mendelssohn, Kant, and Wieland in Germany; Beccaria in Italy—these thinkers held an altogether different view of human reason.

Because this mainstream Enlightenment began in a critique of theological rationalism, its greatest thinkers were, by and large, skeptical about inflated claims for reason, pessimistic about its power to change the human condition, and preoccupied with its contradictions. Against those theologians who pretended to reach the heavens on ladders of syllogisms, these Enlightenment philosophers defended the claims of sensibility and common sense, and built their sciences upon perception, not ratiocination. Yes, they believed ignorance to be slavery and truth to be freedom, but few thought absolute freedom could guarantee truth—hence their stubborn attachment to enlightened monarchy. Yes, they believed progress to be possible and worthy of pursuit, but, following Mendelssohn and Hume, they thought progress only attainable for short periods, and then only through a delicate balance of rational enlightenment and moral cultivation. Yes, they were prone to speak simplemindedly of reason as a calculating faculty, but, along with Kant, they also brooded about madness, melancholy, hypochondria, and the possible self-subversion of reason.

When studying the Counter-Enlightenment critique it is important to have the works of the Enlightenment ready at hand and to refer to them often. It is, to say the least, an enlightening exercise to see how little rapport there so often is between the charges levelled against the modern Enlightenment "project" and the books its authors actually wrote. The reason is not simply that the Enlightenment was, and always has been, diverse. It is also that, as students of human and natural variety, Enlightenment thinkers were highly allergic to "projects." After all, what sort of project can be built on Buffon's *Histoire naturelle*, or on Montesquieu's *Esprit des lois*? What single aim can be discerned in the articles of the *Encylopédie* and the variety of human pursuits illustrated in its luscious plates? The Enlightenment's contempt for medieval and early modern theology, whether merited or not, was a contempt for its naive rationalism, the *tout s'explique* which d'Alembert thought so "childish." It was against this rationalism and the vanity it reflected that the Enlightenment stood, functioning as an anti-object, if anything.

But if this is the case, how did the contrary impression arise? Why is it that so many for so long have seen the works of early modern thinkers as blueprints for laying waste to nature, for turning men into machines, for establishing a homogeneous world-order? The answer is not to be found in interpretative differences, although these subsequently developed. They are, I believe, to be found in motivations. The Counter-Enlightenment turns to Enlightenment philosophy only secondarily, and for extra-philosophical reasons: to discover the roots of a modern "break" or "crisis" which it firmly believes to exist in contemporary society. Without the presumed connection between ideas and social reality, Enlightenment philosophy would hold no more than antiquarian interest for the critics of the modern age. Instead, it is subjected to intense questioning as these critics seek to discover, not its logical inconsistencies or moral blindness, but rather the word that ultimately became deed. It turns out that the Counter-Enlightenment's primary interest is not in books or ideas. Its primary interest is in history.

III.

Appealing to history is a temptation for any doctrine seeking to establish itself against rivals. The first great thinker in the tradition to understand this temptation and its dangers was St. Augustine. In the first four centuries of our era, Christian theology found itself in extremely polemical relation with Roman religion and Hellenistic philosophy, and so succumbed to temptation and appealed to history as a way of settling arguments. The most curious work to come out of this historical turn in theology was Eusebius's *Demonstration of the Gospel*. Eusebius presents a providential history of mankind that begins with creation, passes through Jewish history, reaches a climax in the crucifixion, and ends with the crowning of Constantine, who unites the glory of pagan Rome with the revealed mission of the Christian Church. Eusebius's chronicle was convincing so long as Rome stood. When Rome fell, the verdict of history was reversed, and Christianity was charged with having corrupted Roman virtue and initiated a new, regressive era in world history. Augustine's *City of God* is a long response to this historical charge. It is a brilliant, thoroughly successful defense because Augustine undercuts the presuppositions of both the pagan philosophers and his theological predecessors by denying that world history is God's courthouse. The Christian message, he says, exists outside of time; the salvation promised us is a release from history, not its culmination.

What the fall of Rome was to early Christian theology, the French Revolution was to the Enlightenment. Yet the modern age never produced a St. Augustine; it produced Hegel instead. And ever since Hegel, our judgment of the Enlightenment has been a historical judgment. It has been suggested that the Enlightenment itself bears some responsibility for historicizing its message. But while this may be true of thinkers like Condorcet and Turgot, we must remember that the mainstream of the Enlightenment was rather pessimistic about the course of history. Voltaire's pronouncement about the Lisbon Earthquake—"il y a du mal sur la terre"—gives us a sense of how little the Enlightenment expected from providence. Athens, Rome, and Renaissance Florence were held up as models to be emulated if modern man was to rise out of barbarism; they were not perceived as historical stages which had already been surpassed. The historical schemes of Hume, Mendelssohn, and d'Alembert were allegories meant to inspire thinkers and statesmen alike, to awaken the hope that Enlightenment was again possible.

Hegel was hardly alone in seeing the Revolution as the beginning of a new age, nor was he alone in thinking that the Enlightenment had prepared it. Novalis, Tocqueville, and Constant, who had very different views of the Revolution, all held the Enlightenment responsible for it. But Hegel gave the Enlightenment an altogether greater significance by conceiving of it as a necessary way-station that had to be surpassed in man's journey to self-conscious Spirit. Psychologically, Enlightenment was an expression of human "negativity," the drive to self-assertion that makes consciousness dissatisfied with all positively given content and seeks to give that content itself. Negativity was *the* human characteristic, so in one sense the Enlightenment expressed something essential about human nature. But, according to Hegel, because the eighteenth-century Enlightenment set out to replace a naive Christian faith with a naive faith in man's own powers—in Hegel's phrase, attempted to "bring heaven to earth"—it doomed man to psychological disappointment and political terror. Hegel's Enlightenment is the dissatisfied Enlightenment, *die unbefriedigte Aufklärung*. And since man seeks satisfaction above all, he is destined to surpass the Enlightenment and find his philosophical resting place in Science (as Hegel understood it), and his political resting place in the modern bureaucratic state. From this standpoint it is a very small step indeed to assert that whatever came in the wake of the Enlightenment historically must be its philosophical and political *Aufhebung*.

Hegel was not a Counter-Enlightenment thinker in any superficial sense. He even managed to inspire an Enlightenment heresy called left-Hegelianism, one variety of which dominated many hearts and minds, and much of the globe's surface, until quite recently. However, in a more profound sense Hegel did shift the balance in favor of the Enlightenment's critics by transforming the idea of Enlightenment as a timeless ideal into that of Enlightenment as a bounded period through which a historical process could be seen to be working, and according to which it could be judged.

Hegel's conception of Enlightenment has had such wide influence that even those who consider themselves free from him find themselves depending on him when it comes to the critique of modernity. Three elements to the critique, whether in its early Romantic or later radical form, are of Hegelian origin, and all are questionable.

The first is the overestimation of the Enlightenment's significance. The Counter-Enlightenment thinker finds himself in the curious position of having to treat the Enlightenment as a success—indeed, as a smashing success—if his critique of the Enlightenment's social effects are to have force. An Enlightenment thinker, however, brought back from the grave and made to survey the bloody tapestry of modern history, might reach a different conclusion. He might say that the Enlightenment had had no effect, that it had failed. There was a period in European history when a number of thinkers, though by no means all, revived an old notion of enlightenment that was free from political or theological conventions, and modified this notion to make it serve the practical ends of mankind as a whole. This period, whatever one thinks of it, came to an end. Other periods followed in which different thinkers thought other thoughts and pursued different ends. And human beings continued to live as they always had, certainly no better, possessed of new machines and powers, but not more enlightened. The heavens opened and then they closed.

The critic of modernity points to this same tapestry and charges the Enlightenment with being the loom on which it was woven. If the Enlightenment thinker accepts that the tapestry is horrifying, but denies weaving it, the critic is forced to defend a hypothesis about historical responsibility. That hypothesis, in its simplest form, is the old diachronic fallacy, *post hoc ergo propter hoc*. This is the shaking stone upon which the Counter-Enlightenment builds its case against the modern age. However sophisticated the critic or the dialectic he employs, he must make this diachronic assumption if his critique is to have force. The Enlightenment must appear to be responsible for whatever followed, even for those forces which sought to extinguish the Enlightenment. This assumption, once made, is extremely powerful and even permits the Counter-Enlightenment thinker to resolve the antinomies discussed earlier by affirming the theses and antitheses simultaneously. He does this by deriving a genealogy of modern thought in which each thesis is said to be the historical precondition of each antithesis. For example, irrationalism is explained as a reaction to the Enlightenment's rationalism, religious reenchantment as the product of its disenchantment, and total politicization as the consequence of a prior depoliticization. Such genealogies can be presented as a process of "secularization," as a "dialectic," as an account of the growing "waves" in the modern stream of thought, or as the history of a modern "forgetfulness" of Being. All such genealogies derive, explicitly or not, from Hegel. And, like Hegel's own, they are utterly convincing—until, that is, we consider the other genealogies, which are equally convincing because equally irrefutable.

The second element taken from Hegel is the synchronic assumption that the real and the rational are bound together in history. "Das Denken ist Dingheit, Dingheit ist Denken" (*Phenomenology of Spirit*, §576). This connection is thought to be a dynamic relation, in which ideas arise in reaction to contradictions within existence, and then help to reshape existence in the next historical stage. The Romantic Counter-Enlightenment often presented itself in this light, as having arisen in justifiable reaction to the hard, cold world created by Enlightenment. But if we take the Romantics' assertion seriously and examine the worlds they actually came from, we find remarkably little enlightenment there. Were the Counter-Enlightenment a genuine reaction to the world created by the Enlightenment, it should have grown up in Great Britain or America. Instead, it was born in Germany and flourished among disgruntled Catholics in France, Spain, and Italy. Like "anti-Semitism without Jews," the Counter-Enlightenment seems to flourish whenever and wherever its object is absent.

The radical critique of modernity that grew up after the First World War could hardly assume that the real and the rational were one. Instead, it made the more powerful assumption that the real is irrational, and that this irrationality is a necessary, if unintended, consequence of the modern "project" conceived by the Enlightenment. If a genealogy of modern thought could solve the antinomies and show that Enlightenment was responsible for its intellectual opposite, it could also be extended to show how Enlightenment ideas were responsible for its social opposite—that is, for creating a world which the Enlightenment itself would have judged unenlightened. *Post hoc, propter hoc*, the Enlightenment is taken to be the source of every political, technological, aesthetic, even psychological development of the modern age. This extraordinary assertion has given rise to an enormous literature which today dominates the debate over modernity. Some of these works, like Reinhart Kosellek's *Kritik und Krise*, are written as tragedies; others, like Horkheimer's and Adorno's *Dialektik der Aufklärung*, are unwitting works of farce. But their synchronic and diachronic presuppositions are the same, and they both derive from Hegel.

The third element of the critique of modernity which Hegel helped to inspire is not a presupposition about the nature of history, but rather an eschatological hope about history's ultimate destination. If the Enlightenment is taken to be a historical process that issues in crisis, it is understandable that some will expect a resolution of that crisis in an overcoming of the Enlightenment. This overcoming can be conceived in any number of ways—as a historical return, as a historical leap forward, or as a leap out of history altogether—and each of these may be conceived, not as the opposite of Enlightenment, but as a "higher" or "truer" Enlightenment. Writing during the French Terror, Novalis expressed these eschatological hopes in apocalyptic terms, writing that "true anarchy begets religion and from the destruction of everything positive it raises its glorious head as the maker of a new world." Writing in the afterglow of the Napoleonic conquests, Hegel expressed these hopes in mythical terms as a "Calvary of World Spirit." One might have expected the catastrophe of the Great War to have dashed all eschatological hopes, but just the opposite occurred: among Jewish, Catholic, and Protestant thinkers alike the hope for a new world beyond the modern Enlightenment was reborn. It led one great thinker to believe that a new world would be ushered in by men wearing brown shirts; it led lesser ones to think it had been prophesied in a little red book. The Counter-Enlightenment's critique of modernity does not necessarily imply any one of these eschatological views, but it always ran the risk of encouraging them, and had almost no resources to quell them.

Eschatological hopes such as these do not originate with Hegel. They are as old as dissatisfaction with the human condition, which is to say, as old as the human race. Nor was Hegel the first to discover the disconsolations of philosophy, or the first to put a philosopher on trial. Hegel's novelty rests entirely on his historical conception of these problems. That is why Benedetto Croce's question—"what is living, and what is dead, in the philosophy of Hegel?"—can only be a preliminary question for us. For even if we conclude that the novelty of Hegel's philosophy was precisely its weakness, we still must confront the phenomena Hegel sought to explain. To the extent that the Counter-Enlightenment critique of modernity rests on Hegel's, it contains something dead for us, but also something very alive.

IV.

I began by suggesting that we take the Counter-Enlightenment more seriously than it takes itself. Recently the critics of modernity have come under new criticism themselves, on the principle that turnabout is fair play. A number of thinkers who see themselves as defenders of the Enlightenment today, and especially of its political ideas, believe we can settle our accounts with the Counter-Enlightenment by pointing out its logical errors, its rhetorical strategies, its anti-liberal animus, or the errors of political judgment made by its leading figures. These sorts of arguments are legitimate and usually true. But when we choose to meet an enemy on his own turf, we must always beware of descending to his level. *Verfassungspatriotismus* may be a political virtue, but *Aufklärungspatriotismus* is not a philosophical one. Taking the Counter-Enlightenment truly seriously, in the spirit of the Enlightenment itself, would mean doing something more.

To begin with, it would mean examining the Counter-Enlightenment in a non-historicist light. Ever since the French Revolution the critique of modernity has been carried out as a historical critique, which means that, to be consistent, the Counter-Enlightenment has had to historicize both the Enlightenment and itself. If the Enlightenment was something new under the sun, then so was the Counter-Enlightenment. But if we reject this historical presupposition, that still leaves the possibility—a very good possibility—that the Enlightenment and Counter-Enlightenment alike express something non-historical or eternal in human experience. The greatest critics of modernity, Rousseau and Nietzsche, give that very impression. Whatever they thought of modern man, their real target was an ancient man, Socrates, who equated knowledge with virtue and happiness. Their quite different anti-Socratisms depend less on their readings of history than on their deep reflections about the nature of the human soul and the nature of human interaction in society. Enlightenment for them was a permanent possibility, and therefore a permanent threat to a good life. Even Hegel treats this as an eternal, if historically developing tension, which is what makes his *Phenomenology of Spirit* the most intense, dramatic portrait of man's eternal struggle with Enlightenment in our philosophical literature.

There are, of course, Enlightenments and Enlightenments. Socrates is not St. Thomas, and neither is Kant. But so long as we focus our attention on differences between these Enlightenments, we will overlook the important fact that each was stalked by its own Counter-Enlightenment. The charges levelled against Socrates, Thomas, and Kant all revolved around the same three problems I mentioned earlier: the relation of reason to morality, to the sacred, and to political authority. It seems that Nietzsche was right: the human striving for Enlightenment, what he called the will to truth, is accompanied by an equally strong will to ignorance. The voice of this eternal Counter-Enlightenment can be heard in the myths of Prometheus and Daedalus, in the biblical accounts of Eden and Babel, and in the parable of the Golem. Long before Rousseau's *Émile* the Hebrew Bible taught that "in much wisdom is much grief, and he that increaseth knowledge increaseth sorrow" (Ecclesiastes 1:18). Long before Nietzsche, St. Paul gave a "yea and amen" to ignorance, which would be echoed by Augustine, Tertullian, Luther, and Pascal. Paul writes: "For it is written, I will destroy the wisdom of the wise, and will bring to nothing the understanding of the prudent. Where is the wise? Where is the scribe? Where is the disputer of this world? Hath not God made foolish the wisdom of this world? For after that in the wisdom of God the world by wisdom knew not God, it pleased God by the foolishness of preaching to save them that believe ... The foolishness of God is stronger than men" (1 Corinthians 1:19–21, 25). What critic of modernity, what prophet of postmodernity, has stated the eternal challenge to Enlightenment in stronger terms?

Nietzsche worried that the will to ignorance was being driven out of the soul by the force of Enlightenment. He was too pessimistic. Every Socrates in our tradition gets his Aristophanes, if not always the one he deserves. The critique of modernity developed by the Counter-Enlightenment plays this Aristophanic role in the thought of our times. To the degree that it understands itself and its enemy historically, it falls into confusion and self-contradiction. But this should not distract us from looking beyond this limited horizon, beyond the debate over the modern age, and seeking a confrontation with this eternal Counter-Enlightenment. Any philosophy wishing for genuine enlightenment must be attentive to the permanent questioning of its own worth and to the power of this will to ignorance. These questions can and should be answered; this will can and should be tamed. But as students of Enlightenment we must also be students of Counter-Enlightenment, for what we seek is enlightenment about ourselves.

2 | Isaiah Berlin's Enlightenment and Counter-Enlightenment

Robert Wokler

Isaiah Berlin often compared himself to a tailor, who only cuts his cloth on commission, or to a taxi driver who goes nowhere without first being hailed,[1] a journeyman philosopher, rather like Locke's philosophical underlaborer, so frequently invoked in the tradition of Oxford analytical philosophy. One such commission, from Scribner's *Dictionary of the History of Ideas*, led him to produce the essay on "The Counter-Enlightenment" in 1973 which is commonly said to mark the invention of that term, at least in English.[2] In fact, the expression was not at all invented by Berlin. It is perhaps odd that the French, whose eighteenth-century *philosophes* bequeathed the Enlightenment to the world by way of spreading that infection abroad, have never had a term for it at all and hence no term for the Counter-Enlightenment either. In the English language, the term *Enlightenment* seems to have made its first appearance in the late nineteenth century in English commentaries on Hegel, a few decades before the expression *Scottish Enlightenment* came to be invented, and fully 100 years before anyone had heard of the *Enlightenment Project* conceived by Alasdair MacInytre in his book *After Virtue* more than three decades after the launch of the Manhattan Project.[3] It was of course the Germans, whose detractors still insist it never had one, who invented the term the *Enlightenment (Die Aufkärung)* in the 1780s, by way of a series of *Berlinische Monatsschrift* essays which embraced Wieland's, Reinhold's, Mendelssohn's, and, most famously, Kant's treatment of the subject, and who around a century later also introduced the term *Gegen-Aufklärung*—Counter-Enlightenment—to European social thought and intellectual history.[4]

Berlin's coinage of 1973 is not even the first minting of the expression in English, since the term Counter-Enlightenment appeared fifteen years earlier in William Barrett's *Irrational Man*, where Barrett states, not without some justice, that "Existentialism is the counter-Enlightenment come at last to philosophical expression."[5] For all I know, the term has an even longer pedigree in English. Now that what passes for civilization has been transcribed on disk, it might be helpful if some computer hack were to trace every one of its published uses prior to 1973. Berlin's essay on the subject in the Scribner *Dictionary of the History of Ideas* rehearses the doctrines of a familiar cast of characters who had engaged his attention before: Hamann, to whom he had devoted a chapter of his collection, *The Age of Enlightenment*, in 1956;[6] Vico, on whom he had already published an essay in 1960 in a collection on eighteenth-century Italy;[7] Herder, on whom he had contributed an essay for a Johns Hopkins Press collection on the eighteenth century, subsequently published as an article in *Encounter* in 1965;[8] and de Maistre, the subject of an essay Berlin largely completed by 1960 but first published in Henry Hardy's edition of *The Crooked Timber of Humanity* thirty years later.[9] It would not be until 1977 that he first turned his attention to Jacobi.[10]

Although the term Counter-Enlightenment is now associated with Berlin more than with any other scholar or thinker, we ought to bear in mind that before the mid-1970s, by which time he had long retired from the Chichele Professorship of Social and Political Theory in Oxford and had also left his subsequent position as President of Wolfson College, that expression, and the ideas which it encapsulated, had virtually no bearing at all upon his academic reputation. His initial writings on Hamann, Vico, and Herder, if read at all, were received with much the same enthusiasm as had greeted David Hume's *Treatise of Human Nature* 240 years earlier.[11] At least until he was in his seventies Berlin's fame rested chiefly on four other works: his not altogether flattering intellectual biography of Marx;[12] his contributions to the philosophy of history in the essay "Historical Inevitability" and in his treatment of Tolstoy in *The Hedgehog and the Fox*;[13] and, in the field of political theory, his "Two Concepts of Liberty,"[14] much the most widely discussed of all the inaugural lectures given by professors of politics in the English-speaking world in the twentieth century. It was by virtue of his defense of the idea of "negative" liberty in particular that Berlin, already in his fifties, came to be regarded as the supreme advocate among contemporary political philosophers of a notion of modern liberty, which Benjamin Constant had contrasted with the ideal of ancient liberty in *his* celebrated treatment of the subject in 1819[15] and which, by way of John Stuart Mill, was to form the kernel of modern liberalism itself. Berlin came in the late twentieth century to be regarded as liberalism's foremost advocate—or its chief apologist, according to its detractors. In Perry Anderson's critiques of British national culture in the *New Left Review*, for instance, or, more recently, Quentin Skinner's own inaugural lecture in Cambridge, it was the alleged vacuousness of Berlin's liberalism that was subjected to closest scrutiny.

One might have imagined that, in the years following his retirement, Berlin's political philosophy would have ripened sufficiently to begin its natural course of decay; on the contrary, however, his work on the Counter-Enlightenment has enhanced his standing over the past twenty-five years, invigorating keen interest in new circles, most notably among communitarians who had earlier found his liberalism unpalatable. Thanks in large measure to the editorial labors of Hardy, works which Berlin drafted or broadcast more than thirty years ago make him appear less a defender of modern liberalism than a skeptical critic of the universalist pretensions of modernity, a sage of disparate cultures who recognized the inescapable conflict and incommensurability of their values, thereby apparently making common cause with the antifoundationalist detractors of the metanarratives of modernity, and becoming—from his unlikely perch at the Albany or Athenaeum—"a Savile Row postmodernist," as Ernest Gellner portrayed him.[16]

Perhaps even more than his liberalism had done before, it is Berlin's pluralism that now forms the mainspring of his reputation; and while that idea figures prominently in his essay on Montesquieu, first published in the *Proceedings of the British Academy* in 1955, and in three eloquent paragraphs addressed to it which form the conclusion of his "Two Concepts of Liberty,"[17] it is largely through his elaboration and embellishment of his notion of the Counter-Enlightenment that his pluralism has come to be seen as the mainspring of his political philosophy as a whole.[18] I say "elaboration and embellishment" because his original contribution on the subject was as much ignored as had been his earlier studies of Hamann, Herder, and de Maistre from which it was distilled. In 1976 Berlin reassembled and expanded two of those earlier essays as a book, the last that he would edit himself, entitled *Vico and Herder*,[19] which for the first time occasioned the scholarly attention that had previously been devoted only to his writings in other disciplines. Here we find these preeminent spokesmen of the Counter-Enlightenment portrayed not only as critics of some of the most central tenets of Enlightenment philosophy but also, in anticipating the divide between the *Naturwissenschaften* and *Geisteswissenschaften* that would come to inform the historiography and social sciences of the next two centuries, the pre-French Revolutionary post-modernists of their day.[20]

Here we find historicized conceptions of human nature opposed to the timeless principles of natural law.[21] Here, through Vico's notions of *verum ipsum factum* and Herder's putative conception of *Einfühlung* or empathy, we can detect a species of understanding, of *Verstehen*, only accessible to persons able to penetrate a scheme of things subjectively, with an insider's grasp of how it comes to be what it is.[22] Here we find our contemporary notions of culture, of the spiritual dimensions of human activity represented in the arts, in legal systems, languages, and myths.[23] Through Herder, in particular, we confront ideas of communal identity, of language and the arts as forming the essence of man's species-being, of a celebration of multiplicity and difference, which Berlin termed populism, expressionism, and pluralism, respectively.[24] In casting as profoundly radical and original two provincial and, in certain respects, reactionary figures of the eighteenth century—each largely unappreciated by his contemporaries in the international republic of letters—Berlin managed to pluck from the peripheries of the age of Enlightenment the seeds that would subsequently come to transform it, without ever having to channel a course through those ideological swamps that other commentators interested in the same subject associated above all with the influence of Rousseau.

In *The Magus of the North*—in part inspired by the chapter on Hamann in *The Age of Enlightenment* but which Hardy in fact assembled from papers dating from the mid-1960s for the Woodbridge Lectures at Columbia—Berlin added that Hamann, in his defense of the particular, the intuitive, the concrete, and the personal, denounced the opposite attributes of the Enlightenment and all its works and thereby proved the founder of modern anti-rationalism and romanticism and the forerunner of Nietzsche and the existentialists.[25] These themes were also to inform the Mellon Lectures Berlin delivered in Washington in 1965, finally published in 1999 as *The Roots of Romanticism*, with a recording of the last lecture in its original form appended as a compact disk.[26]

The Roots of Romanticism, incidentally, which Berlin himself never completed, also forms the unfinished *magnum opus* of Moses Herzog in Saul Bellow's novel, published one year before Berlin presented his lectures, that refers to many of the same persons, including Rousseau, Kant, Hegel, Tolstoy, and de Maistre, who were to figure in Berlin's own cast of characters, as well as the Hotel Pierre, in New York, where Berlin often resided when in America. One way of reading *The Roots of Romanticism* is by intercalating Berlin's inchoate lectures at appropriate points of Bellow's novel, so that by way of the compact disk one book may be said to complement the other, with Herzog thus the first fictional figure in world literature to have undergone transubstantiation, through Berlin passing over to the other side and thereby acquiring his own voice.

Several of the reviews of his *Vico and Herder* Berlin found profoundly dispiriting. While friends and admirers, like Patrick Gardiner and Hayden White, commended his scholarship,[27] other philosophers and historians of ideas found major faults in his arguments and took him to task. Arthur Scouten, writing in *Comparative Literature Studies*, and Hans Aarsleff, in the *London Review of Books*, in particular, incurred his wrath. They challenged the main thrust of his argument about the Counter-Enlightenment, Scouten partly on account of Berlin's exaggerating the extent to which Herder had parted company from the *Encyclopédistes*,[28] Aarsleff mainly with respect to Berlin's apparent ignorance of seventeenth- and eighteenth-century anthropological linguistics, in the light of which Vico and Herder, separately and together, ought to have been portrayed as disciples of Enlightenment philosophy rather than as critics.[29] In acid replies to each author, Berlin valiantly defended his scholarship, insisting, especially against Aarsleff, on the profound originality of Vico and the depth of the influence of Hamann upon Herder.[30]

Two other reviewers, William Walsh, writing in *Mind*, and Arnaldo Momigliano, in *The New York Review of Books*, troubled him even more. Can it really be the case, as Berlin had claimed on behalf of Herder, that to explain the meaning of an activity in its local context was also to endorse it?, asked Walsh. How can a genetic explanation form a justification? We are not required to agree that whatever is, is right.[31] Momigliano, from the perspective of an historian of the classical tradition, pursued the same point in a different way. The philosophies of Vico and Herder, the second born in the year the first had died, must not be conflated, he argued, since Vico remained deeply immersed in the values of Christian and classical culture, whereas Herder's fascination with Orientalism inclined him instead towards modern racism. In any event, Berlin appeared to overlook the implications of his reading of these two main protagonists of the Counter-Enlightenment. The crucial question to be asked in each case, Momigliano insisted, was that if we accept Berlin's acount of their attachment to pluralism, how then are we to escape the conclusion that they were also relativists? Before we celebrate their vitality, let us pause to take stock of where such pluralism would lead.[32]

Momigliano was personally well-acquainted with Vico's classical sources and references, but in contrasting the ancient Vico with the modern Herder, and in imputing a relativist stance not only to Vico and Herder but, by implication, also to Berlin himself, he appears to have fallen under the influence of Leo Strauss, whose colleague he had become at the University of Chicago since 1959, after having earlier been a close companion of Berlin at All Souls College, Oxford. Strauss and Momigliano were expatriate Jews, refugees from Fascist powers, who were convinced that Central and Eastern Europe's descent into Fascism and Western Europe's appeasement of it had been prefigured by modern social science's abandonment of the universalist and absolutist principles of classical or Christian civilization. The Counter-Enlightenment doctrine of relativism that Berlin appeared to applaud was denounced by them as lending warrant to the most catastrophic crisis of modernity, thereby making it conceptually and then historically and practically possible. For Strauss, in particular, the relativism entailed by value-free modern social science had opened the prospect of the Holocaust and the extermination of the Jews.[33] Alexander Pope's couplet from his *Essay on Man* had correctly encapsulated our dilemma. In the world of modernity, whatever is, is indeed right.

Berlin did not reply in print to the reviews of Walsh and Momigliano as he had done with respect to those of Scouten and Aarsleff, but in 1979 he accepted an invitation of the International Society for Eighteenth-Century Studies to speak at its Congress of the Enlightenment at Pisa, just a few miles from his summer home in Liguria. There, at a session over which Momigliano himself presided and which I attended—virtually his last public appearance in any academic setting—he supplied his answer to the imputation that his heroes of the Counter-Enlightenment had been heralds of relativism and all its dreadfully attendant consequences. His talk was entitled "Alleged Relativism in Eighteenth-Century European Thought," and it was published, in 1980, in the *British Journal for Eighteenth-Century Studies*; a revised version appeared a decade later in Hardy's edition of *The Crooked Timber of Humanity*.[34]

"A distinguished and learned critic has wondered if I fully appreciate the implications of the historical relativism of Vico and Herder which, unacknowledged by them ... constituted a problem which has persisted to this day," Berlin remarked. "If we grant the assumption that Vico and Herder were in fact relativists ... the point made by my critic was valid. But I now believe this to be a mistaken interpretation of Vico and Herder, although [and here he may be referring to some remarks about relativism which he had made in his original treatments of these writers] I have in my time contributed to it myself." "True relativism," he continued, in so far as it entails fundamental doubt about the possibility of objective knowledge, is derived from other and later sources—from the metaphysics of Schopenhauer and Nietzsche, from social anthropology, from Marx and Freud. It is a nineteenth-century doctrine, not consistently put forward by any influential thinker of the eighteenth century, he claimed.[35] Vico and Herder, he now contended, were pluralists rather than relativists; they believed not in the absence of objective ends but in their variety, their multiplicity, and sometimes conflict. Relativism, he maintained here, was not the only alternative to universalism.[36] The Counter-Enlightenment had confronted Enlightenment monism not by way of the potentially sinister trappings of a nineteenth-century ideology but by invoking the liberating principles of pluralism. It was in this manner that Berlin restated the central theme of his concluding section on "The One and the Many" in his *Two Concepts of Liberty*, except that whereas previously it had been various forms of *monism* which had given rise to the "slaughter of individuals on the altars of the great historical ideals," as he had put it,[37] conceptual responsibility for that dreadful outcome had now been passed even more to *relativism*.

If the Counter-Enlightenment was fundamentally pluralist, the Enlightenment must of course have been its opposite—uniformitarian, undifferentiated, homogenous, and monolithic. In mapping the richly pluralist dimensions of the Counter-Enlightenment, Berlin, all too frequently for my liking, portrayed the Enlightenment as if, as he put it in *The Roots of Romanticism*, it could be boiled down to three fundamental principles, which also, incidentally, constitute the Ionian fallacy, as he elsewhere describes it,[38] and indeed virtually the whole of our Western intellectual tradition so enthusiastically bludgeoned into well-merited obsolescence on Berlin's behalf by John Gray.[39] These principles are, first, that all genuine questions can be answered; second, that all the answers are knowable; and third, that all those knowable answers must also be compatible.[40] That, in short, is what might be termed Berlin's version of the Enlightenment Project, and for his communitarian, postmodernist, or pluralist admirers it has proved quite sufficiently devastating to license their hammering of the last nail into the Enlightenment's coffin.

It is of course true that a richer and more sympathetic portrait of the age of Enlightenment in general can be culled from Berlin's writings, particularly in the last paragraph of his introduction to Enlightenment thinkers where he praises their intellectual honesty and the courage of their campaigns against injustice and ignorance,[41] and perhaps above all in his *Conversations* with Ramin Jahanbegloo, published in 1992, where he speaks of himself as a liberal rationalist who, despite their dogmatism, subscribes fundamentally to the liberationalist values of Voltaire, Helvétius, d'Holbach, Condorcet, and the Enlightenment in general. "They were against cruelty," he remarks there, "they were against oppression, they fought the good fight against superstition and ignorance. ... So I am on their side." [But] "I am interested in the views of the opposition," he continues, not because [I] greatly admire them but because "clever and gifted enemies often pinpoint fallacies" of the Enlightenment and expose some of its "political implications" as "inadequate" and, "at times, disastrous."[42] It is just this last proposition, we might note, that forms the central thesis of Jacob Talmon's *Origins of Totalitarian Democracy* of 1952, in fact inspired by (an unmentioned) Harold Laski in which Talmon instead acknowledges a debt to Berlin's "stimulating suggestions," as he puts it.[43]

For those of us who work in diverse fields of eighteenth-century studies and also greatly admire his achievement, Berlin's invention of a monolithic Enlightenment with just three legs is more than a trifle embarrassing, particularly since it was only assembled so that it might be deconstructed in the manner of Procrustes and thereby point the way to a richer understanding of the diverse threads that constitute its opposite. It makes little sense, I believe, for a pluralist to set aside his own principles when addressing Enlightenment thinkers, who to my mind for the most part characteristically espoused the values with which Berlin confronts them no less tenaciously than he did. In depicting the Enlightenment as if its centrally guiding thread was an absolutist commitment to the pursuit of truth by way of science, Berlin appears to join both Carl Becker, whose *Heavenly City of the Eighteenth-Century Philosophers* he praises in his *Roots of Romanticism*,[44] as well as Richard Rorty, whose portrayal of an Enlightenment doctrine of mind which mirrors nature is drawn upon a similarly Procrustean bed.[45]

According to Becker in particular, the *philosophes* of the eighteenth century had simply turned inside out the Christian absolutism which they decried, substituting the pursuit of earthly happiness in place of the unworldly salvation of our souls, thereby demolishing the city of god only to rebuild it on the terrestrial plain.[46] The Enlightenment can thus be portrayed as having loved the thing it killed and of taking on its mantle in the very act of destroying it, by substituting a rationalist form of arcane dogmatism for another, based on faith.[47] Berlin was to my mind far too wise and learned to be seduced by such nonsense.

Even among those *philosophes* of whom it might be said that this was their preeminent objective, the pursuit of scientific truth in the Enlightenment did not take the form of belief in the one and only true religion by another name. Of all major eighteenth-century thinkers, Montesquieu was perhaps the most tenacious supporter of the proposition that the laws of nature and the operations of the human mind must be understood in the same way. No one in the Enlightenment subscribed more plainly to physicalist explanations of social behavior and culture, and Rorty's account of mind as nature's mirror in fact describes the central thrust of Montesquieu's philosophy perfectly. Yet from that monolithic perspective on both the natural and human sciences, there springs no universalism or cosmopolitanism of any kind. Above all his contemporaries, Montesquieu was specially sensitive to the local variety, specificity, and uniqueness of social institutions, customs, and mores. His *Esprit des lois* might well have been subtitled "A Study of Difference." His *Lettres persanes* ought to be required reading in any course of comparative literature devoted to the subject of "Otherness," as indeed should be Swift's *Gulliver's Travels* and Voltaire's *Candide*.

A postmodernist definition of the Enlightenment in terms of its deconstruction of Christian dogmas by way of critical theory would, I believe, more aptly describe that century-long intellectual movement which was inspired by the Revocation of the Edict of Nantes in 1685 and the Glorious Revolution in England three years later than do the uniformitarian strictures of Becker and Rorty. From Berlin's own pluralist perspective, the advent of that fresh approach may be said to be marked by the passage from Bossuet's *Histoire universelle* to Fontenelle's *Pluralité des mondes*. No one who read the voyages assembled by the abbé Prévost in his collection, which added so much to that produced by Samuel Purchas in the previous century, could fail to notice how disparate were the cultures of mankind throughout the world, and how diverse their social institutions. No one who read about the Egyptian or Hebrew chants in Burney's *General History of Music* or about Persian or Chinese tunes in Rousseau's *Dictionnaire de musique* could any longer be persuaded that the Western scale and its harmonies were universally appreciated.

Accounts relating real or imaginary journeys to exotic worlds, or singing the praises of a primitive golden age, circulated as widely, and often among the same readers, as did Enlightenment treatises on the natural sciences and on the progress of civilization. Europe's spiritual and political hegemony over the rest of the world was not appreciated at all but in fact fiercely opposed in a great many anticolonialist classic works of eighteenth-century philosophy and anthropology, from Rousseau's *Discours sur l'inégalité* to Diderot's *Supplément au Voyage de Bougainville* to the Abbé Raynal's *Histoire des deux Indes*. Even while expressing optimism with respect to the increasingly secular development of the human race as it rose from barbarism to civilization, the proponents of the Enlightenment Project characteristically displayed a profound pessimism about the imperialist nature of Western Christendom. Instead of denouncing the Enlightenment's rationalist and universalist pretensions, its detractors would do better to investigate the skeptical empiricism which informed the doctrines of its leading advocates, from Bayle to La Mettrie and d'Holbach, who framed fundamentally liberal objections to the bigotry of sacred knowledge as uncovered by revelation and to the universalism of blind faith.[48]

These commonplace truths, which warrant reiteration only because they are so infrequently remembered by most modern, postmodern, and communitarian critics of Enlightenment philosophy, were well known to Berlin. Although it had sometimes been gained secondhand and was seldom reliably stored for invocation in scholarly footnotes, Berlin's erudition was vast and his command of the literature in eighteenth-century fields in which I was working myself was as broad as that of any person I ever met while completing my doctorate at Oxford; and it was generally deeper on account of the fact that his own philosophical interests more closely approximated the ideas in the texts we discussed than those of my tutors with just literary backgrounds, whose grasp of the intellectual context of an eighteenth-century work sometimes obscured their penetration of its meaning.

When I conveyed to Berlin my thoughts about the *Querelle des Bouffons* of the mid-1750s,[49] he not only pointed me towards commentators who had addressed this musical dispute's seventeenth-century precursors but also corrected some doubtful eighteenth-century Italian prose I had transcribed that was in need of such attention. Berlin's own essay on Montesquieu in *Against the Current* sheds genuinely fresh light upon that central thinker, perhaps the most central thinker, not of the Counter-Enlightenment but of the Enlightenment itself. Although the tone of Aarsleff's objections to Berlin's account of Herder strikes me as excessively severe, I feel more than a little inclined to agree with his contention that the intellectual gulf between Herder and Hamann is vast, and I am pleased to find from recent scholarship on Herder (of which Berlin could not have been aware) that many crucial passages of Herder's *Ideen*, his masterpiece, were drawn directly from Adam Ferguson and, more distantly, Montesquieu.[50] As Berlin himself reports at length, moreover, Hamann read Hume meticulously and was greatly persuaded by his account of the nature of belief and reason.[51] All of which, to my mind, suggests that much of what has come to pass for the Counter-Enlightenment properly figures within the Enlightenment and not outside it.[52]

With the exception of the caricatures of that intellectual movement which he drew for the purpose of highlighting what he supposed was its opposite, Berlin's sympathies, style, and almost the whole corpus of his writings strike me as cast in an Enlightenment mold. This really is the principal thesis I wish to convey here—that Berlin was a *philosophe* of enlightened disposition *malgré lui*,[53] whose life and work together display the spirit of enlightenment at virtually every juncture apart from where he contrived to address that subject. However postmodern he might have come to appear by virtue of the recent diffusion of lectures he conceived thirty or forty years before his death, it is hard to imagine this admirer of the analytical precision of Austin's prose impressed by the lectures on ontology which rendered Heidegger in Freiburg "the secret king of philosophy" of an utterly different kind, although I suppose that he would have regarded Derrida's alleged charlatanry an insufficient reason to deny him an honorary degree, at any rate from Cambridge.[54] Gray describes the main thrust of his philosophy as *agonistic* in its liberalism,[55] but the combative nature of his imagery is an altogether milder affair than the traumatic notion of *Geworfenheit*—of being thrown—that lies at the heart of the human predicament described by Heidegger and out of which have sprung postmodernist notions of a decidedly coarser species than Berlin's bespoke variety from Savile Row.[56]

As for "difference" and "otherness," I suspect that no philosopher of the twentieth century was more peripatetic but at the same time comfortably at home in every culture of the three continents he visited regularly in which he was welcomed. Throughout the night of his spiritual apotheosis in the company of Anna Akhmatova, depicted so brilliantly in Michael Ignatieff's biography, it was she who spoke incessantly of the inner world and dark intensity of Dostoyevsky and other writers who had labored on Russian soil, Berlin who instead invoked the more luminous subtleties of Turgenev among exiled artists who had worked abroad.[57] No nineteenth-century figure was to command his admiration more than Herzen, that ebullient Westernizer among dour Slavophiles, that cosmopolitan Russian abroad, that generous spirit of enlightenment from a dark-eyed nation in a still benighted age, whom he describes as a kind of Russian Voltaire of his day.[58] When Berlin addressed the greatest literary masterpiece of his native language, Tolstoy's *War and Peace*, it was not the rich tapestry of the social life of the Russian peasantry and aristocracy portrayed there which engaged his attention most, but rather Tolstoy's theory of history, his respect for Rousseau and other thinkers of the French Enlightenment, his contempt for "unintelligible mysteries" drawn from "mists of antiquity," his hostility to the cant of the freemasons. The Tolstoy he most admired, cast in his own image, he describes as a skeptical realist who stood in lifelong opposition to dogmatic authoritarianism.[59]

In several respects, and above all in his comprehensive mastery of the Enlightenment *oraison funèbre* or funeral oration which comprises so many chapters of his *Personal Impressions*,[60] Berlin was the spiritual descendant of both d'Alembert and Condorcet, permanent secretaries, in the late eighteenth century, of the *Académie française* and *Académie des sciences*, respectively. When, for instance, he congratulated Lewis Namier on his production of an excellent book—"all the better for being short,"[61] he added—his wit could glisten with the sparkle of Voltaire. But to my mind, in his ideals, his enthusiasms, his spontaneity, his vitality, his mimicry of others, his genial self-abasement fuelled by genuine self-doubt, he was more like Diderot than anyone I ever knew. By dint of his own *Einfühlung* with diverse past and present thinkers Berlin managed to make their ideas vivid and compelling, without having to adopt them as his own. Such transitivity or clairvoyance was much sought and greatly prized by the *philosophes* of the Enlightenment I know best. No academic figure of our time was better suited or more attracted to the delights of the linguistic turns of the eighteenth-century *salon*.

Even with respect to his nationalism and Zionism, Berlin strikes me as a child of the Enlightenment. At least in the English-speaking world, communitarians today, including many who found themselves drawn more to Berlin's pluralism than to his liberalism, have been mainly concerned with the cultures of ethnic minorities in parts of the world conquered and colonized by Europeans, or with the loss of spiritual bonds of fraternity in societies predominantly held together by market mechanisms alone. Berlin, by contrast, focused on the identity of a community that colonized but never gained security in Europe, and although a practicing Jew with a command of Hebrew sufficient to enable him to lecture in that language, he never displayed the slightest interest in Jewish theology and scarcely any in Jewish culture and the arts. However remarkable their achievements, the greatest of Jewish artists—Heine and Mendelssohn, for instance—he judged manifestly inferior to Goethe and Beethoven, respectively, if only because Heine and Mendelssohn had all too conspicuously attempted to scale the summits of just German culture, whereas Goethe and Beethoven, he contended, had produced poetry and music of universally sublime character which had transcended the national identities of their composers.[62] Though he traveled frequently to Israel, the Wailing Wall of the Temple Mount in Jerusalem—famously described by his devoutly observant relative, Yeshayahu Leibowitz, as the *Kotel* recast as a *Dis-kotel*—bore scant mystical significance for him. As passionate as was his commitment to Zionism, he loathed the extremism of Menachem Begin and the Irgun,[63] which he regarded as a band of terrorists, and although he seldom spoke in public on such matters, he was convinced that the existence of a Jewish state—that last child of a European *Risorgimento*, as he sometimes put it[64]—did not exclude but on the contrary necessitated the establishment of a Palestinian state as well. "Home is the place where, when you have to go there, they have to take you in," Robert Frost had once said,[65] and Berlin concurred. What was necessary above all else, to his mind, was that in a world in which Jews cannot but remain perpetual strangers, destined never to be truly naturalized, there must somewhere be a refuge or homeland for them too, not one in which they should all be obliged to live, but one to which they might one day have to flee.

These are questions which have bedeviled Jews throughout the history of their diaspora. But from the late seventeenth to the late eighteenth century, in the great schisms of Catholic and Calvinist Europe which gave rise to a different diaspora that inspired the pleas of toleration of Spinoza, Bayle, Locke, and others—which to my mind lie at the heart of the only intellectual movement of the period that might correctly be termed "The Enlightenment Project"[66]—these issues were pursued in fresh ways, and for the Jews in a new idiom, in the language of civil and human rights. Here, in the context of an eighteenth-century debate about Jewish identity, assimilation, and incorporation in the state, pursued with renewed vigor after the French Revolutionary enfranchisement of the Jews—not least by Marx—lies the proper context for an understanding of Berlin's Zionism.

I must not, however, fail to introduce the fly in this ointment. If the Enlightenment constitutes the background of Berlin's Zionism, its fundamental tenets, contrary to the central thesis I have just put forward, do not spring at all from Enlightenment ideals of toleration. Those ideals—encapsulated most famously by Voltaire in his *Lettres philosophiques* where he describes a London Stock Exchange comprised of men who before they worship their different gods in their separate churches negotiate in a common currency, of which the only infidels are traders who go bankrupt[67]—do not and cannot embrace Berlin's Zionism. For Voltaire and most other *philosophes* of the Enlightenment, the Jews only required the protection of the rule of law by civil powers uninterested in matters of faith. For Berlin, the Jews must be empowered to return to a land in which they alone constitute the predominant community. When writing about such matters with respect to the eighteenth century, Berlin was impressed not by the *Plea for the Toleration of the Jews* compiled by Moses Mendelssohn, grandfather of the composer, translator of Rousseau and, by virtue of his learning and humanity, one of the foremost luminaries of the German Enlightenment. He was struck instead by the provocative and in some respects even anti-Semitic diatribe produced by Hamann, who regarded the mere toleration of differences as a denial of their importance—a genuinely postmodernist claim. When pursuing the same themes in the mid-nineteenth century in his essay on the "Life and Opinions of Moses Hess," he hailed as a masterpiece Hess's treatment of *Rome und Jerusalem*, in which Hess denounced as inconsistent a belief both in enlightenment and in the Jewish mission in exile, on account of its endorsing the ultimate dissolution and the continued existence of Judaism at the same time.[68] Here, wrote Berlin, was a work which preached Zionism more than thirty years before the term had been invented, all the more powerfully persuasive today than it had proved in the course of Hess's own lifetime, in view of its warning to Germany's assimilated Jews that they would one day suffer a cataclysm of greater magnitude than any they could conceive.[69]

In 1932, in the same year that Becker's *Heavenly City of the Eighteenth-Century Philosophers* was published, Ernst Cassirer, one of the first Jewish rectors of a German university, produced as well his *Philosophie der Aufklärung*, which in large measure articulates his own defense of a noble tradition of German Enlightenment, including Leibniz, Wolff, and Baumgarten, in the face of contemporary barbarism.[70] But while Cassirer was drafting his work, the Weimar Republic he served—in effect modern Germany's own Enlightenment Project—was itself in its death throes. A few months after the publication of *Die Philosophie der Aufklärung*, the institutions which had protected the civil rights of assimilated Jews vanished with the Republic's dissolution, and as a consequence Bertolt Brecht, Albert Einstein, Walter Gropius, Wassily Kandinsky, Thomas Mann, Paul Tillich, Bruno Walter, and many other luminaries of twentieth-century science and culture, as well as Cassirer, were forced into exile.[71] In an essay on "Jewish Slavery and Emancipation" which first appeared in *The Jewish Chronicle* in 1951 and has only just been published again, Berlin remarked that while the Jews had taken every conceivable step to adapt and adjust themselves in the societies in which they had sought to be naturalized, their efforts had all "proved unavailing."[72] The extermination of European Jewry had established the hopelessness of true assimilation, he adds in his *Conversations* with Jahanbegloo.[73] That perception above all else sustained his Zionism. It marks the most decisive break of his attachment to the principles of the Enlightenment I know, to my mind much more striking than his depiction of its three-legged uniformitarian faith in his portrayal of the Counter-Enlightenment.

I should like finally to comment briefly on just one matter which I believe to be intimately connected with this subject, although it was not addressed directly by Perry Anderson when he first raised it in his own fashion in an essay on "Components of the National Culture," which appeared in the *New Left Review* in the summer of 1968.[74] Readers of this collection who can should cast their minds back to that period of our history which, by way of the Prague Spring and the student uprising in France in May, seemed for many left-wing commentators at the time a fresh and then subsequently a false dawn. Almost as if to recapitulate celebrated lines about a specter haunting Europe occasioned by the revolutions of 1848, Anderson begins his text as follows: "A coherent and militant student movement has not yet emerged in England," he writes. "But it may now be only a matter of time before it does."[75] Why was England so bereft of a radical political culture, he wondered, such as had arisen in Germany, Italy, and France? The principal reason, he explained, was the absence of a theoretical center in England, which had never produced a classical sociology or national tradition of Marxism. And one of the main factors which explain England's "listless mediocrity" and "wizened provincialism" in such matters, as he put it, was that since 1900 it had been subjected to a wave of immigrants from Eastern and Central Europe whose "elective affinity" for a quiescent society and unsystematic and untheoretical social sciences had impeded the development of a political culture such as could be found, in 1968, in Germany, Italy, and France. Whereas dissident radicals, or "Reds," who fled the instability of Central Europe settled elsewhere—the Frankfurt Marxists in America, for instance, Lukács in Russia, and Brecht and Mann in Scandinavia—England had by a process of natural selection proved attractive only to the "Whites," which had thus ensured that the mantle of intellectual authority progressively passed from Victorian families bearing the name Macaulay, Trevelyan, Arnold, Huxley, Stephens, Wedgwood, or Hodgkin, to Germans like Eysenck; to Austrians such as Wittgenstein, Popper, Gombrich, and Klein; to Poles like Malinowski and Namier; and to Russians like Isaiah Berlin.[76]

I must not comment too lengthily here on this curious tableau of enduring complacence made possible by England's attraction of expatriate academics from Central and Eastern Europe, cloned with suitably acquired characteristics. Let me note only that, while distinguishing "Reds" from "Whites," Anderson never once mentions the word "Jew," nor does he take stock of anything to do with Judaism which might explain why these expatriates abandoned their homes abroad. If when fleeing Russia Berlin's parents had settled instead in Germany, Italy, or France and stayed there, it is more than likely that I should not have had this tale to tell. Unless it was Chaim Weizmann, no political leader of any people in the contemporary world so commanded Berlin's esteem as Winston Churchill. Even more than Franklin Roosevelt, if only because it seemed to his own followers whom he rallied to his cause that success was so unlikely, Churchill's "greatest service to mankind" had been to show that it was "possible to be politically effective and yet benevolent and humane."[77]

Berlin died on November 5, 1997. He was virtually the last survivor of that generation of immigrants whose ascendancy over higher education in Great Britain Anderson so much lamented. He had precious little in common, ideologically or temperamentally, with other luminaries of that White rather than Red emigration—with Hayek, Eysenck, or Popper, for instance—who collectively are held to have steered the English nation through its long slumber while less ideologically hamstrung radical students on the Continent revolted. His Zionism, like his liberalism, was undogmatic. He formed no school and had no followers. He flourished in a civic culture which was not his own without ever abandoning his native identities or the exotic languages of his youth. He was a Russian Jew who had come to feel at home abroad, the first Jewish Fellow of All Souls and the only holder of the Order of Merit and President of the British Academy whose two grandfathers, an uncle, an aunt, and three cousins had been shot, quite possibly by the associates of a very elderly Latvian citizen of Australia whom the British Home Secretary felt minded to deport but not detain when alerted of his presence in England around three years ago.[78] A few weeks before Berlin's death, John Pocock had delivered the first of a series of lectures in his honor at Oxford, which he had conceived as both paying his tribute and articulating their differences.

Exactly one week after his passing, Quentin Skinner gave his inaugural lecture as the Regius Professor of Modern History in Cambridge, "Liberty before Liberalism," in which he addressed and sought to correct the concept of negative liberty introduced by Berlin's own inaugural lecture forty years earlier.[79]

With respect to Berlin's approach to the reading of texts in political theory and the history of ideas, Pocock and Skinner in their different ways point to *décalages* or breaks which are both epistemic and generational. In view of the number of columns of print that followed the demise of Britain's preeminent academic pillar of the establishment, some of which in other circumstances might have been devoted to reporting Skinner's lecture, there is a sense in which Berlin's death could accurately be described, in the words of Norman Mailer on the passing of Truman Capote, as "a good career move." But although he was eighty-eight years old, his demise shook me and many other persons throughout the world very deeply indeed. I was reminded of the Jewish child portrayed so affectionately in Louis Malle's autobiographical *Au Revoir les enfants*, whose dazzling command of Schubert at the piano just before his deportation gave his classmates a glimpse of another world in their midst which they had never known firsthand, of all that was best in European civilization, brought to them and then taken away by all that was worst. Not only by the sheer humanity of his writings and the exuberant cadences of his style, but by virtue even of the circumstances of his presence in England, Berlin was, to my mind, the very epitome of the spirit of enlightenment.[80]

NOTES

1. Ramin Jahanbegloo, *Conversations with Isaiah Berlin* (London: Peter Halban, 1992), pp. 95–6.
2. Philip P. Wiener (ed.), *Dictionary of the History of Ideas* (New York: Charles Scribner's Sons, 1968, 1973), vol. 2, pp. 100–12.
3. In French, the expression "les lumières" refers to the authors of Enlightenment ideas as well as to their doctrines' collective character. Thanks to Rivarol and others, the term achieved a certain currency in the course of the French Revolution, and in the second half of the nineteenth century, partly by way of Taine's surveys of the origins of contemporary France, what in English around the same time came to be described as the "the Age of Enlightenment" was encapsulated in French as "le siècle des lumières." On the inauguration in English of the expression *The Enlightenment*, see John Lough, "Reflections on Enlightenment and *Lumières*," in the *British Journal for Eighteenth-Century Studies* 8 (1985), pp. 1–15, and especially James Schmidt, "Inventing the Enlightenment: Anti-Jacobins, British Hegelians, and the *Oxford English Dictionary*," forthcoming in 2003 in the *Journal of the History of Ideas*. The modern imagery of the age of *The Scottish Enlightenment* owes much to James Mc-Cosh's *The Scottish Philosophy* of 1875 and, above all, Henry Grey Graham's *Scottish Men of Letters* of 1901, but it was first conceptualized within the eighteenth century by Dugald Stewart. With respect to the expression *The Enlightenment Project*, I am unaware of any published instances before the appearance in 1981 of Alasdair MacIntyre's *After Virtue: A Study in Moral Theory* (London: Duckworth) (see chs. 5–6. pp. 49–75).

4. Norbert Hinske and Michael Albrecht (eds.), *Was ist Aufklärug? Beiträge aus der Berlinischen Monatsschrift* (Darmstadt: Wissenschaftliche Buchgesellschaft, 1973), Ehrard Bahr, *Was ist Aufkärung? Thesen und Definition* (Stuttgart: Reclam, 1974), and James Schmidt (ed.), *What is Enlightenment? Eighteenth-Century Answers and Twentieth-Century Questions* (Berkeley and Los Angeles: University of California Press, 1996). For *Gegen-Aufklärung*, see Friedrich Nietzsche's *Nachgelassene Fragmente* of the spring and summer of 1877, in Nietzsche, *Werke: Kritische Gesamtausgabe* (Berlin: Walter de Gruyter, 1967–), sect. 4, vol. 2, p. 478, 22[17]: "Es giebt kürzere und längere Bogen in der Culturentwicklung. Der Höhe der Aufklärung entspricht die Höhe der Gegen-Aufklärung in Schopenhauer und Wagner."
5. William Barret, *Irrational Man: A Study in Existential Philosophy* (New York: Doubleday, 1958), p. 244.
6. Isaiah Berlin, *The Age of Enlightenment*, forming vol. IV of the *The Great Ages of Western Philosophy* (Boston: Houghton Miflin, 1956), ch. 8, pp. 271–5.
7. Isaiah Berlin, "The Philosophical Ideas of Giambattista Vico," in *Art and Ideas in Eighteenth-Century Italy* (Rome: Edizioni di Storia e Letteratura, 1960), pp. 156–233.
8. Isaiah Berlin, "Herder and the Enlightenment," in Earl R. Wasserman (ed.), *Aspects of the Eighteenth Century* (Baltimore: Johns Hopkins University Press, 1965), reprinted in *Encounter*, 25 (no. 1, July 1965), pp. 29–48 and (no. 2, August 1965), pp. 42–51.
9. Isaiah Berlin, *The Crooked Timber of Humanity: Chapters in the History of Ideas*, ed. Henry Hardy (London: John Murray, 1990), pp. 91–174.
10. Isaiah Berlin, "Hume and the Sources of German Anti-Rationalism," in G. P. Morice (ed.), *David Hume: Bicentennial Papers* (Edinburgh: Edinburgh University Press, 1977), reprinted in Berlin's *Against the Current: Essays in the History of Ideas*, ed. and with a bibliography by Henry Hardy, with an introduction by Roger Hausheer (London: Hogarth Press, 1979); see especially pp. 181–5.
11. "It fell dead-born from the Press," remarked Hume in his autobiography, recapitulating a line from Pope's *Epilogue to the Satires*.
12. Isaiah Berlin, *Karl Marx: His Life and Environment*, first published by Thomas Butterworth in London in 1939, of which four editions and over ten translations had been published by 1978.
13. Isaiah Berlin, "Historical Inevitability," Auguste Comte Memorial Trust Lecture no. 1 (London: Oxford University Press, 1954), and *The Hedgehog and the Fox* (London: Weidenfeld and Nicolson, 1953).
14. Isaiah Berlin, "Two Concepts of Liberty" (Oxford: Clarendon Press, 1958), most recently published in Berlin, *Liberty*, ed. Hardy (Oxford: Oxford University Press, 2002).
15. Stephen Holmes, *Benjamin Constant and the Making of Modern Liberalism* (New Haven: Yale University Press, 1984), ch. 1, "The Anatomy of Liberty," pp. 28–52, and Lionel Gossman's contribution to this volume.
16. Ernest Gellner, "Sauce for the Liberal Goose" (review of John Gray, *Isaiah Berlin*, London: Harper Collins, 1995), *Prospect* (November 1995), p. 61.
17. Isaiah Berlin, "Montesquieu," in his *Against the Current*, pp. 142, 144, and 157–8, and his "Two Concepts of Liberty," in *Liberty*, pp. 212–17.

18. Berlin's pluralism was, to my mind, inspired ultimately by his reading of both Herder and John Stuart Mill, although its connections with later philosophical doctrines have still to be traced. I am unconvinced by Michael Ignatieff's allusion in this regard (see his *Isaiah Berlin: A Life*, [London: Chatto & Windus, 1998], p. 336, n. 4) to James Fitzjames Stephen's *Liberty, Equality, Fraternity* of 1873, and I suspect that ideas associated with pluralism would in Berlin's own lifetime have come to his notice more by way of such distinctions as were made by W. D. Ross in 1930 in his account of *The Right and the Good*. Kingsley Martin, in his biography of *Harold Laski* (London: Victor Gollancz, 1953) describes what he terms "the pluralist movement" prevalent in London in the 1920s (see pp. 71–2 and 74), whose decentralist and syndicalist principles have scant connection with Berlin's pluralism. In the final chapter of *Isaiah Berlin*, Gray argues (see pp. 141–56) that value-pluralism and liberalism are inconsistent ideals, notwithstanding Berlin's endeavors to derive one from the other. But in his *Conversations* with Jahanbegloo (see p. 44) Berlin himself describes these principles as incompatible, even though he subscribes to each of them.
19. Isaiah Berlin, *Vico and Herder: Two Studies in the History of Ideas* (London: The Hogarth Press, 1976), and Berlin, *Three Critics of the Enlightenment: Vico, Hamann, Herder*, ed. H. Hardy (London: Pimlico, 2000).
20. Berlin, *Three Critics of the Enlightenment*, pp. 8–12, 13–16, 30–40, 111, 131–2, 143, and 169.
21. Berlin, *Three Critics of the Enlightenment*, pp. 57–62 and 212–13.
22. Berlin, *Three Critics of the Enlightenment*, pp. 14, 34–9, 131, 212, 233, 318, and 360.
23. Berlin, *Three Critics of the Enlightenment*, pp. 10, 55–6, 64–7, 73–8, 108, 192–6, and 314–15.
24. Berlin, *Three Critics of the Enlightenment*, pp. 15–16, 168–172, 176–7, 179–80, 189, 208–9, 224–5, and 231–9.
25. Isaiah Berlin, *The Magus of the North: J. G. Hamann and the Origins of Modern Irrationalism*, ed. H. Hardy (London: John Murray, 1993), and *Three Critics of the Enlightenment*, pp. 283–4 and 328–9. As Hardy explains in his preface (p. 246), this text has been salvaged for readers partly by way of a machine relic found in the National Science Museum and the expertise of staff at the National Sound Archive, which together made possible the reconstitution of "Dictabelt" recordings—now a defunct technology—embracing passages for which no original manuscript or typescript survived.
26. Isaiah Berlin, *The Roots of Romanticism*, the A. W. Mellon Lectures in the Fine Arts, 1965, ed. Henry Hardy (London: Chatto and Windus, 1999).
27. White, books in review, *Political Theory*, 5.1 (February 1977), pp. 124–7, and Gardiner, review essays, *History and Theory*, XVI.1 (1977), pp. 45–51. While largely welcoming Berlin's scholarship, William Dray, however, in a critical notice, *Canadian Journal of Philosophy*, IX.1 (March 1979), pp. 179–82, doubts whether Berlin had managed to establish Vico's and Herder's significance for readers today. Among commentaries of a predominantly descriptive rather than evaluative character, see, for instance, John Michael Krois, book reviews, *Philosophy and Rhetoric*, 10.4 (Fall 1977), pp. 276–80, and James C. Morrison, "Three Interpretations of Vico," including assessments as well of Ferdinand Fellmann's *Das Vico-Axiom* and Leon Pompa's *Vico*, offering interpretations

strikingly different both from Berlin's and each other's, *Journal of the History of Ideas* XXXIX.3 (1978), pp. 511–18.
28. Scouten, book reviews, *Comparative Literature Studies*, XV.3 (1978), pp. 336–40 (especially p. 338).
29. Hans Aarsleff, "Vico and Berlin," collectively reviewing *Russian Thinkers*, *Concepts and Categories*, *Against the Current*, and *Personal Impressions*, as well as *Vico and Herder*, in the *London Review of Books*, 5–18 November 1981, pp. 6–7, succeeded by his published letter in retort to Berlin's response of 3–16 June 1982, pp. 4–5. I greatly value Aarsleff's friendship and regard his command of seventeenth- and eighteenth-century linguistics and philosophy as virtually unrivaled in the world of historical scholarship today. But, to my mind, his occasional rebuke of linguists and philosophers whose purportedly inflated self-esteem and standing he takes to be unmerited distracts from the strength of his arguments. Other critics, none more than Christopher Hitchens in an egregiously ill-tempered review of Ignatieff's biography, have not hesitated to accuse Berlin of appeasement, inactivism, or charlatanry. "Here is the rich man's John Rawls," remarks Hitchens (in the *London Review of Books*, 26 November 1998, p. 11), his aptitude for irony "conditioned ... by his long service to a multitude of masters."
30. Isaiah Berlin, "Professor Scouten on Herder and Vico," *Comparative Literature Studies*, XVI.2 (June 1979), pp. 141–5; and "Isaiah Berlin responds to the foregoing criticisms of his work" and "Isaiah Berlin writes," *London Review of Books*, 5–18 November 1981, pp. 7–8, and 3–16 June 1982, p. 5.
31. W. H. Walsh, book reviews, *Mind*, vol. LXXXVII, no. 346 (April 1978), pp. 284–6 (especially p. 286).
32. Arnaldo Momigliano, "On the Pioneer Trail," *The New York Review of Books*, 11 November 1976, pp. 33–8 (especially pp. 34 and 38).
33. Leo Strauss, *Natural Right and History* (Chicago: University of Chicago Press, 1953), introduction, pp. 2–6, and "Progress or Return? The Contemporary Crisis in Western Civilization," dating from 1952, first published in *Modern Judaism* (1981), pp. 17–45, and reprinted in Strauss, *Jewish Philosophy and the Crisis of Modernity*, ed. Kenneth Hart Green (Albany: State University of New York Press, 1997), pp. 87–136. On Berlin's assessment of Strauss, see Jahanbegloo, *Conversations with Isaiah Berlin*, pp. 31–2.
34. *British Journal for Eighteenth-Century Studies*, 3 (1980), pp. 89–106, and Berlin, *The Crooked Timber of Humanity: Chapters in the History of Ideas* (London: John Murray, 1990), pp. 70–90. Berlin's revisions first appeared in L. Pompa and W. H. Dray (eds.), *Substance and Form in History: A Collection of Essays in Philosophy of History* (Edinburgh, 1981).
35. Berlin, *The Crooked Timber of Humanity*, pp. 76–8.
36. Berlin, *The Crooked Timber of Humanity*, p. 85.
37. Berlin, "Two Concepts of Liberty," in *Liberty*, p. 212.
38. The "Ionian fallacy," as he termed it, was first discussed by Berlin in 1950 in his essay on "Logical Translation" published in the *Proceedings of the Aristotelian Society*. It is treated in some detail by Claude Galipeau on pp. 50–58 of his *Isaiah Berlin's Liberalism* (Oxford: Clarendon Press, 1994).
39. John Gray, *Enlightenment's Wake: Politics and Culture at the Close of the Modern Age* (London and New York: Routledge, 1995), and my review,

"Laying the Enlightenment to Rest," *Government and Opposition*, 32 (1997), pp. 140–5.
40. Berlin, *The Roots of Romanticism*, pp. 21–2. Variants of the same argument appear in "The Decline of Utopian Ideas in the West," in *The Crooked Timber of Humanity*, pp. 24–5, and in "Hume and the Sources of German Anti-Rationalism" in *Against the Current*, pp. 162–4.
41. Berlin, *The Age of Enlightenment*, introduction, pp. 28–9.
42. Jahanbegloo, *Conversations with Isaiah Berlin*, pp. 70–1.
43. Jacob L. Talmon, *The Origins of Totalitarian Democracy* (London: Secker & Warburg, 1952), preface, p. vii.
44. Berlin, *The Roots of Romanticism*, p. 32.
45. Richard Rorty, *Philosophy and the Mirror of Nature* (Princeton: Princeton University Press, 1980).
46. Carl H. Becker, *The Heavenly City of the Eighteenth-Century Philosophers* (New Haven: Yale University Press, 1932), pp. 29–31.
47. On this theme, see especially my "The Enlightenment, the nation-state and the primal patricide of modernity," in Norman Geras and Robert Wokler (eds.), *The Enlightenment and Modernity* (London: Macmillan Press, 2000), pp. 161–2.
48. I have drawn the last three paragraphs largely from my own "Multiculturalism and Ethnic Cleansing in the Enlightenment," in Ole Peter Grell and Roy Porter (eds.), *Toleration in Enlightenment Europe* (Cambridge: Cambridge University Press, 2000), pp. 81–2.
49. See my "*La Querelle des Bouffons* and the Italian Liberation of France: A Study of Revolutionary Foreplay," *Studies in the Eighteenth Century*, 6, special issue of *Eighteenth-Century Life*, 11 (1987), pp. 94–116.
50. I have in mind here Wolfgang Pröss's edition of Herder's *Ideen zur Philosophie der Geschichte der Menschheit* (München: Hanser, 2002).
51. Berlin, *Three Critics of the Enlightenment*, pp. 281 and 328.
52. On this point, if I read him correctly, I largely subscribe to Aarsleff's interpretation of a central tradition of Enlightenment linguistics and philosophy, inspired by Leibniz and embracing Locke, Condillac, and Süssmilch, which he takes to have been misconstrued by other commentators, sometimes, as with regard not only to Berlin but also Noam Chomsky, because he regards them as skewed by nineteenth-century perspectives on the course of European intellectual history.
53. I have borrowed this remark from Mark Lilla.
54. In 1992 Jacques Derrida was awarded a highly contested honorary doctorate from Cambridge, by way of an unprecedented vote forced mainly by the university's philosophers, triumphing with 336 votes in his favor against 204.
55. See especially the sixth chapter of Gray's *Isaiah Berlin*, pp. 141–68.
56. Martin Heidegger, *Sein und Zeit*, seventh edition (Tübingen: Max Niemayer Verlag, 1953), p. 348, and Ernst Cassirer, *The Myth of the State* (New Haven: Yale University Press, 1946), p. 293.
57. Ignatieff, *Isaiah Berlin: A Life*, ch. 11, pp. 148–69.
58. Isaiah Berlin, "A Remarkable Decade. IV: Alexander Herzen" (first published in *Encounter* in the mid-1950s), in *Russian Thinkers*, ed. Henry Hardy and Aileen Kelly, with an introduction by Kelly (London: Hogarth Press, 1978), p. 189.

59. Isaiah Berlin, *The Hedgehog and the Fox* (London: Weidenfeld & Nicolson, 1953), pp. 46 and 79.
60. See especially Berlin's commemorations of L. B. Namier and J. L. Austin in his *Personal Impressions*, ed. Henry Hardy, with an introduction by Noel Annan (London: Hogarth Press, 1980), pp. 63–82 and 101–15.
61. As recounted by Simon Schama at a meeting commemorating Berlin's life and work held in New York's Harvard Club in 1998.
62. Isaiah Berlin, "Jewish Slavery and Emancipation," in *The Power of Ideas*, ed. Henry Hardy (London: Chatto & Windus, 2000), pp. 169–70.
63. Ignatieff, *Isaiah Berlin: A Life*, p. 234.
64. Isaiah Berlin, "The Origins of Israel" (first published by the Anglo-Israel Association in 1953), and "Jewish Slavery and Emancipation," in *The Power of Ideas*, pp. 150 and 164.
65. Avishai Margalit, "Address delivered at the Commemoration in the Sheldonian Theatre, Oxford on 21st March 1998," and Margalit, "The Crooked Timber of Nationalism," in Ronald Dworkin, Mark Lilla, and Robert B. Silvers (eds.), *The Legacy of Isaiah Berlin* (New York: New York Review of Books, 2001), pp. 151–2.
66. See my "Multiculturalism and Ethnic Cleansing in the Enlightenment" in *Toleration in Enlightenment Europe*, pp. 69–85.
67. See the sixth of Voltaire's *Lettres philosophiques*. This text, incidentally, on account of its description of Presbyterians who only preach through their nose when they return to Scotland where they constitute the majority, might be said to form the Enlightenment's reply to Alasdair MacIntyre's *After Virtue*.
68. Isaiah Berlin, "The Life and Opinions of Moses Hess," in *Against the Current*, pp. 237–40, and *Three Critics of the Enlightenment*, pp. 296–7 and 309.
69. Isaiah Berlin "Moses Hess," in *Against the Current*, pp. 245 and 249.
70. On the circumstances surrounding the composition of Cassirer's work and its defense of the German Enlightenment, see especially my "Ernst Cassirer's Enlightenment: An Exchange with Bruce Mazlish," in *Studies in Eighteenth-Century Culture*, 29 (2000), pp. 335–48, and Kent Wright, "'A Bright Clear Mirror': Cassirer's *The Philosophy of the Enlightenment*," in K. M. Baker and P. H. Reill (eds.), *What's Left of Enlightenment? A Postmodern Question* (Stanford: Stanford University Press, 2001), pp. 71–101. Berlin reviewed the English translation of Cassirer's *Philosophie der Aufklärung*, first published in 1951, in the *English Historical Review*, 68 (1953), pp. 617–19.
71. Peter Gay, *Weimar Culture: The Outsider as Insider* (Westport, Conn.: Greenwood Publishers, 1968), p. xiv.
72. Berlin, *The Power of Ideas*, p. 165.
73. Jahanbegloo, *Conversations with Isaiah Berlin*, p. 21.
74. Perry Anderson, "Components of the National Culture," *New Left Review*, 50 (July–August 1968), pp. 3–57.
75. Anderson, "Components of the National Culture," p. 3.
76. Anderson, "Components of the National Culture," pp. 7–8 and 15–19.
77. Isaiah Berlin, "Winston Churchill in 1940," "President Franklin Delano Roosevelt," and "Chaim Weizmann," in Berlin, *Personal Impressions* (London 1981), pp. 16, 31, 52–3 and 62.
78. Konrad Kalejs, allegedly a member of the Arajs Kommando Unit responsible for the murder of thousands of Latvian Jews during the Second World War,

returned to Australia in January 2000 after a long stay in a retirement home in Leicestershire. He died in Melbourne the following year.

79. Quentin Skinner, *Liberty before Liberalism* (Cambridge: Cambridge University Press, 1998), pp. 113–16.

80. These remarks, initially prepared in January 2000 for the Oxford Political Thought Conference and the Tel Aviv symposium on "Isaiah Berlin's Counter-Enlightenment" from which this collection is drawn, were also delivered the following March as a public lecture at the Central European University in Budapest and subsequently for the political theory seminar at Harvard University directed by Harvey Mansfield. In their original format, and virtually without annotation, they were published in the second *Jewish Studies Yearbook* of the Central European University in 2002. I am grateful to Joshua Cherniss, Henry Hardy, Roger Hausheer, Joseph Mali, and Wolfgang Pröss for supplying me with several leads and references.

3 | Enlightening the Enlightenment

Roger Hausheer

Isaiah Berlin never left the world in any doubt about where he stood vis-à-vis the eighteenth-century Enlightenment and its legacy. Broadly speaking, he saw himself as one of its proponents and continuators. "The intellectual power, honesty, lucidity, courage and disinterested love of the truth of the most gifted thinkers of the eighteenth century," he once wrote, "remain to this day without parallel. Their age is one of the best and most hopeful episodes in the life of mankind."[1] But, like any genuine friend or sincere family member, Berlin could be as unsparing towards those morally and intellectually close to him, whether contemporary or dead and gone, as he was profoundly well-informed about their innermost character and habits. He seemed to believe that among the most precious gifts available to human beings, painfully difficult to give but still more painfully difficult to accept, is the truth about themselves. In any event, he placed the highest possible value upon self-knowledge. And since both love and hate in their very different ways sharpen human vision, he did not hesitate to abandon the rose-tinted spectacles of intimacy and affection for the remorseless telescopes and microscopes and the deadly instruments of night-time vision wielded by the enemy. *Sapere aude!* Kant's slogan for the Enlightenment probably never had a more faithful practitioner.

But one of the consequences of Berlin's almost Nietzschean daring and passion for hunting down and stating the truth *quand-même*, is that the Enlightenment also never had a friend and supporter with fewer illusions about it or with a profounder knowledge of its potentially fatal weaknesses. And it is precisely this ruthless engagement with the Enlightenment that has given rise to so much misunderstanding about Berlin and the Enlightenment. His almost preternatural bent for sliding into the skins and acquiring the eyes and hearts of its most savage and effective opponents, and then retailing their worlds *in toto* with consummate literary skill and moral and mental conviction in short, sharp, vibrantly memorable essays rather than interminable gray tomes, has misled many an erudite but unwary critic friendly to the Enlightenment into identifying Berlin as one of its most subtle and insidious enemies. Likewise, there have been, and are, enemies of

Enlightenment reason and universalism who have seen in him one of their *confrères*. In what follows I shall clarify a little this curious and highly complex relationship.

Before doing so, some biographical and quasi-sociological considerations might be in place. With the exception of Rousseau, no doubt, and to a much lesser degree, perhaps, Diderot, the great leaders of the French Enlightenment were on the whole socially secure and firmly rooted in what they took to be the cosmopolitan (i.e. French) civilization of their place and time. They were French, they were upper class if not aristocratic, they were universal. Problems of identity, status, and position were much less likely to arise for them, if at all. The pattern of their allegiances tended therefore to be correspondingly simpler, more homogeneous and unified, and their vision of the world and of the human past, present, and future more harmonious and serene, for all that many were engaged in a fierce and dangerous battle against the *ancien régime*. Nor had the world yet gone through the harrowing collective educational process of the French Revolution, the Russian Revolution, the great European Wars, and mass industrialization. By contrast, the tug and pull of Berlin's three major allegiances and identities was among the most important formative factors of his life and gave him an early existential jolt out of any comfortable rut. He felt himself, and in his life revealed himself to be, at one and the same time fully a Jew, a Russian, and an Englishman.[2] It was perhaps this early collision in the heart and mind of a supremely intelligent and sensitive man that first stimulated his active interest in the cluster of central human problems that preoccupied him all his life, and were instrumental in leading him to disengage himself from some of the principal Enlightenment positions. To him such positions were palpably too smooth, simplistic, rational, universalistic, and, for the most part, blandly optimistic. His own early life was profoundly disrupted by one of the two great political storms of the twentieth century, and his early middle years were dominated by his experience of the war and his work as a political analyst attached to the British Embassy in Washington, and then in Moscow. Also, though he rarely spoke of this, no account of his life can leave out the persecution and loss of many close relatives in the Nazi Holocaust and under Soviet tyranny. There is therefore an authentic quality to everything he says about the great issues of our time that is often lacking in the writings of academic practitioners of social and political thought. And if, as he claimed, he is indeed essentially an Enlightenment figure, he should be seen as one who is older and wiser than his eighteenth-century forebears.

In addition to these outward circumstances, which were so propitious to his intensive study of the perennial human problems, there was his unique intellectual temperament, his astounding capacity for what might perhaps be termed objective empathy, or what Keats called "negative capability." He possessed qualities of mind and heart of a type best exemplified by some of the great creative writers, like Shakespeare or Balzac. This creativity is evident not just in the all-embracing sweep of his vision, or in his inexhaustible sense of detail and nuance, but also and above all in his uncanny ability to enter into and recreate, to *become*, as it were, some of the central figures he studied and wrote about. It was this capacity for a kind of higher mimicry, for self-transposition into the minds and temperaments of radically differing types in other times and places, which made of him a master navigator of the modern condition: a man who set out to explore and map, objectively and exactly, the oceanic depths and continental contours of the European mind from the Enlightenment onwards.

I.

Berlin's early philosophical development was strongly influenced by the dry, ahistorical, analytical empiricism of the British tradition. His own account of the informal dialectical clashes between himself and his friends, Ayer and Austin among others, involving minute technical points and sharply astringent logic, is very revealing.[3] But in marked contrast with his Oxford philosophical colleagues, he had from the start displayed a boundless curiosity about the endless diversity of human life. This interest in history, literature, and the arts, in politics and social life, in gossip and intimate self-revelation, in every conceivable expression of human existence and behavior, grew with time. In contrast to most of his philosophical contemporaries, he moved easily in the medium of the major European languages and their literary and philosophical cultures. He was driven by an almost Faustian desire to taste at first hand the teeming variety of human existence. This very Jewish passion for knowledge for its own sake, for the pursuit of truth in all its manifestations, was the prime motive for his abandonment of pure philosophy in the 1950s. He announced that "I gradually came to the conclusion that I should prefer a field in which one could hope to know more at the end of one's life than when one had begun; and so I left philosophy for the field of the history of ideas, which had for many years been of absorbing interest to me."[4]

Already in the course of writing his book on Marx in the 1930s, Berlin had encountered the scientific, naturalistic, sociological approach of the thinkers of the French Enlightenment.[5] As an empiricist and a believer in rationalist methods himself, he was bound to find something agreeable and superficially attractive about their approach. The sweeping away of theology and metaphysics, superstition, tradition, and blind authority, were a major part of the general critical activity in which he and his friends saw themselves as being engaged. There was after all something not unconvincing about the Comteian schema of the progress of human knowledge: first came mathematics, then physics and astronomy, followed in turn by chemistry, biology, psychology, sociology, and so on up the scale to the scientific study of ever higher levels of complexity and organization; each successive stage requiring and building upon its predecessor, to form the seamless whole of the completed edifice. Why should there not be a science of man, history, and society on a par with the Newtonian system in physics? Indeed Comte's eighteenth-century predecessor, Condorcet, had explicitly looked forward to the day when there would be a naturalistic sociology to study human beings as the life sciences study bees and beavers.[6] And indeed it was this scientific rationalist Enlightenment programme that had formed the principal intellectual inspiration of the French Revolution. Yet for all that the Revolution swept like a cleansing storm through Europe, transforming the old order and liberating whole groups and classes of human beings (and unleashing hitherto repressed areas of the collective psyche), it did anything but achieve its positive goal of a lasting, stable, rational social organization based on liberty, equality, fraternity throughout the civilized world. Indeed, a great part of the work of Comte and even of Marx can be understood as an attempt to find out where the

French Revolution went wrong and to discover methods and principles of a still more rational, still more scientific kind, that would guarantee success the next time round.

But by the time Berlin came to write his book on Marx, it was at least absolutely clear to him that the most recent heir of the scientistic Enlightenment tradition, namely the Bolshevik Revolution built upon Marxist-Leninist principles, had spawned an oppressive iron dictatorship which made even the excesses of the French Revolutionary era pale by comparison. Berlin was thus among the very few Western intellectuals who, from the very start, could see that there was something radically amiss—and generally something askew in principle—at the heart of this entire approach to the study of man, society, and human history.[7] But what exactly was it?

II.

As always, Berlin finds answers to the problems that trouble him in an attentive study of the relevant portions of history. It was while working on Marx that he was brought into contact with the whole tradition of eighteenth- and nineteenth-century thought in German-speaking lands, and it was immediately apparent to him—as it had been to the great German intellectual historians who are his true precursors[8]—that a great part of the most original and revolutionary thinking in those times and places developed in reaction against the French Enlightenment spirit and its later progeny. One wave after another of writers, thinkers, movements, and schools of thought, had rebelled against the entire rationalist, universalistic, scientific outlook. To treat human beings naturalistically as nothing but objects of science was to offend against the most important truth about them, namely that they are free and creative, and was guaranteed to provoke a furious response from those so treated. Thus, it was to the enemies of the Enlightenment—and the more violent, sharp-sighted, and systematically critical, the better they were—that Berlin was now drawn, half in terror and half in admiration, but always with an ultimate inner detachment, seeking insight into the causes of the foundering of a general movement with whose overall ambitions for greater clarity and light, reason and humanity, he was in total sympathy—even if he had himself begun to entertain the most serious doubts over some of its dogmatic, unexamined assumptions about the nature of human beings.[9]

Among the basic assumptions of the rational, scientific, Enlightenment approach to the world, both of nature and of man, is the belief that everything can and should be studied with objective detachment as inert material which can be exhaustively described, classified, or brought under covering causal laws. For the purposes of scientific investigation, the world is conceived of as possessing no independent life of its own outside the system of scientific laws that govern its behavior, or beyond the exhaustive classificatory schema into which it falls. Whether it is Newtonian physics accounting for the movements of physical bodies or Linnaean botany meticulously describing plants, such methods of study explicitly rule out and exclude the unaccountable, the unpredictable, the undescribable. They are by their very nature fixed and deterministic. In the case of physics, for example, which for the Enlightenment was the science par excellence, there can be absolutely no question of final causes or purposes, of things possessing inner lives and consciously pursuing ideals, but only of causal regularities. (Here I am of course referring to classical physics of the kind that inspired eighteenth-century thinkers.) No doubt Aristotle was guilty of anthropomorphism when he attributed final causes to literally everything in the universe, including the universe itself; but the nefarious general tendency of the thinkers in the new tradition—which had first emerged in the Renaissance, which was most powerfully embodied in the sciences established by Galileo and Newton, and which, through the French Enlightenment and after, had come to dominate literally every field of human thought and investigation—was to eliminate final causes not just from those areas where they do not properly belong, but from the scheme of things altogether, even from that corner of the universe where they originate and are specifically at home, namely the human realm. The austerity of this approach, not to say its absurdity, comes out very clearly when we try to adopt it in the study of human history and culture. When it comes to dominate political practice, tragedy is the inevitable result.

More generally still, as Berlin saw it (and he returned to this again and again in his writings), the new scientific world-picture, purged of purposive categories of all kinds, as well as the generalized Enlightenment view that grew out of it, rested upon three central presuppositions common to systematic Western thought since the time of Plato. The first is that the cosmos and everything in it, including human beings, represents a single harmonious whole whose structure is objectively given and exists independently of any and all observers; the second, that with sufficient intelligence and determination we can discover the appropriate methods and procedures for establishing what this structure is, and thereby gain answers to all our questions both of theory (concerning fact, the way things are in the widest sense) and of practice (concerning values and how we should live and act both as individuals and larger groups); and finally, that once we have discovered these fixed truths about the ultimate and unvarying structure of things we will find ourselves in possession of a neat, seamless, logically coherent body of knowledge, where no proposition contradicts another. It was these monolithic presuppositions that Berlin spent so much of his life worrying and writing about. At times he attacked them directly in his own voice; at other times he exposed their shortcomings in ways that were necessarily historical and indirect, for example, by subjecting to sympathetic but unsparing critical examination the ideas of some of their most formidable opponents. In performing his task, Berlin has, as it were, conducted a gigantic campaign in which the specifically human realm of values—where freedom, choice, self-conscious purposive action, self-understanding, self-creation, and self-interpretation are the defining core of things—is decisively liberated from the alien rule of science and generalizing methods. This is the reason he set such store by the existence of some types of radical, nondeterministic freedom and inveighed against the hard-boiled determinism of Holbach and Helvétius and their modern successors. His penetrating essay, "From Hope and Fear Set Free,"[10] for example, represents in this respect a resounding blow to one of the central orthodoxies running through the greater part of Western philosophy from the ancient Stoics to the present day, an orthodoxy which reached its high point in the writings of some of the major Enlightenment thinkers.

Equally powerful is Berlin's defense of freedom at a collective and historical level, a preoccupation which informs his passionate and celebrated essay

"Historical Inevitability." It is an interesting question whether any of the major Enlightenment thinkers was without his own more or less deterministic theory of history. In any event, Berlin attacks all deterministic theories of history, whether metaphysical like those of Hegel and his idealistic heirs, or positivistic like those of Comte and his many contemporary successors to the present day, or those which, while being wholly materialist, nevertheless combine elements of both, such as Marxism. In all of these human history is seen as obeying an unalterable pattern. Such views are partly inspired by the success of the natural sciences in their respective spheres, partly by a misapplication of the deep-rooted category of teleology (according to which all things are not merely as they are, but, like individual human beings, also pursue purposes), and not least by the perennial desire of human beings to abdicate personal responsibility. With great thoroughness and acuity Berlin exposes all these positions as being utterly dogmatic and unempirical. And it might be noted parenthetically that the history of the past decade or more has scarcely belied his judgment.

Always, however, whether dealing with deterministic theories of history or with the question of individual free will as such, Berlin points to a much more general and much deeper set of arguments against the thesis that our lives are determined either as isolated individuals or as functions in the processes of historical wholes. These arguments take us to the very core of his vision of man and of the essence of human nature, and furnish a major key to his peculiar approach to human studies. Very few modern thinkers since Kant have been quite so intensely aware of the truth that to understand human beings and their knowledge of themselves and their world one must first understand the central constitutive categories that motivate them. After Kant it became a commonplace that there is a framework of categories by which we and our world are in some sense bounded, and that these categories establish absolute limits of and for human life. We perceive, think, sense, feel, and act within and in terms of these categories, and while by virtue of philosophical reflection we can become aware of them, they cannot, as constitutive categories—that is, the foundations upon which everything else rests, including scientific theories—be made the objects of study by empirical science without fatal circularity. There are not many thinkers who are much preoccupied with peering intently into their own inner subjectivity, and those who are find it hard to sustain for any period of time. This reflexive act of self-dwelling, this turning back of the inner eye upon itself, of which Kant (some would add Descartes) was the systematic pioneer and by far the greatest master—can be extended in two main directions. It can be pressed deeper and deeper into the realm of subjectivity itself, revealing its basic structures with increasing depth and refinement, as Husserl, Heidegger, Bergson, Merleau-Ponty, Sartre, and others have sought to do; or it can explore the emergence in the historical realm of some of the deepest presuppositions about what we are (and should be) as human beings, as thinkers from Vico and Herder to Dilthey, Windelband, Troeltsch, Meinecke, and others have done. In any event, none of these thinkers, not even Kant in any straightforward sense, despite his famous essay of that title, can easily be categorized as an Enlightenment thinker or as adopting Enlightenment methods. For they depart too sharply from Enlightenment scientific naturalism as well as from epistemological monism and value universalism for that.

While Berlin's great (and, in the English-speaking world, incomparable) contribution has lain largely in conceptual archeology in the historical sphere, what he says, however obliquely and impressionistically, about the reflexive subject is also of the first interest. As intensely as any German *Lebens-* or *Existenzphilosoph* from Jacobi to Heidegger or Bollnow, but with far less portentousness and metaphysical fog, Berlin indicates that we all possess as humans a primordial sense of reality, a being in being, which is prior to all further thought, reflection, and rational analysis, including predictive science, and upon which these rest. The pages where this conviction shines forth clearly—for example, in "Historical Inevitability," in the last two or three sections of "The Hedgehog and the Fox," in "The Sense of Reality," and in various other places—are among the most luminous Berlin ever wrote.[11]

This primitive sense of some form of primal subjective being or agency that precedes all else is a very strong theme in Berlin. It seems to be for him the ultimate root both of our conviction that we are free beings in some absolutely nondeterministic sense and also constitutive of our essential human nature at the very deepest level. Indeed, so basic is it, that our entire moral vocabulary rests upon it, and basic terms like responsibility, praise, guilt, remorse, regret, desert, and others, stand or fall with it. We literally cannot think it away or else we will at the same time think away so much of our humanity, of our bedrock sense of what it is to be a human being in the world, that the attempt to do so is an impossibility—an impossibility of a type not merely logical or psychological, but *sui generis* and deeper than either. To seek to explain in causal or any other terms this not-further-analyzable "categorial" awareness is like trying to balance the base of the mountain on its summit. There is a peculiarly compelling, almost Sartrean, existential agony in those pages of "Historical Inevitability" where Berlin struggles in vain to envisage a world where everything, including the thoughts which are trying to envisage it, is determined through and through. He is living through the nightmare as he tries to state it.

There are then very compelling reasons why human beings cannot be studied just as natural objects exhaustively explainable by natural science or the disciplines modeled on it. In "The Concept of Scientific History" in particular, Berlin offers a comprehensive survey of the principal ways in which history differs from science, and spells out in detail the reasons why a science of history on a par with, say, Newtonian physics is a conceptual impossibility.[12] This essay, taken together with "Does Political Theory Still Exist?,"[13] offers something like a program for the type of history of ideas which he advocates. For human beings interpret themselves in terms of very general models and their associated categories. Some of these are as old as humanity itself and so virtually universal. Others change, and sometimes quite radically, through historical time. The Western tradition of political thought, for example, has seen a succession of such models. As a model or models come to seem antiquated, or are seen to do too little justice to the altering patterns of experience, they are replaced by others. Such models often overlap or clash; but one thing is certain, and that is that no single model, no matter how deep, penetrating, and sophisticated, can ever encompass the whole of experience once and for all. Each is exclusive and at best casts light on a portion of human life for a period of time. But unlike scientific theories which have been superseded, such systems of concepts and categories remain of permanent interest and value.

For each opens its own special doors to human self-understanding, and it should be a central preoccupation of both philosophers and historians of ideas in each generation (and a part of the education of any civilized human) to ask critical normative questions of these models in relation to the unique problems of their own day. Berlin spent his entire adult life engaged in this activity and, not surprisingly, came up with some very remarkable and deeply transforming results.

III.

Virtually all of Berlin's work in the history of ideas revolves around what he sees as the greatest revolution in our concepts and categories since the Renaissance and the Reformation: the rebellion against monism in all fields of human thought and action. This does not of course entail a crude chronological break—first universal monism, then suddenly universal pluralism. For he is very careful to allow that there were skeptics and relativists from antiquity onwards, but they were largely marginal and did not deflect the main rationalist current.[14] The full statement of anti-monist positions and their immense practical impact had to wait for later thinkers, and even now the full implications of these for theory and practice are still working themselves out with unforeseeable consequences. Moreover, as Berlin often notes, the monist presuppositions of two millennia which were at the core of the French Enlightenment still (more or less) dominate our contemporary culture, though they now exist uneasily side by side with, and are perhaps increasingly succumbing to, the powerful pluralistic (and relativistic) currents released by the Counter-Enlightenment and German Romanticism.[15]

A major part of Berlin's work in the history of ideas has been to identify some of the principal moments in this process. Among the thinkers who most powerfully exemplify (albeit unaware of the vast consequences of what he was doing) the earliest shifts in our conceptual bedrock is Machiavelli.[16] According to Berlin, Machiavelli was probably the very first to juxtapose starkly two coherent, all-embracing, objectively valid but mutually exclusive systems of morality: the Christian ethics of his time and ours which aim at the perfection of the individual life and preach meekness, self-abnegation, and renunciation of this life for the next; and those of the Greek polis and Republican Rome which aim at the power and glory of the body politic and aspire to self-assertion and self-fulfillment in this life. The critical consideration is that no criteria exist for choosing between these two equally valid but totally incompatible systems. It is this, and not Machiavelli's "Machiavellianism," which, according to Berlin, has exercised the civilized world ever since. In the early modern world it marks the first irreparable fracture in the belief in a single universal structure of values binding on all mankind.

It is this concern of Berlin's with the massive collective shift in mind-sets that makes Vico an object of such inexhaustible fascination to him.[17] On Berlin's interpretation of him, this strange, isolated genius, born long before and long after his time, traced unerringly all the chinks in the monist edifice into which the revolutionary movements of the coming two hundred years were to drive fatal wedges. Vico was the first to state explicitly that human beings do not possess an unalterable essence; that they understand their own works and the world of history which they themselves make, in a way in which they cannot understand the world of external nature; that there is therefore a distinction to be drawn between the knowledge which we acquire of things and actions from the inside (as their creators and agents), and that which we acquire of them from the outside by observation, experiment, and scientific inference; that a society or culture has a pervasive pattern by which all its products are marked or "coloured," and that cultures move through identifiable phases of growth and development from childhood through maturity to old age; that all human institutions and activities, even the most severely practical and utilitarian, are never just that, but also vital forms of self-expression; that therefore timeless principles and standards in art or life are not available and that every human manifestation should be judged by the canons of its own time and place, of the specific phase reached by its own culture; that finally a new distinction among the varieties or types of human knowledge must be added to the two types traditionally distinguished (a priori-deductive and a posteriori-empirical), namely a form of "inner" knowledge by which we enter into the mental universe of other ages and peoples by what Vico calls *fantasia* or acts of reconstructive imagination. The implications of all this for Berlin's own conception of intellectual and cultural history will be very apparent: the works of Vico are the womb from which sprang the cardinal distinction between the sciences and the humanities, a distinction which has suffered a curious neglect in the Anglo-Saxon world. (Apart from Collingwood and Berlin, who has taken it seriously?) This is the seed of the doctrines of *Einfühlen* and *Verstehen* later developed by Herder and after him by the great German historicists, Dilthey, Windelband, Troeltsch, Simmel, Scheler, Meinecke, Max Weber, and their many colleagues. No modern thinker has thrown more light upon the historical genesis and precise philosophical status of that distinction than Berlin, with more than a hint that failure on a grand scale by our uncompromisingly technological civilization to appreciate it for what it is constitutes one of the major and rapidly growing ills of our times. However that may be, the fatal consequence that follows from it for monism is that if an unbridgeable gap exists between the natural sciences and humanistic studies, and if the latter can therefore never in principle be reduced to the former, then a breach has been made in the two-thousand-year-old dogma that all knowledge must form a seamless, systematically interconnected whole. The Enlightenment and neo-positivist dream of a unified science of all there is is a creature that belongs properly in the realms of philosophical mythology.

It is above all in the German-speaking world of the second half of the eighteenth century that Berlin sees the great antinomian revolt first beginning to take a real hold on life, with incalculable theoretical and practical consequences. The writers of the *Sturm und Drang* movement of the 1770s, for example, Lenz, Klinger, Gerstenberg, Leisewitz, and the very young Goethe, in their chaotic and turbid plays (and lives) railed against all forms of social and political organization; and in every sphere of human life rejected rules as such, not because they were unjust, or authoritarian, or irrational, but because, as rules, they addressed the general, which is a fiction, and not the concrete, which alone is true. But it was above all the great counter-rationalist Hamann who was the first to say all this very consciously.[18] Systematic abstraction of any kind filled him with blind rage. Scientific hypotheses and generalizations had for him at very best an instrumental value; they could not yield unassailable knowledge. Such knowledge was always concrete and specific, given to us only by the senses and by spontaneous imagination, instinct, and insight. The lover and the poet understand the world, not the scientist. Everything worth knowing is known by direct perception alone—by our immediate, not-further-analyzable sense of reality. Hamann's theory of language, which struck Berlin with especial force, and according to which language does not map the objectively given features of a preexistent timeless reality but rather creates its own unique world in place and time (with the implication that there are as many worlds as there are languages), has a remarkably modern (and for that matter, postmodern) ring.[19]

No one felt the impact of Hamann's original vision more forcibly than Herder, who for Berlin is of absolute central importance.[20] For Herder uncovered some of the major categories that have literally transformed the modern world, and thereby made a permanent contribution to human self-understanding. He is the true originator of three utterly novel ideas: populism, or the belief that men can realize themselves fully only when they belong to an identifiable group or culture with roots in a common language, tradition, custom, and common historical memories; expressionism, or the notion that all men's works "are above all voices speaking," forms of expression or communication, which convey a total vision of life; and finally pluralism, which renders logically incoherent the belief in a universally valid, ideal path to human fulfillment sought with varying degrees of success by all men at all times and places. After these two seminal thinkers, Vico and Herder, nothing was ever to be quite the same again.

IV.

From the first quarter of the nineteenth century onwards, particularly in the German lands, a new and immensely powerful image bound itself upon the European imagination. Berlin threw much light on this development in essays such as "The Apotheosis of the Romantic Will"[21] and "The Counter-Enlightenment,"[22] as well as in his posthumously published Mellon Lectures, *The Roots of Romanticism*,[23] which contains his most sustained account of it. Successive waves of German writers and thinkers went to greater and greater lengths in their rejection of the entire notion of objectivity as such. In this they left figures like Vico and Herder far behind. This rejection pertained not only to the realms of ethics and aesthetics, but also to the very existence of the external world, objective reality itself. A radical shift of categories occurred, a great revolution of the spirit, where will usurps the function of intellect, and free, quasi-artistic creation replaces scientific discovery. Though this shift began in the sphere of literature, art, and music, and in relations between people in private life, it soon overflowed into politics and social life with (ultimately) catastrophic results. The central figure in this scenario for Berlin was Fichte. His voluntarist philosophy of the absolute ego that creates literally everything inaugurated an epoch. Poets, philosophers, artists, statesmen, and divines were intoxicated by it. The heroic individual imposing his will on nature or society became the dominant model. The notion of the self as an active, creative principle freely generating its own values and goals and the material—nature—upon which it operates, came to inform many and very diverse moral, artistic, and political movements.

From the heroic and defiant figures of Schiller's early plays and poems and the tragic heroes of Kleist, to the works of Tieck, Arnim, and Hoffmann, we have ever more insistent attacks on the objective system builders. In Tieck especially, whose plays and novellas play fast and loose with time, space, and causality, Berlin sees the true originator of the Theatre of the Absurd. In the works of Hoffmann, where all things become totally fluid, suspended in a state of perfect virtuality and where no boundaries exist, and anything may turn into anything else, we see unmistakable premonitions of full-blown early twentieth-century German Expressionism. Again, Fichte's image of man as a demiurge inspired Carlyle and Nietzsche and had a fateful impact on the ideologies of Fascism and National Socialism. Even the Marxist doctrine of the dignity of labor, and the heroic, Romantic vision of man as a creative being, united together with his fellows in a vast collective assault upon nature with a view to molding it to human ends, owes something to this current of ideas. Voluntarism, dynamism, self-assertion dominate the scene. This, surely, is the birthplace of Fascism, pragmatism, existentialism, subjectivism, relativism, and many later currents of counter-rationalist, counter-Enlightenment thought. Here the will finally triumphs over the intellect, knowledge is demoted to the status of hand-servant to our practical purposes, and the world is but the image cast by our total life-projects. Above all, heroism and martyrdom, the absolute status of integrity, sincerity, authenticity, and the unique light within, are the values around which lives are henceforth lived. Ends are created, not discovered. The truth or falsehood of an ideal is no longer thought to be important, or even to be a question at all.

In particular, this is the birthplace of nationalism, a subject to which Berlin devoted some of his most prescient essays.[24] As a coherent doctrine, it emerged for the first time in the modern world in the pages of Herder: for him, and those Germans he influenced, the archenemy was French universalism and materialism. Berlin sees Herder's thought as, on the one hand, a comprehensive rejection of the doctrine that universal rational rules governing theory and practice could be discovered, and, on the other, a traumatic reaction on the part of the Germans to the condescending attitude towards them of the politically, culturally, scientifically, and militarily superior French. This natural response of wounded pride on the part of a backward people vis-à-vis a more advanced one is an early and typical case of an attitude which was to become increasingly prevalent in the nineteenth century, and has become a worldwide syndrome in our own time. Yet in the case of Herder the sense of nationhood and of belonging to a continuous culture and language is still benign and in some sense universal: he does not subscribe to the idea of the unavoidability of conflict among nations and believes that they can (and should) exist peacefully and productively side by side. The Enlightenment element in his outlook is still strong. But it is when the free, creative Fichtean self of the German Romantics—initially identified with the inspired individual artist—takes on collective forms (as tends to happen with a kind of inner logic which Berlin explores in "Two Concepts of Liberty"[25]), and becomes identified with a nation, race, or culture, or some other supra-personal entity, that clashes to the death occur. Each such separate "self" creates and pursues its own independent goals. These it will seek to realize—and against all comers. In the absence of universal rational criteria of adjudication, of universal moral standards or norms, the war of all against all inevitably ensues. This is aggressive nationalism with a vengeance, and from there to Fascism and National Socialism it is but a short step.

V.

No one grasped this great mutation of ideas more fully than Berlin. No one traced its principal twists and turns with greater skill and erudition. And no one, it has to be admitted, entered into the minds and hearts of some of its major figures with greater empathy and understanding. When he writes, for example, about one of the great harbingers of Fascism, de Maistre, his words might sound almost like an ardent apologia.[26] And so evident is his admiration and even affection for, say, the life and work of the outrageously obscurantist archreactionary, Hamann, that the incautious could (and do) easily fall into the error of supposing that Berlin himself belongs to the irrationalist camp. But as we noted at the beginning of this essay, he repeated again and again, in conversation and in print, that he had been all his life a staunch supporter of the Enlightenment and what it stands for. What then is his own relationship to this vast body of Counter-Enlightenment ideas and doctrines which, after all, he spent much the greater part of his intellectual life unearthing and analyzing? In a sense, his work was a gigantic exercise in genealogy—his own, that is. For despite his protestations of Enlightenment leanings, it is apparent to anyone even on a cursory reading of his writings, that he himself has at least a hybrid place on the great Romantic genealogical tree he delineated, and that his own is, at best, a highly modified Enlightenment position.

At the risk of a good deal of oversimplification, perhaps the following can be said. There are five main ways in which the Counter-Enlightenment's arguments against the underlying assumptions of Western rationalism, and especially against the French Enlightenment (and its modern descendants), have radically modified, and might force us to abandon, these assumptions that have dominated Western civilization for two hundred years and more.

In the first place, these thinkers, beginning especially with Vico and Herder, undermined the two-thousand-year old rationalist faith in a single system of timeless norms binding on all men at all times and places. But where the full-blown Romantics and their progeny tended towards subjectivism and relativism, and thereby undermined the monist faith even more radically than could have been dreamt of by Vico or Herder, the latter, each in his own way, subscribed to a form of value pluralism which allowed for the flowering of a vast variety of value systems within a common human horizon. These systems may conflict with and exclude one another; values within any one system may prove uncombinable; and the consciousness of the single individual may be riven by values that are at war with one another. Yet so long as these outlooks, attitudes, and ways of life are such that we can accept, perhaps only after a great effort of imagination, that they were right for those people in those times, places, and general circumstances—and provided they do not offend against our core sense of what it is to be human—then they must be admitted into the great family of possible moral universes. It is this that Berlin has identified as objective value pluralism and it is this to which, albeit in a highly sophisticated and evolved form, he subscribes.

In the second place—and this follows from the above—the insights of these thinkers blow to pieces that faith common to so many Enlightenment thinkers and those who later carried their flag that somewhere there is one single, static, unitary pattern, floating in the future or buried in the past, which will embrace the whole of mankind. The very notion of Utopia is thereby shown to be not so much something which it is difficult (or even impossible) to realize in purely practical terms, as rather something literally inconceivable, a sheer logical impossibility, the nature of human values being what it is.

Thirdly, in "Two Concepts of Liberty," which has set the framework for all serious discussion of liberty over the past four decades (and may come to serve the liberalism of the future much as Mill's "On Liberty" has served that of the past one and a half centuries), Berlin has used these insights to develop a doctrine of liberty which is both profound and highly original (despite its obvious roots in Constant, Herzen, and Mill). In addition to all the standard liberal arguments for individual liberty, he urges that there is one consideration above all others which confers unique claims on what he identifies with great sharpness as "negative" liberty. It is that in a world where values, by their intrinsic character, are guaranteed to collide and clash and, in extreme cases, to fight it out to the death, rational solutions to problems in these areas will remain impossible in principle. Hence the rule of experts and specialists so dear to the majority of thinkers in the enlightened, mainstream Western tradition is an idle and dangerous dream. Tragic clashes and agonizing choices, so far from being pathological anomalies waiting for their cure, are a normal, ineradicable feature of the human condition. That being so, it follows that the maximum possible freedom from interference—and the consequent maximization of freedom of choice—for individuals and groups, always allowing for the claims of basic social order and some very basic values like justice, is more likely to promote human flourishing and fulfillment and mitigate frustration and pain, than any of the more "rational," "enlightened," "scientific" alternatives. Hence Berlin's eloquent plea for "negative" liberty. Hence, too, his cautionary words against "positive" liberty. The latter, he makes clear on several occasions, is a profoundly genuine and central value but, with its almost invariably monist claims, its voluntarist motives, and its collectivist implications, can all too often convert liberty into its opposite. The outcome can be oppressive tyranny where every person and every action is forced into its allotted slot in the frictionless whole. The totalitarian dictatorships of the twentieth century made this danger very plain. Both Hitler and Stalin said, and probably really believed, that they were liberating their peoples.

Fourthly, in Berlin's view Herder, and after him the Romantic revolt generally, brought to light what probably amounts to a permanent historical category, namely, the notion of "belonging," and above all of belonging to a nation. The Enlightenment, Marx, and most liberal internationalists since their time, have tended to regard the idea of nation and nationalism as a deformation of the human world and not as a natural and integral part of it. Following Herder, and developing some of his most novel insights, Berlin—virtually alone among liberal thinkers of any stature in the twentieth century—paid serious and not unsympathetic attention to this exceedingly complex human manifestation. Herder—in propounding the seminal ideas that flow from his conception of "belonging," which he was the very first thinker to formulate explicitly, namely, as the deep need of human beings for membership in a continuous cultural and historical community, rooted in its own geographical territory—literally discovered what we are increasingly being compelled to recognize as a fundamental and unaltering human requirement. If the coherent thesis built up by Berlin out of Herder's scattered insights is right, then the need to belong to, and acquire and express one's identity in and through, a concrete historical community, is a universal need which is just as deep and imperious as the need for food, drink, clothing, shelter, and procreation: deprivation of it may not prove immediately fatal, but in the long run it will wreak inevitable havoc. In a world of settled normality, nations, communities, and groups would, for Herder, in the ideal case coexist side by side in a state of happy and creative self-absorption, uninvaded, and untroubled by invidious comparisons with culturally or materially "superior" neighbors. But this deep, and even now only very partially recognized, human need has enemies of two main types: those that spring from the destructive universalizing and "reifying" tendencies of Western science and technology and Enlightenment standards generally; and those arising from radical disruption of the community by conquest, invasion, alien rule, or, in the extreme case, by expulsion from its ancestral territory and dispersal to live as an alien minority among other nations. These are the principal factors that trigger those pathological convulsions of national self-awareness that now scar the entire globe. This happened perhaps for the very first time, at any rate in the modern world, with the French domination of Germany for several centuries, ending in a climax during the Napoleonic Wars and the invasion of German territories. That led to some of the key insights developed by German thinkers into the perennial nature and needs of human communities, insights brought to light in the only way they can be, historically and from within, traced and described in terms of general categories that define human beings as such, those emerging and evolving most general features of the human lot which the history of ideas as practiced by Berlin exists to identify and record. To give but one example of something that occurred in our own time and is remarkably analogous to the early German experience, the nationalist-fundamentalist revolution in Iran, provoked by the too-rapid introduction, under the Shah, of Western outlooks and technology into a medieval, theocratic society, wrought an eruption that was wholly unpredicted by any of the conventional social scientists, for all their elaborate empirical soundings and statistical techniques; and yet it contains absolutely nothing to surprise the student of the collective learning process which Berlin so brilliantly describes. For good or evil, ancient regional and cultural identities are everywhere reawakening today. Berlin is one of the few thinkers who can equip us to analyze and understand them for what they are.

Finally, the roots of Berlin's own approach to acquiring knowledge of human beings are firmly planted in the great rebellion of the Counter-Enlightenment. No one is more aware of the variety of types of knowledge and understanding, and of their irreducibility to a single standard or pattern, nor of the immense harm that is done by the blind application to every aspect of human existence of a model that is successful in one area of experience, as, for example, of Newtonian physics by the French Enlightenment. Indeed, among the most important results of his investigations is the knowledge that the unthinking imposition upon human beings of abstract schemas drawn from alien disciplines has been both the greatest stumbling block to human self-understanding and also one of the greatest sources of human suffering. Quite independently of Adorno, Horkheimer, Habermas, and the Frankfurt School, but with vastly greater clarity and conceptual precision, Berlin has exposed the genuinely inhuman and oppressive implications of some very influential aspects of Enlightenment thought and of its Marxist and scientific successors. From first to last he was an impeccable empiricist, and on this issue, in true empiricist fashion, he subjects the Enlightenment tradition, its thought and action, to the most devastating testing available, namely, the ferocious reaction against them over the past two hundred years and more by all those human individuals and groups which have in one way or another been exposed to them. If the historian had a laboratory, this would be it. No better method exists for exposing flaws in rationalistic constructions zealously imposed on unwilling human beings.

Wherever these Enlightenment nostrums break down irretrievably before the Romantic onslaught, Berlin is prepared to concede that it must give ground. Something is all too clearly amiss with the proposed remedies. Moreover, on a very constructive note, he wants to make a virtue of necessity and to learn from the mistakes, to enlighten the Enlightenment, and to revise and enrich such key notions as "man," "human nature," "society," "culture," "history," "knowledge," "understanding," and so forth, in the light of its defeats. All these terms acquire a deeper and richer resonance than they ever had in the eighteenth century. The result is a net increase in our knowledge of what human beings are and can be (and, perhaps most importantly, cannot be made to be). In this sense, then, his intention is continuous in spirit with that of the Enlightenment, whatever radical breaks he may find it necessary to make with some of its more rigidly unempirical assumptions.

Out of this "dialectical" clash between Enlightenment and Counter-Enlightenment, then, Berlin, while poignantly aware of the savagery and violence its more extreme manifestations have caused, seeks nevertheless to salvage a great enlargement of the human spirit. In particular, it is to Vico and Herder, the German Romantics, Schlegel, Schleiermacher, and Schelling (and also no doubt to their heirs, Dilthey, Windelband, Troeltsch, Rickert, and Meinecke), that we may trace the origins of his own acute sense of those priceless forms of knowledge which we have exclusively in the purely human realm—empathy, insight, imaginative understanding, and the capacity to transpose ourselves into the lives of other human beings and to share in what they value most, regardless of the medium of expression or action. These, surely, constitute much the most sacred and valued part of our lives. Berlin refines and develops the notion of *"Verstehen"* in this sense, especially in his work on Vico, with incomparable sharpness and clarity, utilizing to the full the scrupulous logical techniques he acquired when a young man as one of the founders of Oxford philosophy.

And by a curious paradox, in tracing the earliest origins of the Counter-Enlightenment, and in analyzing and describing some of its most radical consequences in their fullest form and in their relevance to our own day, he made himself in a sense both the genealogist and consummator of that elusive but long-awaited "Newtonian Revolution" in the human studies desiderated precisely by Kant and by the thinkers of the French Enlightenment (and their descendants down almost to the present). To present Berlin as some kind of not-yet-recognized Newton in the field of the human studies would rightly be dismissed as uncritical adulation. Yet it is perhaps not too fanciful to see him as representing the summation of a series of developments, which began in the late eighteenth century, passed through the hands of a chain of thinkers, principally in the German-speaking world, and came to their fullest fruition in him. Taken together, these thinkers, who revolted in various ways and degrees against the Enlightenment ambition of treating man exclusively as an object of science like any other, attained by tortuous routes for the humanities what Newton and others were able to do for the sciences of nature by more direct paths. By turning their backs upon what they took to be the false start made by the official Enlightenment approach in this respect, they helped pave the way for an alternative approach which, in the figure of Berlin, has at last succeeded in perceiving clearly what makes the humanities the humanities and prevents them in principle from ever being homogenous with the natural sciences. The rational study of man, viewed essentially from the outside in naturalistic terms as the Enlightenment would have it, as a physical, biological, natural-historical, anatomical, neurophysiological object (all of which, it must be stressed, Berlin applauds as among the greatest triumphs of modern science), and to some degree as a psychological, sociological, anthropological, and economic animal, too, has rested upon relatively secure foundations for some time.

But here at last the study of that which makes humans most specifically human is also placed upon a rational footing and at the same time freed from the profound and damaging misconceptions by which it had so long been bedeviled. That is the study of man as a free, autonomous, consciously purposive, unpredictably creative, self-interpreting and self-transforming species, whose proper element is history and whose nature is revealed, not timelessly once and for all from the outside, but in his most basic, all-informing, developing and evolving—and sometimes violently transformed and clashing—concepts and categories, which are known, and can only be known, as it were, "from within." This has the effect, surely, of rendering the human sciences—now purified of extraneous elements both natural-physical and theological-metaphysical—as autonomous and as rationally self-transparent as they can ever be made. Their intellectual and spiritual dignity is revealed to be at least as great as that of the natural sciences, if not much greater. And the type of history of ideas which Berlin did so much to perfect, and of which he was by general consent one of the greatest masters, opens up a whole field of rational investigation in which so much is waiting to be done. The history of ideas, as Berlin himself used often to observe, is full of paradoxes. That a prime goal of the Enlightenment should eventually have been achieved by winding paths it would have found it impossible to conceive, and by intellectual personalities many of whom it would have found it impossible to comprehend, is but one of them—though a major one.

If this interpretation is anywhere near correct, then Berlin is a true patron saint of the Enlightenment, but with this great difference that, unlike the founding fathers and their more legitimate heirs, he alone has passed through the crucible of the Counter-Enlightenment and emerged transformed—shining with the light of Enlightenment more radiantly than ever. Indeed, one might go further, and feel tempted to declare him an intellectual colossus: one of the half-dozen or so deepest and most wide-ranging, most consistent and most penetrating, most richly generous and humane social and political thinkers to emerge since the Enlightenment, standing squarely within its ranks—a great seminal figure whose true status is only gradually dawning.

Notes

1. Isaiah Berlin, Introduction to *The Age of Enlightenment: The Eighteenth Century Philosophers*, selected, with and introduction and interpretive comments by Isaiah Berlin (New York: Houghton Miffin, 1956), p. 29.

2. Isaiah Berlin, "The Three Strands in My Life," *Jewish Quarterly* 27 [2–3] (Summer/Autumn 1979), pp. 5–7.
3. Isaiah Berlin, "J. L. Austin and the Early Beginnings of Oxford Philosophy," *Personal Impressions*, ed. Henry Hardy, with an introduction by Noel Annan (London: Hogarth Press, 1980), pp. 101–15.
4. Isaiah Berlin, *Concepts and Categories: Philosophical Essays*, ed. Henry Hardy, with an introduction by Bernard Williams (London: Hogarth Press, 1978), p. xii.
5. Isaiah Berlin, *Karl Marx: His Life and Environment*, 4th ed. (London: Oxford University Press, 1978), pp. 27–33.
6. Isaiah Berlin, "Historical Inevitability," in *Four Essays on Liberty* (London: Oxford University Press, 1969), pp. 42–43.
7. Ramin Jahanbegloo, *Conversations with Isaiah Berlin. Recollections of an Historian of Ideas* (London: Phoenix, 1992), pp. 8–13; and "Conversations with Russian Writers," *Russian Thinkers*, ed. Henry Hardy and Aileen Kelly, with an introduction by Aileen Kelly (London: Hogarth Press, 1978), p. 212.
8. I remember once after lunch with Berlin at his home in Headington House sometime in early 1992 his saying, in a remarkable aside, after we had talked a bit about Dilthey, Windelband, and particularly Rickert, "Well, perhaps I am really a German thinker who writes in English." For all his very Humean characteristics, singled out among others by Stuart Hampshire, "Nationalism," in *Isaiah Berlin: A Celebration*, eds. Edna and Avishai Margalit (London: The Hogrinth Press, 1991), there is more than a grain of truth in his remark. My forthcoming intellectual biography of Berlin will enlarge on this topic.
9. See Jahanbegloo, *Conversations with Isaiah Berlin*, pp. 70–1.
10. Isaiah Berlin, "From Hope and Fear Set Free," in *Concepts and Categories*.
11. Isaiah Berlin, "Historical Inevitability," pp. 69–73; "The Hedgehog and the Fox," in *Russian Thinkers*, pp. 74–80; and "The Sense of Reality," in *The Sense of Reality: Studies in Ideas and their History*, ed. Henry Hardy, with an introduction by Patrick Gardiner (London: Chatto and Windus, 1996), pp. 16–28.
12. Isaiah Berlin, "History and Theory: The Concept of Scientific History," *History and Theory* 1 (1960), pp. 1–31, repr. as "The Concept of Scientific History" in *Concepts and Categories*.
13. Isaiah Berlin, "Does Political Theory Still Exist?" (1962), repr. in *Concepts and Categories*.
14. Isaiah Berlin, "The Counter-Enlightenment," in *Against the Current: Essays in the History of Ideas*, ed. and with a bibliography by Henry Hardy, with an introduction by Roger Hausheer (London: Hogarth Press, 1979), pp. 2–3.
15. Isaiah Berlin, "The Romantic Revolution," in *The Sense of Reality*, pp. 191–3, and Jahanbegloo, *Conversations with Isaiah Berlin*, pp. 158–159.
16. Isaiah Berlin, "The Originality of Machiavelli," in *Studies on Machiavelli*, ed. Myron P. Gilmore (Florence: Sansoni, 1972), pp. 149–206, repr. in *Against the Current*.
17. Isaiah Berlin, *Vico and Herder: Two Studies in the History of Ideas* (London: Hogarth Press, 1976).
18. Isaiah Berlin, *The Magus of the North: J. G. Hamann and the Origins of Modern Irrationalism*, ed. Henry Hardy (London: John Murray, 1993).
19. See the appendix to *The Magus of the North*, pp. 129–132.
20. Berlin, *Vico and Herder*, pp. 149–205.

21. Isaiah Berlin, "The Apotheosis of the Romantic Will," in *The Crooked Timber of Humanity: Chapters in the History of Ideas*, ed. Henry Hardy (London: John Murray, 1990).
22. Isaiah Berlin, "The Counter-Enlightenment," in *Against the Current*.
23. Isaiah Berlin, *The Roots of Romanticism*, the A. W. Mellon Lectures in the Fine Arts, 1965, ed. Henry Hardy (London, Pimlico, 2000).
24. Isaiah Berlin, "Nationalism," in *Against the Current*; and "The Bent Twig," in *The Crooked Timber of Humanity*.
25. Berlin, "Two Concepts of Liberty," pp. 149–54.
26. Isaiah Berlin, "Joseph de Maistre and the Origins of Fascism," in *The Crooked Timber of Humanity*.

4 Berlin, Vico, and the Principles of Humanity

Joseph Mali

Late in his life, Isaiah Berlin wrote a short review-essay on Peter Burke's *Vico* contribution to the Past Masters series of Oxford University Press.[1] The essay, which was published posthumously under the title "The Reputation of Vico," was Berlin's last attempt to justify Vico's reputation as a genius whose "originality" was fully appreciated, if at all, only long after his time.[2] As Berlin would have it, Burke's contention that Vico was not a "forerunner" of our times but rather "a typical Neapolitan scholar and thinker of his time" aligned him with those who failed to appreciate Vico's "originality."[3] This apparent fallacy in Burke's positive assessment of Vico outweighed the "many merits" that Berlin otherwise found in his book, all the more so because, for Berlin, "originality"—the ability to think "against the current"—was the singular quality that distinguished those thinkers whom he deemed really important to the history of ideas, even if, as in the case of Vico, they themselves were rather insignificant in it. What made Vico, along with thinkers such as Hamann or Sorel, who were likewise rather marginal in their times, into the most "original" past masters of our modern cultural history was their opposition to the dominant "monistic" ideologies in Western civilization. For Berlin these comprised all those ethical and political doctrines that sought to reduce the moral and cultural plurality of human life to some ultimate unity or verity, be it the "true religion" of the Judaeo-Christian canonists, the "natural law" of the human scientists, or the "perfect society" of the Marxists. Yet much as he admired the "originality" of Vico and his fellow protagonists of the "Counter-Enlightenment," Berlin well saw that their rejection of rationality and all other norms and forms of universality rendered them prone to all sorts of misapprehensions and accusations. Berlin recalls one typical reaction to his own evaluation of Vico as "the most original philosopher the Italians have produced"[4]:

> I remember well how, one evening at dinner at Harvard some years ago, my friend and hero Gaetano Salvemini turned upon me and denounced my interest in Vico's writings. "Vico," he declared, "was a fraud. Vico was a charlatan. Croce [at this point Salvemini took a deep breath and then puffed it outwards] blew him up like that, like that! Vico has been translated into English. English is an honest language.

Now everyone will see through this pretender, nothing will be left of him, nor, I hope, of Croce either.[5]

Reflecting on this incident some forty years later,[6] Berlin could safely conclude that Salvemini's augury "was not destined to be fulfilled." Berlin should have added, of course, that it was largely due to his own efforts that Vico has acquired his great reputation as one of the greatest "past masters" in modern intellectual history, at least among scholars outside Italy. The latest Vico-bibliography of "Works in English from 1884 to 1994"[7] attests to the fact that the current celebration of Vico began around 1960, the year in which Berlin published his first major essay on Vico.[8] According to Giorgio Tagliacozzo, the indefatigable promoter of the remarkable Vico-*Rezeption* in our times, Berlin's essay on "The Philosophical Ideas of Giambattista Vico" was the main catalyst behind this latest and grandest stage in "Vico's Resurrection": "No other similarly comprehensive and innovative study of Vico's thought, setting it in its philosophical context and relating it to modern social disciplines, existed before Berlin's essay or would appear anywhere during the decade it so auspiciously inaugurated."[9] When Berlin republished this essay, with minor revisions, as the first chapter in his book *Vico and Herder* in 1976, Vico had already become a cultural hero for scholars in the humanities and social sciences, who have commonly come to praise him as the main discoverer of almost all of our modern—all too modern—disciplines.[10] Berlin not only initiated this process of recognition among modern theorists—for modern artists had already rediscovered Vico through Joyce—but he also propagated it beyond academic circles: in November 1970 he published a long essay on Vico in the *New York Times Magazine*, the lively title ("One of the Boldest Innovators in the History of Human Thought") and style of which ensured that a large public became familiar with Vico's name and main ideas.[11] The thriving Vico industry of the last three decades, which is duly monitored in the annual *New Vico Studies*, and the recent republication of Berlin's own *Vico and Herder*, defy Berlin's somber conclusion in that book that Vico "is constantly rediscovered and as constantly laid aside. He remains unreadable and unread."[12] Yet, the enthusiastic reception of Vico as a great "modern thinker" inevitably led to some oddities and even absurdities, as, for example, on those occasions when Vico has been associated with modern thinkers whom he would never have understood and who, all too often, have never bothered to understand him. And then, of course, there have always been those who hated Vico.

Recalling the incident with Gaetano Salvemini during the dinner at Harvard, Berlin remarks, without further comment, that this great Italian scholar and anti-Fascist fighter came to hate Vico so intensely because he regarded him a "political reactionary." At the time of that conversation this association was still very vivid. For just several years earlier, in March 1944, during the bicentennial commemoration of the death of Giambattista Vico, Giovanni Gentile, the leading intellectual of Italian Fascism, delivered a public speech in which he hailed Vico as the true founder of the Fascist movement in Italy.[13] And yet, the fact that Vico's legacy in Italy was acclaimed both by political reactionaries like Gentile and revolutionaries like Gramsci, or by both de Maistre and Michelet in France; that it inspired Marxists like Labriola and Lafargue as well as Revisionists like Sorel and Pareto—indicates that the reception of Vico—as is the case with other enigmatic thinkers like Machiavelli, Rousseau, or Nietzsche—has often been largely determined by ideological interpretations. In his comments on this ambivalent legacy Berlin mentions that Vico had been represented as a "forerunner of Fascism," but also, and more resoundingly, as a "proto-Marxist," as a "Catholic apologist," "pragmatist," "existentialist," and as much else—all of which means, for Berlin, that Vico faced the "particular danger that attends the fate of rich and profound but inexact and obscure thinkers, namely that their admirers tend to read too much into them, and turn insensibly in the direction of their own thoughts."[14] Berlin goes on to cite some famous examples of modern thinkers who fashioned their own Vico in this way, and we in turn may apply his acute observation to Berlin himself and consider whether Berlin had not "read too much" of his own thought into Vico, thereby perhaps making of Vico much too modern a thinker, a champion of Berlin's own ethical and political creeds of liberalism or pluralism—creeds that Vico could not possibly have held.

Some critical reviewers of Berlin's *Vico and Herder* were alert to this apparent methodological fallacy in Berlin's interpretation, as, in fact, was Berlin himself. Much as he tried to dissociate himself from the Crocean tendency to perceive Vico as the "forerunner" of Hegelianism, Marxism, historicism, and similar "isms," Berlin often referred to Vico as an "originator" or "anticipator" of all kinds of later modern theories. He was particularly eager to promote Vico over against all the major German schools of *Geisteswissenschaft* in the nineteenth century: not only did he claim that Vico had actually discovered the very notion of *Geisteswissenschaft*, but he also implied that Vico had thought up, in all but names, the conceptual categories of Schelling's *Mythologie*, Hegel's *Phänomenologie*, Marx's *Ideologie*, or Weber's *Wissenssoziologie*. It seems that Berlin was as much impressed as amused by Michelet's observation, which he repeatedly and approvingly cited (even in his last essay), that "these illustrious Germans might have remembered that they had all formerly lived in Vico. All the giants of criticism are already contained, with room to spare, in the little pandemonium of the *New Science*."[15] Berlin may have had some personal, and perhaps not quite rational, motivations for this counter-German motion, but his basic association of Vico with the German tradition of *Geisteswissenschaft*, and, above all, his persistent attempt to portray Vico as the real creator of the new hermeneutic methodology in the humanities and social sciences, summed up in the assertion that "Vico virtually invented the concept of understanding—of what Dilthey and others call '*verstehen*,'"[16]—makes clear what, in his view, was Vico's most important intellectual achievement. Whatever Vico himself may have meant by the term "new science" (*scienza nuova*)—and he in fact consigned it merely to "philology," the old humanistic art which traditionally entailed the formal interpretation of words in classical works and which he sought to improve by the new sciences of etymology and mythology—Berlin rightly saw that in order to achieve that professional task Vico had forged a whole new theory of understanding human beings in past or foreign cultures through their literatures, pictures, and gestures, by probing deeper than philologists had hitherto done, beyond words into images, beyond theories into stories, back to what James Joyce must have meant in this famous evocation in *Finnegans Wake*: "The Vico road goes round and round to meet where terms begin."[17]

Along with Joyce and many other modern discoverers of Vico, Berlin drew his interpretation, and much inspiration, from this famous oration in the *New Science*:

But in the night of thick darkness enveloping the earliest antiquity, so remote from ourselves, there shines the eternal and never failing light of a truth beyond all question: that the world of civil society has certainly been made by men, and that its principles are therefore to be found within the modifications of our own human mind. Whoever reflects on this cannot but marvel that the philosophers should have bent all their energies to the study of the world of nature, which, since God made it, He alone knows; and that they should have neglected the study of the world of nations, or civil world, which, since men had made it, men could come to know.[18]

The latter part of this passage has often been quoted and discussed by theorists of the human sciences, who have commonly come to regard it as one of the most significant contributions to the formation of their methodology.[19] Following Croce, Collingwood, and other Idealists, they commonly celebrate Vico as the first and foremost opponent of Descartes and all other Positivists. According to that version, Vico began his campaign of liberation already in his early metaphysical and theological treatises with his epistemological notion that *verum et factum convertuntur sunt*, namely that perfect knowledge is possible only *per causas*, and hence attainable only by the creator's own knowledge of what he or she has made. Berlin largely concurs with this interpretation of the oration. He readily found in its resounding conclusion the first and best confirmation of his own humanistic conception of history as a spontaneous and largely autonomous process of human creation through self-assertion. Yet, whereas most other commentators on Vico's famous oration have either ignored or misread its first part (and in any case failed to follow its syllogistic construction, which would have required them to draw Vico's philosophical conclusion from his historical assumptions) Berlin pays as much attention to its opening declaration, starting with its cryptic references to the mythic times in which Vico claims to have made his monumental discovery. For, as Vico himself testified and as Berlin reiterates, the decisive moment in the creation of his new science of humanity was when Vico managed to decipher the "poetic characters" by which the ancient mythmakers had made up their "human institutions": "This discovery, which is the master key of this Science, has cost the persistent research of almost all our literary life, because with our civilized natures we [moderns] cannot at all imagine and can understand only by great toil the poetic nature of these first men."[20] Elsewhere Vico elaborates more clearly how these "poetic characters"—above all the first mythological figure of Jove—had forced themselves on their own makers: "In their monstrous savagery and unbridled bestial freedom there was no means to tame the former or bridle the latter but the frightful thought of some divinity, the fear of whom is the only powerful means of reducing to duty a liberty gone wild."[21] As Berlin would have it, this reconstruction of the mental configuration by which (as Vico cunningly put it) "man becomes all things by not understanding them (*homo non intelligendo fit omnia*)"[22]—is the first theory of "alienation and reification."[23] In Vico's words:

> In such fashion the first men of the gentile nations, children of the nascent mankind, created things according to their own ideas. But this creation was infinitely different from that of God. For God, in his purest intelligence, knows things, and, by knowing them, creates them; but they, in their robust ignorance, did it by virtue of a wholly corporeal imagination. And because it was quite corporeal, they did it with marvelous sublimity; a sublimity such and so great that it excessively perturbed the very persons who by imagining did the creating, for which they were called "poets," which is Greek for "creators."[24]

What renders Vico's achievement so great, then, and so truly modern, is not merely the application of the old theological and the new philosophical notion of *verum/factum* to history, namely the simple realization that men themselves had made their history, but rather the more acute realization of *how* they had made it: by their human, all too human, faculties of mythopoeic imagination (*fantasia*), memory (*memoria*), and creative invention (*ingenium*). In that way, Berlin elaborates, "Vico transformed this notion [*verum/factum*] and gave it immensely greater scope and depth (and increased its dangerously speculative character) by extending it to the growth in time of the collective or social consciousness of mankind, particularly at its pre-rational and semi-conscious level, to the dreams and myths and images that have dominated man's thoughts and feelings from his earliest beginnings."[25]

Among the many "new sciences" that Berlin ascribed to Vico's *New Science* he prized above all the invention of "historical anthropology."[26] Vico, he argued, was the "begetter" of this methodology which is captured in the axiom, "Doctrines must take their beginning from the matters of which they treat."[27] Berlin rightly saw that with this assertion Vico initiated a genealogical turn in the historical sciences of the Enlightenment, for he thereby challenged the main naturalistic assumption of the age, namely the belief in the fixity of human nature beyond any culture. While contemporary philosophers of history like Voltaire or Hume could still maintain, with Machiavelli, that "if the present be compared with the remote past, it is easily seen that in all cities and in all peoples there are the same desires and the same passions as there always were,"[28] Vico saw that our great classical ancestors were very different from us:

> From these first men, stupid, insensate, and horrible beasts, all the philosophers and philologists should have begun their investigations of the wisdom of the ancient gentiles ... And they should have begun with metaphysics, which seeks its proofs not in the external world but within the modifications of the mind of him who meditates it. For since this world of nations has certainly been made by men, it is within these modifications that its principles should have been sought.[29]

According to Berlin, by "modifications" Vico "appears to mean what we should mean by the stages of the growth, or of the range or direction, of human thought, imagination, will, feeling, into which any man equipped with sufficient *fantasia* (as well as knowledge acquired by rational methods) can 'enter.' "[30] This rendition of *modificazioni*, which confines them to the "metaphysical" and other mythopoeic creations of "the mind" (*mente*) and all but ignores the more physical creations that men had made in the "external world," is congenial to Berlin, who tended to perceive the study of history in humanistic and rather idealistic terms. His objection to the very notion of "scientific history" was mediated by his reading of Vico, as well as by his reading about Vico, primarily, it seems, the writings of his teacher—and the one who introduced him to Vico—R. G. Collingwood, who required from the historian a certain capacity for empathetic identification of (and with) other human agents, an introspection of both self and others that could lead to a "re-enactment" of their peculiar situations, intentions, and actions.[31] In any case, Vico's injunction to regain the mental "modifications" of the *primi uomini* implied, for Berlin, "that the way to understand such men and their worlds is by trying to enter their minds, by finding out what they are at, by learning the rules and significance of their methods of expression—their myths, their songs, their dances, the form and idioms of their language, their marriage and funeral rites. To understand their history, one needs to understand what they lived by, which can be discovered only by those who have the key to what their language, art, and ritual mean—a key which Vico's *New Science* was intended to provide."³² Vico thereby instated a new interpretive methodology that consists in what Berlin calls "reconstructive imagination."

Some critical readers of Berlin's essays on Vico, notably Leon Pompa and Perez Zagorin, took him to task for having imputed to Vico this hermeneutical, and, in their view, quite mystical, notion of "empathetic" historical interpretation.³³ Vico, as they read him, preached and practiced a new scientific methodology of historical interpretation that was utterly positivistic, modeled on the Baconian-Newtonian conception of empirical inquiry into reality that was bound, and could be found, by physical rather than metaphysical laws. Insofar as Vico claimed to have discovered the "order of human institutions" or the laws of an "ideal eternal history traversed in time by every nation in its rise, development, maturity, decline, and fall" his *New Science* of history appears to be not as anti-mechanistic and anti-deterministic as Berlin presents it.³⁴

Vico indeed modeled his *New Science* on the new mathematical-physical sciences. He may have borrowed the title *scienza nuova* from Galileo's *Dialoghi delle Nuove Scienze*. More importantly, inasmuch as his aim was to discover the origins of human history in some fundamental "institutions," or, to use the terms he had used in the title of the first edition of his major work—to set up a *New Science concerning the Principles of Humanity*—his work may have owed even more to Newton.³⁵ For the key term "Principles" in this original title, as well as in the title of the last edition, clearly alludes to Newton's *Principia*. Like most of his contemporaries, Vico did not need to read Newton's *Principia* in order to get its literal meaning: "These principles," Newton wrote, were not some "occult qualities" which cannot be observed and tested, like metaphysical entities, but are those physical properties and forces—like the cohesion of bodies, inertia, or gravity—which form and govern the movements of all natural things in the world, and might therefore be rightly called the "general Laws of Nature."³⁶ In the *New Science*, Vico sought to establish these principles accordingly. Setting out from the assumption that "the nature of institutions is nothing but their coming into being at certain times and in certain guises," Vico then sought to discover "in the deplorable obscurity of the beginnings of the nations and in the innumerable variety of their customs" the "principles of humanity," namely, those primal capacities of human beings which, much like Newton's "principles of nature," have formed and govern their social life and history.³⁷ What are these "principles of humanity" and how does Vico claim to have found them?

According to Pompa and like-minded positivists, it would seem that Vico developed a systematic analytical methodology similar to the hypothetico-deductive model of "covering laws" in the natural sciences. Accordingly, the "principles" he invoked were to be found in the permanent physical realities that determined human life and history, either in man (physiological and biological compulsions) or outside him (geographical conditions). Berlin rejected this interpretation, even though he, too, noted the affinity between Vico's *New Science* and the new natural sciences.³⁸ Against the positivists, however, Berlin maintained that even if Vico had initially molded his work on Newton's scientific methodology, he eventually inverted its premises: he came to realize that his new science of humanity was not only more "certain" than the science of nature—because it relied on a more intimate knowledge of its object—but that it was also more "true" because it processed a better kind of knowledge, namely that possessed by the one who made the object of knowledge. In Berlin's words: "In history we are the actors; in the natural sciences mere spectators. This is the doctrine, above others, on which Vico's claim to immortality must rest. For upon it rests the crucial distinction between *Geisteswissenschaft* and *Naturwissenschaft*. The battle over this distinction has continued unabated until well into our own day."[39] And in order to retrieve the actors' knowledge we must indeed "enter," as Berlin likes to paraphrase Vico, the "minds" of the historical actors whom we study, yet not by any mystical feats of intuitive "empathy" or speculative identification with "those quite wild and savage" brutes, whom indeed "we cannot at all imagine," but rather by methodical investigation of those mental expressions which we "can comprehend if only with great effort," precisely as modern psychologists or anthropologists do when they interpret dreams or myths.[40] As Berlin elaborates: "Myths, according to Vico, are systematic ways of seeing, understanding, and reacting to the world, intelligible fully perhaps only to their creators and users, the early generations of men," but, at the same time, they are also "for modern critics the richest of all sources of knowledge of the physical and mental habits and the social ways of life of their creators."[41]

Consequently, and quite uniquely among philosophical commentators on Vico's *New Science*, Berlin paid due attention to Vico's own definition and actual execution of his *New Science* as a philological, and not only philosophical, investigation of human affairs. Although he wrote much on Vico's "philosophical" conception of knowledge, Berlin rightly recognized that underlying his conception of *verum/factum* were some concrete "philological" observations on human life and history. This dual vision is neatly worked out in his book *Vico and Herder*, which contains two complementary essays on both the philosophical and the philological-historical aspects of Vico's theory of knowledge. In the second essay, "Vico's Theory of Knowledge and its Sources," Berlin pursued the important studies of John Pocock and Donald Kelley on the "historical revolution" of legal scholarship in early modern Europe and was able to show how Vico could have derived many of his most insightful philosophical notions from this domain.[42] In any case, Berlin insists that "the truly revolutionary move is the application of the *verum/factum* principle to the study of history," so as to make clear that even if it is true, as scholars from Croce to Löwith have shown, that Vico could find some clues to that principle in Augustine or in Thomas Aquinas, or (more probably) in Hobbes, his real achievement was having shown in practical and historical terms how men in "earliest antiquity" had actually made *their* world by certain "modifications" which still prevail in *our* world of "modernity." For Vico indicates quite clearly that he had discovered the "truth" about the "civil world" (*mondo civile*)—that is, how men had made it and why, therefore, they (or other men) could come to know it—in some archaic "human creations" (*cose umane*) that have made up and still sustain this "civil world," being thus "its principles," and which, insofar as they are still veritable to us, "are to be found within the modifications of our own human mind." Vico, in other words, claims that in order to know what *our* world really is we must know how men in "earliest antiquity" made *their* world. And this is possible to do because, and only insofar as, we share those same archaic mental "modifications" which enabled ancient men to know and to make this world. These are none other than the myths which still persist in our minds and cultures in a variety of forms—in linguistic metaphors, literary idioms, religious rites, moral rules, political institutions, national traditions, and similar human creations.

Following on these astute observations Berlin was thus able to realize that the actual method of inquiry that Vico had in mind, and around which he constructed his entire *New Science*, was in fact—and by Vico's own definition—"historical mythology." Vico's assertion that "history cannot be more certain than he who creates the things also narrates them"[43] intimates what scholars in the humanities and social sciences have nowadays come to call "the narrative construction of reality"; when applied to history, it means that in order to explain historical events it is imperative to grasp the ultimate narratives of the agents involved in events—their myths:

> It follows that the first science to be learned should be mythology or the interpretation of fables; for, as we shall see, all the histories of the gentiles have their beginnings in fables, which were the first histories of the nations. By such a method the beginnings of the sciences as well as of the nations are to be discovered, for they ... had their beginnings in the public needs or utilities of the peoples and were later perfected as acute individuals applied their reflection to them.[44]

"Mythology, or the interpretation of fables" was, then, the "first science" (*la prima scienza*) of Vico's *New Science*. And he duly turned it into a new science by grounding the classical myths in the actual norms and forms of life of the peoples in ancient civilization, which were, in his view, utterly primitive and imaginative. Long before the emergence of the various interpretive social sciences of the nineteenth century—psychology, anthropology, sociology—Vico had already conceived of the mythopoeic construction of social reality, namely of the fact that inasmuch as men have made up their history according to certain imaginative and narrative patterns in which they do not merely believe but actually live, the explanation of human actions in history must always include—and perhaps even take the form of—an attempt to recover and interpret the subjective meanings of these actions from the point of view of the agents performing them, even if, and especially when, these meanings are immemorial and largely impersonal.

In brief, Berlin came to appraise Vico's *discoverta* of the creative mythopoeic imagination as a "major achievement" in the history of historical studies, because it was a virtual discovery of what we nowadays call "cultural history" as well as of some other modern social sciences: "The door that he opened to the understanding of cultural history by the 'decoding' of myths, ceremonies, laws, artistic images" rendered him, for Marx, the first "writer on social evolution," or, for Berlin, "the begetter of historical anthropology."[45] Berlin celebrates this achievement in the most flamboyant terms, and his appraisal warrants quoting at some length as it discloses the full force and range of his interpretation, the very qualities which, some critics would argue, may have gone beyond a plausible logical, let alone historical, reconstruction of Vico's thoughts:

> Vico is the author of the idea that language, myths, antiquities, directly reflect the various fashions in which social or economic or spiritual problems or realities were refracted in the minds of our ancestors; so that what may appear as profound theological conflicts or impassable social taboos are not what mechanically-minded

thinkers have taken them to be—by-products of material processes, biological, psychological, economic, and so on, although they may be that too—but primarily, "distorted" or primitive ways of recognizing social facts and of reacting to them. He is the author of the view that a rite or symbol or object of worship, from fetishism to modern nationalism, is most correctly interpreted as an expression of resistance to some social pressure, or joy in creation, or admiration for power, or craving for unity or security or victory over a rival group (what later theorists were to call ideologies) which may take diverse forms, mythological, metaphysical, aesthetic—different types of spectacles through which reality is apprehended and acted upon. He was the first to conceive the notion that in this fashion it was possible to achieve a kind of window into the past—an "inside" view—to reconstruct, not simply a formal procession of the famous men of the past, clad in their stock attributes, doing great deeds or suffering some fearful fate, but the style of entire societies which struggled and thought, worshiped, rationalized, and deluded themselves, put their faith in magical devices and occult powers, and felt, believed, created in a fashion which may be strange to us, and yet not wholly unintelligible.[46]

This is vintage Berlin. But is it really Vico? Who, in this passage, is the real "author of the view that a rite or symbol or object of worship, from fetishism to modern nationalism, is most correctly interpreted as an expression of ... what later theorists were to call ideologies"?

It was primarily against this tendency to associate Vico so wholly with the German tradition of *Geisteswissenschaft* and to imbue his original views, however seminal they may have proven to be for later generations, with so many modern meanings and implications, that Peter Burke wrote his study.[47] As noted above, Berlin was very much aware of this apparent methodological fallacy in his interpretation of Vico, and seemingly also in the interpretation of others whom he deemed original and seminal thinkers. His awareness of this problematic was heightened in the wake of the new methodological revision in the history of ideas, the so-called Cambridge School of Pocock, Skinner, and Dunn that became dominant from the late 1960s onward, and reasserted the primacy of contextual considerations in textual interpretations. Whereas Berlin tended to inflate the potential significance of ideas, the new school of thought deflated their actual relevance, restricting them to what their makers could have meant under the prevailing political conditions, practical options, ideological limitations, rhetorical conventions, and all other historical institutions of their times. In the introduction to *Vico and Herder* Berlin responds to this new historiographical policy indirectly but very poignantly:

> The importance of accurate historical knowledge to the understanding of the meaning, force and influence of ideas may be far greater than many unhistorical thinkers, particularly in English-speaking lands, have recognized, but it is not everything. If the ideas and the basic terminology of Aristotle or the Stoics or Pascal or Newton or Hume or Kant did not possess a capacity for independent life, for surviving translation, and, indeed, transplantation, not without, at times, some change of meaning, into the language of very disparate cultures, long after their own worlds had passed away, they would by now, at best, have found an honorable resting place beside the writings of the Aristotelians of Padua or Christian Wolff, major influences in their day, in some museum of historical antiquities ... The importance of past philosophers in the end resides in the fact that the issues which they raised are live issues still (or again), and, as in this case [of Vico and Herder], have not vanished with the vanished societies of Naples or Königsberg or Weimar, in which they were conceived.[48]

While Berlin's general argument for the historicity of ideas is clear, and has been much discussed,[49] it should be noted that, according to Berlin's own testimony, he derived his peculiar conception of "history of ideas" from Vico.[50] The above words make clear that as an historian of ideas Berlin was more interested in "live issues" rather than in "ideas" about them. His professional transition from philosophical to historical studies of "ideas" betrays a deeper intellectual transition from a philosophical to an historical conception of "ideas."[51]

Along with Vico, whom he rediscovered during that crucial transition in the mid-1950s, Berlin came to suspect, and eventually reject, the very idea and ideal of Descartes' "clara et distincta idea."[52] His deep "sense of reality" taught him that such rationalistic and absolutistic norms of truth are unrealistic in social forms of life, where the meanings of words and even of truths are usually determined by practical rather than by theoretical considerations, according to mythical rather than logical categories. Vico had claimed that "truth is sifted from falsehood in everything that has been preserved for us through long centuries by those vulgar traditions which, since they have been preserved for so long a time and by entire peoples, must have had a public ground of truth. The great fragments of antiquity, hitherto useless to science because they lay begrimed, broken, and scattered, shed great light when cleaned, pieced together, and restored."[53] This perception informed Vico's new epistemological conception of "common sense" (*senso comune*): "Human choice, by its nature most uncertain, is made certain and determined by the common sense of men with respect to human needs or utilities ... Common sense is judgment without reflection, shared by an entire class, an entire people, an entire nation, or the entire human race."[54] Vico contrasted this practical knowledge or "consciousness of the certain," which he calls *coscienza*, with the theoretical "knowledge of the true," or *scienza*, and his main effort was to take the former traditional and rather emotional knowledge which we derive from our own experience in common personal and communal affairs and turn it into a *scienza nuova*, literally his *New Science* of whole nations and civilizations. In his essay "Vico's Concept of Knowledge" Berlin thus concluded that in this form of "knowing founded on memory and imagination" Vico overcame the classical distinction between the theoretical and the technical forms of knowledge, those which Gilbert Ryle redefined by the terms "knowing that" and "knowing how," and thereby paved the way for the interpretive social sciences of psychology, anthropology, or sociology, which, much like Berlin's own history of ideas, are concerned with what Vico called "certain" rather than "true" forms of knowledge.[55]

Such notions of the practical, commonsensical, and ultimately mythical construction of social reality were immensely important for Berlin's political philosophy and history of ideas, principally for his rehabilitation of such atavistic notions as "populism," "expressionism," or "nationalism." Berlin found Vico especially pertinent because of his basic assumption that all human associations are (to use a modern expression) "imagined communities," whose members "are naturally impelled to preserve the memories of the laws and institutions that bind them in their societies" by means of "fabulous histories" and other narrative and festive commemorations.[56] For all its apparent conservatism, this was a very realistic and pluralistic theory of society, and as such proved much more conducive to the modern theory of liberalism than all the rationalistic and monistic theories of "perfect society" that proliferated in the Enlightenment. "To a disciple of Vico, the ideal of some of the thinkers of the Enlightenment, the notion of even the abstract possibility of perfect society, is necessarily an attempt to weld together incompatible attributes—characteristics, ideals, gifts, properties, values that belong to different patterns of thought, action, life, and therefore cannot be detached and sewn together in one garment."[57] Berlin's deep antipathy to simplistic explanations and solutions for the "live issues" of the human condition and to all kinds of abstract utopian "visions of perfection," aligned him with Vico, who likewise rejected such delusions: "Philosophy considers man as he should be and so can be of service to but very few, those who wish to live in the republic of Plato and not to fall back into the dregs of Romulus."[58]

Vico's new theory and history of society were designed to explain how the *primi uomini*, who "in their robust ignorance" were plainly "incapable of truth and of reason" and thus unable to deduce and behave according to some rational "law" as Hobbes had assumed, nevertheless managed to create the *mondo civile* by dint of their own mythopoeic capacities. Hence his objection to the natural law theorists from Aristotle through his Stoic and Thomistic followers to the contractual theorists of society in his age, primarily Grotius and Hobbes: they all sought to explain the evolution of human society by "the natural law of the philosophers (or natural theologians) [which] is that of reason," and not by "the natural law of the gentes, [which] is that of utility and force."[59] Berlin disliked Vico's political ideology of "utility and force," but he still detected in that conservative ideology an important innovative methodology:

> A static model like the social contract omits sociological and psychological facts—the survival of the past into the present, the influence of tradition, of inherited habits and shapes they assume; it ignores or distorts the true view of society as something compounded out of many interlaced, altering strands of conscious, semi-conscious and buried memories, of individual and collective reactions and sentiments, of patterns of social life which we speak of as the character of a family, a tribe, a nation, an historical period, the roots of which are all but lost, yet to some degree still remain traceable in the opaque and tantalizing past. Only those who have the imagination and knowledge to trace this process to its origins, and so reconstruct it, can understand its effects in the present or assess its values and prospects.[60]

Ultimately then, Vico's definition of his *New Science* as an investigation that "proceeds by a severe analysis of *human* thoughts about *human* necessities or utilities of social life" and thus becomes "a history of *human* ideas"[61] helped Berlin to redefine what he was aiming for in his own "history of ideas"—the history not only of what men of ideas thought, but also of what they felt, imagined, desired, and expressed in utterances which were not always clear to their contemporaries, and all too often (as in the case of Vico) even to themselves, thus leaving them to be elaborated and fully articulated only by later historians of ideas.[62] Berlin turned to the history of ideas in order to liberate those thinkers who were immersed in this predicament, above all passionate counter-rationalists like Vico, Hamann, Herder, de Maistre, or Sorel, all of whom had, like Berlin himself, given up or gone beyond the clear and distinct "ideas" of philosophy in order to deal with the deeper and darker "issues" of human life and history.

According to Berlin, the single most important "issue" that these thinkers commonly evoked was that of human plurality in history. To Berlin's mind, all the other great issues—of human identity, liberty, and dignity, of equity in society and of the polity—depend on this basic social condition of a plurality of ethical, political, and aesthetical norms and forms of life. This was also the single most important subject of Berlin's own philosophical and political works.[63] In his various studies in the history of ideas he sought to trace the origin and transformations of this notion of "pluralism," and ultimately concluded that, with the sole exception of Machiavelli, it matured only in the eighteenth century, with the intellectual movement of Counter-Enlightenment that rejected the "monism" of the Enlightenment. According to Berlin, its first champions were Vico, Hamann, and Herder who dared challenge the monistic Aristotelian, Christian, and Cartesian conceptions of truth, and countered the latest deterministic theories of natural laws in all human actions and creations, be they in history or in poetry, with their novel observations of cultural singularity and plurality.[64] Leaving aside the empirical and historical problems inherent in this conception—classical and biblical scholars would probably argue for such cultural pluralism in antiquity, Renaissance scholars would surely predate Vico with Pico, and Enlightenment scholars could simply cite Swift's *Gulliver's Travels*, Diderot's *Supplément au voyage de Bougainville*, or Lessing's *Nathan der Weise*—the main problem is whether the very notion of "pluralism," with its distinct modern liberal connotations, was conceivable to any of the thinkers of the Counter-Enlightenment mentioned above. While Herder might rightly be considered a "pluralist" by our standards, the characterization of Vico as such seems odd. Vico was, after all, a supporter of absolutist Catholicism and monarchism, a theoretician and guardian of "order" and "authority," and a conservative scholar who sided with the "ancients" in their battle against the "moderns" in Naples, traits which his fellow-citizen, the radical social historian Pietro Giannone, exposed already in Vico's lifetime. Above all, he was the author of a *New Science*—a work that aspired to be a "rational civil theology" of providential history and reasserted the hegemony of the one and only holy scripture over all other pictures of reality. The full title of this work—*Principles of a New Science concerning the Nature of the Nations, by which are found the Principles of Another System of the Natural Law of the Gentes*—implies that he believed in some alternative yet equally universal "natural laws" that dictate the cyclical motions of man, society, and history. Again, some critical commentators have noted the apparent ideological fallacy in Berlin's interpretation: Arnaldo Momigliano thus remarked that Berlin "must have found in Vico and Herder confirmation and support in his life-long fight for cultural pluralism and respect for minorities," yet then wondered whether this "cultural pluralism" might not have entailed "moral relativism" of which a defender of the Catholic faith like Vico, at least, could not possibly approve.[65]

In his reply to this criticism, Berlin carefully distinguishes between "cultural pluralism" and "moral relativism": the latter form of epistemological skepticism, he claims, was as yet inconceivable to thinkers in the eighteenth century, and in any case would have been unacceptable to thinkers like Vico (and Herder) who did not think that different cultures with their various truths were incommensurable; but they certainly could, and did, espouse (in all but name) some kind of pluralism, "which merely denies that there is one, and only one, true morality or aesthetics or theology, and allows equally objective alternative values or systems of value."[66] Could Vico, then, be better defined as a "moral pluralist"? Berlin seems to support this option when he argues that, according to Vico, we "are urged to look upon life as affording a plurality of values, equally genuine, equally ultimate, above all equally objective; incapable, therefore, of being ordered in a timeless hierarchy, or judged in terms of some one absolute standard."[67]

This liberal assessment of Vico has been strongly contested by Mark Lilla. In his *G. B. Vico: The Making of an Anti-Modern*, Lilla attacks Berlin's presentation of Vico as a moral pluralist, arguing that even if Vico has inadvertently contributed to certain modern pluralistic tendencies he was essentially "anti-modern," an old Catholic apologist in the guise of a new scientist, whose main aim was to reassert the dogmatic theological and political ideology of order and authority, albeit by a novel methodology.[68] Lilla shows, for example, that some of Berlin's most fundamental assumptions about Vico, starting with the first assertion that, for Vico, "the nature of man is not, as has long been supposed, static and unalterable or even unaltered; that it does not so much as contain even a central kernel or essence, which remains identical through change,"[69] must be revised, and ultimately reversed, when checked against Vico's doctrine of some basic propensity to truth (*vis veri*) that has always impelled all human beings, pagans as well as Christians, to believe in God, however variable their routes and rites may have become. This human aspiration to divinity assumes the form of a common law, then, that has imparted a certain unity and continuity to Universal History, and guarantees that we can recognize its metaphysical motivation and destination.

Should Vico, then, be considered at least a "cultural pluralist"? This is certainly the case according to Berlin's definition of the term quoted above, and which continues as follows: "There is a finite variety of values and attitudes, some of which one society, some another, have made their own, attitudes and values which members of other societies may admire or condemn (in the light of their own value-systems) but can always, if they are sufficiently imaginative and try hard enough, contrive to understand—that is, see to be intelligible ends of life for human beings situated as these men were."[70] This is a more plausible option, but it too is quite problematic, because Vico himself does not seem to have conceived of—let alone applied—those liberal terms of cultural equivalency in his *New Science*. Vico, in other words, may have come to recognize "cultural pluralism" as inevitable but not as valuable in itself. Even if we acknowledge, with Berlin, that Vico's pluralistic conception was tacit, better revealed in practical cultural explorations than in any theoretical declarations, the prime example that Berlin cites, again and again, as proof of Vico's implicit recognition of some essential incompatibility and incommensurability of valuable options in cultural history—the so-called "discovery of the true Homer"—hardly sustains the argument that this reinterpretation of the Homeric poetry as primitive and brutal (important as it was for the historicist revision of the common anachronistic renditions of Homer as "sublime poet") intimates a genuine pluralistic conception of multiculturalism.[71] For all his acute perception of a certain "truth" in pagan mythology, and much as he hailed it as a "true narration" (*vera narratio*) of the primal human condition, Vico ultimately judged its poetic creations, however magnificent and efficient they proved in the education of the *primi uomini*, to be, in themselves, utterly "primitive," "barbarous," "false" and "absurd," and in any case always insisted on the priority and superiority of biblical history over against all the classical stories. Vico's declarations on "the essential difference between our Christian religion, which is true, and all the others, which are false"⁷² or on the ethical and political supremacy of contemporary Christian European "perfect monarchies" over all other nations, do not reveal the kind of tolerance that one would expect from a "cultural pluralist;" indeed they reveal that Vico lagged far behind such "monistic" thinkers of the Enlightenment as Locke or Voltaire.

On these premises, Michel Foucault is perhaps not altogether wrong to argue, against all the Counter-Enlightenment claims on Vico's behalf, that Vico was very much a man of the Enlightenment insofar as he shared its basic temporal orientation: "The present may also be analyzed as a point of transition toward the dawning of a new world. That is what Vico describes in the last chapter of the *scienza nuova*; what he sees 'today' is 'a complete humanity ... spread abroad through all nations, for a few great monarchies rule over this world of peoples'; it is also 'Europe ... radiant with such humanity that it abounds in all the good things that make for the happiness of human life.' "⁷³ Moreover, Vico's more fundamental attempts to discover a common "Mental Dictionary for assigning meanings to all the different articulate languages, reducing them all to certain units of ideas in substance,"⁷⁴ or to deduce the universal laws of genetic psychological and historical development of all men and nations,⁷⁵ imply that he shared at least some of the naturalistic presumptions of Enlightenment thinkers, who commonly believed, with Hume, that "there is a great uniformity among the actions of men, in all nations and ages, and that human nature remains still the same, in its principles and operations."⁷⁶

A critical revision of Berlin's "pluralistic" conception of Vico along these guidelines might modify not only some of his "modernistic" interpretations of Vico, but also the more fundamental dichotomic conception of the "Enlightenment" and "Counter-Enlightenment" that Berlin had forged. As the virtual inventor of the term "Counter-Enlightenment"⁷⁷ Berlin could rightly claim, in Humpty Dumpty fashion, that this word means just what he wanted it to mean, namely a reactionary opposition to the Enlightenment, a different yet equivalent form of "counter-revolution." This definition is apt when applied to fanatical thinkers like Hamann or de Maistre. But if the "Counter-Enlightenment" is more generally associated with thinkers such as Vico, Herder, Burke, and likeminded antirationalists, who indeed countered the positivistic ideology and methodology of the Enlightenment—and this is how Berlin actually presents the Counter-Enlightenment in his definitive essay—then we would do better to liken this wayward intellectual movement to the "Counter-Reformation" or with what we nowadays would call "counter-cultural" movements, whose aim is not to denounce what they oppose—the Reformation, culture—as such, but rather to offer alternative theories and practices for their realization. As Charles Taylor suggests, we must come to see the "Counter-Enlightenment" as an immanent aspect of the "Enlightenment" itself, a natural and integral reaction to its process of rational maturation, which, inasmuch as it opens and calls up more archaic sources of experience, is essential to its reinvigoration and permanent continuation.⁷⁸ Recent studies on the various national forms of Enlightenment, or on the so-called "Religious Enlightenment," or, as John Pocock would now have it, on the "Enlightenments" that were viable even to a single author like Gibbon, also offer a useful basis for a revision of Berlin's rather monolithic conception of the Enlightenment and the Counter-Enlightenment.⁷⁹

What is required, then, is a dialectical, not antithetical, conception of the two movements, such as would show how both shared and pursued certain common ideas and ideals of human amelioration, yet did so according to different essential assumptions about human life and history. Whereas the thinkers of the Enlightenment assumed that all men were naturalistic and egotistic but ultimately rationalistic, and thus sought to edify society by an ever more reasonable conception and organization, Vico and his associates in the Counter-Enlightenment believed that all men were both "sociable" yet "weak and fallen,"[80] more imaginative than cognitive, and thus sought to solidify the mythopoeic traditions by which they have made up and still sustain their communities. In order to see where Vico differs most radically from the Enlightenment, then, and where, in fact, his "cultural pluralism" emerges quite clearly in the attempt to establish a new science of man on the cultural creations of "the nations" rather than on the natural reactions of "man," we must return to the passage from Hume quoted above. Hume's reasoning continues as follows:

> Would you know the sentiments, inclinations, and course of life of the Greeks and Romans? Study well the temper and actions of the French and English: You cannot be mistaken in transferring to the former most of the observations which you have made with regard to the latter. Mankind are so much the same, in all times and places, that history informs of nothing new or strange in this particular ... Its chief use is only to discover the constant and universal principles of human nature, by showing men in all varieties of circumstances and situations, and furnishing us with materials from which we may form our observations and become acquainted with the regular springs of human action and behaviour.[81]

Hume's assertion that what counts in the study of men are not transient and different "cultural" creations but rather permanent "natural" reactions, was, on his own admission, an "introduction" of Newton's experimental methodology into human reality.[82] And true to his Newtonian convictions he rules out any "hypothetical" qualities of human nature, that is, nonelemental, nonexperimental, and merely "accidental" manifestations of human actions and creations. As in Newton's *Principia*, so too in Hume's "science of man" the critical and most crucial motion is the reduction of all the phenomenal appearances to eternal "principles." Hume clearly identifies them as, and with, certain "physical desires" in man, the powerful "passions" that rule even the slavish "reason," mere instinctual energies, then, which, to his mechanical reasoning, set in motion the "springs of human action." A brief and final discussion of Vico's notion and demonstration of the "principles of humanity" will make clear how he really achieved his New Science against both the old and the new sciences of man.

As we recall, Vico sought to discover the "principles of humanity" in those "human institutions" which have proven crucial for "the preservation of the human race."[83] Here is his conclusion:

> Now since this world of nations has been made by men, let us see in what institutions all men agree and always have agreed. For these institutions will be able to give us the universal and eternal principles (such as every science must have) on which all nations were founded and still preserve themselves. We observe that all nations, barbarous as well as civilized, though separately founded because remote from each other in time and space, keep these three human customs: all have some religion, all contract solemn marriages, all bury their dead. And in no nation, however

savage and crude, are any human actions performed with more elaborate ceremonies and more sacred solemnity than the rites of religion, marriage, and burial. For, by the axiom that "uniform ideas, born among peoples unknown to each other, must have a common ground of truth," it must have been dictated to all nations that from these three institutions humanity began among them all, so that the world should not again become a bestial wilderness ... These must be the bounds of human reason. And let him who would transgress them beware lest he transgress all humanity.[84]

The validity of Vico's concrete "principles" may be—and has been—contested on empirical grounds. Vico himself cites the counter-examples of Arnauld, Bayle, and Spinoza, and modern readers could certainly produce even better empirical refutations.[85] But such claims miss the essential point of Vico's argument. For what is really novel and important in his notion of the "principles of humanity" is the hermeneutical, not the empirical, claim, namely his assertion that any cross-cultural understanding, to be possible at all, must assume and pursue certain absolute norms, or—to use a modern phrase—"limiting notions" of morality, which determine the range within which various forms of life can be exercised and be recognized as human.[86] Vico makes clear that he opted for these three "civil institutions" because they are, or rather have become, "natural customs" among all the peoples.[87] The moment at which certain customs become natural marks the beginning of humanity, as well as the starting-point of all human sciences, because the appearance of certain rule-governed routines, which are manifestly morally principled, suggest that the human creatures who behave in that way no longer obey their natural instincts but rather submit themselves to their own rules. These customs can thus be followed by us, but this is feasible only insofar as we can relate their rule-governed or "principled" behavior to our own experience, however different that may be. Thus, for example, in order to understand an alien religious belief or rite we must have some kind of religious experience or knowledge. This, then, is Vico's contention: that since the world in which people live is a world of cultural meaning which they themselves have created, in order to understand it we must grasp this meaning for them and in ourselves. The fact that we can do so and usually do implies for Vico that underlying the cultural plurality in which we live there is a common basic and universal morality which we know because we have made it:

> There must in the nature of human institutions be a mental language to all notions, which uniformly grasps the substance of things feasible in human social life and expresses it with as many diverse modifications as these same things may have diverse aspects ... This common mental language is proper to our Science, by whose light linguistic scholars will be enabled to construct a mental vocabulary common to all the various articulate languages living and dead.[88]

Berlin, I think, would have agreed with this conclusion. Much as he accentuated, and celebrated, the essential incompatibility and incommensurability of valuable options in our multicultural predicament, he insisted that "there are, if not universal values, at any rate a minimum without which societies could scarcely survive."[89] Significantly, he developed this theory in three essays that he wrote around 1960, that is, exactly at the time of his first major essay on Vico. His cardinal assumption in these essays was that certain basic "concepts and categories" of human experience must prevail for our knowledge of human affairs to be possible at all.[90] What Berlin means by these "concepts and categories" are not the a priori Kantian categories of time and space, but rather, much like in Vico's lexicon, some common experiential notions that enable us to make sense of human actions. He elaborates:

> The basic categories (together with their corresponding concepts) in terms of which we define men—such notions as society, freedom, sense of time and change, suffering, happiness, productivity, good and bad, right and wrong, choice, effort, truth, illusion (to take them wholly at random)—are not matters of induction or hypothesis. To think of someone as a human being is ipso facto to bring all these notions into play: so that to say of someone that he is a man, but that choice, or the notion of truth, mean nothing to him, would be eccentric: it would clash with what we mean by "man" not as a matter of verbal definition (which is alterable at will), but as intrinsic to the way we think, and (as a matter of "brute" fact) evidently cannot but think ... Thus if I say of someone that he is kind or cruel, loves truth or is indifferent to it, he remains human in either case. But if I find a man to whom it literally makes no difference whether he kicks a pebble or kills his family, since either would be an antidote to *ennui* or inactivity, I shall not be disposed, like consistent relativists, to attribute to him merely a different code of morality from my own or that of most men, but shall begin to speak of humanity and inhumanity.[91]

As we ponder these words, we recall Vico's final words on the "principles of humanity": they "must be the bounds of human reason." Indeed they must, "and let him who would transgress them beware lest he transgress all humanity."

Notes

The essay draws on some notions that I first raised in my study *The Rehabilitation of Myth: Vico's New Science*, Cambridge: Cambridge University Press, 1992. In the *Acknowledgements* I wrote: "Sir Isaiah Berlin read and discussed with me subsequent versions of this study in Oxford, and was always generous with his time and comments; to him I owe not only my greatest scholarly debt, but also my deepest personal gratitude for his support during hard times." I would like to dedicate this essay to Isaiah's memory, with the hope that in this critical engagement with his work I do what he taught me to do with works of great thinkers.

1. Peter Burke, *Vico* (Oxford: Oxford University Press, 1985); Isaiah Berlin, "The Reputation of Vico," *New Vico Studies* 17 (1999), pp. 1–5, with Peter Burke's "Response to Berlin: Vico Disparaged?," pp. 7–10.
2. Among Berlin's previous attempts to defend Vico's "originality" see his disputations "On Vico," *The Philosophical Quarterly* 35 (1985), pp. 281–90, in reply to Perez Zagorin, "Vico's Theory of Knowledge: A Critique," *The Philosophical Quarterly* 34 (1984), pp. 15–30; and his reply to Hans Aarsleff's critical review-essay, "Vico and Berlin," *London Review of Books* 5–18 Nov. 1981, pp. 6–7, published in the same issue pp. 7–8, with an additional comment in the issue of 3–16 June 1982, p. 5.
3. Berlin, "The Reputation of Vico," p. 3. Burke inveighs against the "myth of the forerunner" in *Vico*, pp. 8–9, and subsequent chapters.
4. Berlin's comment in Ramin Jahanbegloo, *Conversations with Isaiah Berlin. Recollections of an Historian of Ideas* (London: Phoenix, 1992), p. 96.
5. Berlin, "The Reputation of Vico," p. 4.

6. There are two good reasons to assume that the conversation took place in 1949: The English translation of Vico's *New Science* by Max Harold Fisch and Thomas Bergin, to which Salvemini refers, appeared in 1948; Berlin and Salvemini were then at Harvard University, where they both worked at the Widener Library and regularly met privately and on social occasions. Michael Ignatieff, *Isaiah Berlin. A Life* (New York: Metropolitan Books-Henry Holt, 1998), p. 191.
7. *Vico: A Bibliography of Works in English from 1884 to 1994*, ed. Molly Black Verene, (Charlottesville, Va.: Philosophy Documentation Center, 1994).
8. Isaiah Berlin, "The Philosophical Ideas of Giambattista Vico," in *Art and Ideas in Eighteenth-Century Italy* (Rome: Edizioni di Storia e Letteratura, 1960), pp. 156–233.
9. Giorgio Tagliacozzo, "Toward a History of Recent Vico Scholarship in English," *New Vico Studies* I (1983), p. 10.
10. Isaiah Berlin, *Vico and Herder. Two Studies in the History of Ideas* (London: The Hogarth Press, 1976). Now reprinted with some bibliographical revisions in *Three Critics of the Enlightenment: Vico, Hamann, Herder*, ed. H. Hardy (London: Pimlico, 2000). The topicality of Vico at the time is evident in the anthologies *Giambattista Vico: An International Symposium*, ed. G. Tagliacozzo and H. White (Baltimore: The Johns Hopkins University Press, 1969); *Vico and Contemporary Thought*, ed. G. Tagliacozzo, M. Mooney, and D. P. Verene, special volumes of *Social Research* 43, Numbers 3 & 4 (1976); *Giambattista Vico's Science of Humanity*, ed. G. Tagliacozzo and D. P. Verne (Baltimore: The Johns Hopkins University Press, 1976). Berlin contributed to the first two publications, and wrote a long review-essay on the third: "Corsi e Ricorsi," *Journal of Modern History* 50 (1978), pp. 480–9.
11. Isaiah Berlin, "One of the Boldest Innovators in the History of Human Thought," *The New York Times Magazine*, 23 November 1970, pp. 75–100. Republished in Isaiah Berlin, *The Power of Ideas*, ed. Henry Hardy (Princeton, N.J.: Princeton University Press, 2000), pp. 53–67.
12. Berlin, *Vico and Herder*, p. 95.
13. Henry S. Harris, *The Social Philosophy of Giovanni Gentile* (Urbana, Ill.: University of Illinois Press, 1960), pp. 286–7.
14. Berlin, *Vico and Herder*, p. 95.
15. Jules Michelet, Preface to *Histoire romaine*, quoted by Berlin from the English translation of Max Harold Fisch in his Introduction to *The Autobiography of Giambattista Vico*, tr. M. H. Fisch and T. G. Bergin (Ithaca, N.Y.: Cornell University Press, 1963), p. 78, in *Vico and Herder*, p. 94; "One of the Boldest Innovators," *The Power of Ideas*, p. 66: "Giambattista Vico and Cultural History," in *The Crooked Timber of Humanity: Chapters in the History of Ideas*, ed. Henry Hardy (London: John Murray, 1990), pp. 62–3; "The Reputation of Vico," p. 3.
16. Berlin, *Vico and Herder*, p. 107.
17. James Joyce, *Finnegans Wake* (London: Viking Press, 1939), p. 452.
18. Giambattista Vico, *The New Science*, tr. M. H. Fisch and T. G. Bergin, (Ithaca, N.Y.: Cornell University Press, 1968), par. 331.
19. For comprehensive reviews of earlier formulations of this notion see Benedetto Croce, *The Philosophy of Giambattista Vico*, tr. R. G. Collingwood (London: Howard Latimer, 1913), pp. 279–301; Rodolfo Mondolfo, *Il*

"*verum-factum*" *prima di Vico* (Napoli: Guida, 1969); Karl Löwith, *Vicos Grundsatz: Verum et factum convertuntur: Seine theologische Prämisse und deren säkulare Konsequenzen* (Heidelberg: Carl Winter Universitätsverlag, 1968). For a forceful attempt to reassert Vico's originality see Max H. Fisch, "Vico and Pragmatism," in *Giambattista Vico: An International Symposium*, pp. 401–24.

20. Vico, *The New Science*, par. 34.
21. Vico, *The New Science*, par. 338.
22. Vico, *The New Science*, par. 405.
23. Berlin, *Vico and Herder*, p. 61.
24. Vico, *The New Science*, par. 376.
25. Berlin, *Vico and Herder*, p. 26.
26. Berlin, "Vico and Cultural History," pp. 60–3. See also "Isaiah Berlin in Conversation with Steven Lukes," *Salmagundi* 120 (1998), pp. 87–8.
27. Vico, *The New Science*, par. 314.
28. Niccolò Machiavelli, *Discourses on the First Ten Books of Titus Livius*, tr. L. J. Walker (London: Routledge & Kegan Paul, 1950), I.39.1.
29. Vico, *The New Science*, par. 374.
30. Berlin, *Vico and Herder*, p. 27.
31. Berlin, "The Concept of Scientific History," in *Concepts and Categories: Philosophical Essays*, ed. Henry Hardy, with an introduction by Bernard Williams (Oxford: Oxford University Press, 1978), pp. 131–4; "The Pursuit of the Ideal," in *The Crooked Timber of Humanity*, p. 8. For some pertinent critical observations on the idealistic tendencies in (what might be called) the Collingwood-Berlin School of Vico studies, see Cecilia Miller, *Giambattista Vico. Imagination and Historical Knowledge* (London: MacMillan, 1993), pp. 29–32, 139–42.
32. Berlin, *Vico and Herder*, pp. xviii–xix.
33. Leon Pompa, *Vico: A Study of the New Science*, 2nd ed. (Cambridge: Cambridge University Press, 1990), pp. 223–30; Perez Zagorin, "Vico's Theory of Knowledge: A Critique," *The Philosophical Quarterly* 34 (1984), pp. 15–30.
34. Vico, *The New Science*, par. 163, 238, 245.
35. Max. H. Fisch, "Introduction" to *The New Science*, XIX–XX.
36. Isaac Newton, *Opticks*, repr. of 4th edition (London: G. Bell & Sons, 1931), pp. 401–2.
37. Vico, *The New Science*, par. 147, 344.
38. Berlin, *Vico and Herder*, pp. xx–xxi.
39. Berlin, *Vico and Herder*, p. 67.
40. Vico, *The New Science*, par. 338. Berlin defends his notion of "reconstructive imagination" against Pompa's criticism in *Vico and Herder*, footnotes to pp. 32–3, and in his response to Zagorin's critical essay in "On Vico," *The Philosophical Quarterly* 35 (1985), pp. 281–90.
41. Berlin, *Vico and Herder*, pp. 52–3.
42. Isaiah Berlin, "Vico's Theory of Knowledge and its Sources," *Vico and Herder*, pp. 99–142; originally published as "Sulla teoria del Vico circa la conoscenza storica," in *Lettere italiane* 17 (1965), pp. 420–31.
43. Vico, *The New Science*, par. 349.
44. Vico, *The New Science*, par. 51.
45. Berlin, "Giambattista Vico and Cultural History," p. 62.

46. Berlin, *Vico and Herder*, pp. 56–7.
47. Burke, "Vico Disparaged?," p. 7, referring to his *Vico*, pp. 78–80, 93–4.
48. Berlin, *Vico and Herder*, p. xvi.
49. Roger Hausheer, "Introduction" to Isaiah Berlin, *Against the Current: Essays in the History of Ideas*, ed. and with a bibliography by Henry Hardy, with an introduction by Roger Hausheer (Oxford: Oxford University Press, 1981), pp. xvi–xxv; Claude J. Galipeau, *Isaiah Berlin's Liberalism* (Oxford: Oxford University Press, 1994), pp. 26–34.
50. Isaiah Berlin, "The Pursuit of the Ideal," pp. 8–10; Jahanbegloo, *Conversations with Isaiah Berlin*, pp. 72–82.
51. Berlin's essays signal the transition from the philosophical "history of ideas" of scholars like Lovejoy, Cassirer, Kristeller, or Koyré that flourished in the 1930s and 1940s, to the more historical and hermeneutical trends that emerged in the 1960s. See the programmatic essay of Donald R. Kelley, "Horizons of Intellectual History: Retrospect, Circumspect, Prospect," *Journal of the History of Ideas* XLVIII (1987), pp. 143–69.
52. Berlin, *Vico and Herder*, pp. 9–12.
53. Vico, *The New Science*, par. 356–7.
54. Vico, *The New Science*, par. 142.
55. Berlin, "Vico's Concept of Knowledge," in *Against the Current*, pp. 111–19.
56. Vico, *The New Science*, par. 201–2.
57. Berlin, "Vico and the Ideal of the Enlightenment," in *Against the Current*, p. 129.
58. Vico, *The New Science*, par. 131.
59. Vico, *The New Science*, par. 394, 1084.
60. Berlin, *Vico and Herder*, pp. 40–1.
61. Vico, *The New Science*, par. 347.
62. Among many assertions of this view see, for example, Isaiah Berlin, "The Concept of Scientific History," pp. 103–42, esp. pp. 132–3. See also Berlin's reflections on his transition and vocation in Jahanbegloo, *Conversations with Isaiah Berlin*, pp. 23–31.
63. For a vibrant exposition of Berlin's political philosophy along these lines see John Gray, *Isaiah Berlin* (Princeton, N.J.: Princeton University Press, 1996).
64. Isaiah Berlin, "The Counter-Enlightenment," in *Against the Current*, pp. 4–13.
65. Arnaldo Momigliano, "On the Pioneer Trail" (Review of Berlin's *Vico and Herder*), *New York Review of Books*, 11 Nov. 1976, p. 33–8.
66. Isaiah Berlin, "Alleged Relativism in Eighteenth-Century European Thought," in *The Crooked Timber of Humanity*, p. 87.
67. Berlin, "Alleged Relativism in Eighteenth-Century European Thought" p. 79.
68. Mark Lilla, *G. B. Vico: The Making of an Anti-Modern* (Cambridge, Mass.: Harvard University Press, 1993), pp. 1–6.
69. Berlin, *Vico and Herder*, p. xvi.
70. Berlin, "Alleged Relativism in Eighteenth-Century European Thought," p. 79.
71. Berlin, "Vico and the Ideal of the Enlightenment," pp. 120–29; "Giambattista Vico and Cultural History," pp. 63–8; "Alleged Relativism in Eighteenth-Century European Thought," pp. 78–9.
72. Vico, *The New Science*, par. 1092, 1110.

73. Michel Foucault, "What is Enlightenment?", tr. C. Porter, in *The Foucault Reader*, ed. P. Rabinow (London: Penguin, 1984), p. 34, citing Vico, *The New Science*, par. 1089, 1094.
74. Vico, *The New Science*, par. 445.
75. Vico, *The New Science*, par. 241–2.
76. David Hume, *An Enquiry Concerning Human Understanding*, ed. L. A. Selby-Bigge (Oxford: Oxford University Press, 1902), p. 83.
77. See Berlin's remark in Jahanbegloo, *Conversations with Isaiah Berlin*, pp. 69–70.
78. Charles Taylor, "The Immanent Counter-Enlightenment," in *Canadian Political Philosophy: Contemporary Reflections*, ed. R. Beiner and W. Norman (Oxford: Oxford University Press, 2001), pp. 386–400.
79. See, for example, *The Enlightenment in National Context*, ed. R. Porter and M. Teich (Cambridge: Cambridge University Press, 1981); David Sorkin, *Moses Mendelssohn and the Religious Enlightenment* (London: Peter Halban, 1996); J. G. A. Pocock, *Barbarism and Religion*, vol. I: *The Enlightenments of Edward Gibbon 1737–1764* (Cambridge: Cambridge University Press, 2000).
80. Vico, *The New Science*, par. 2, 129.
81. Hume, *An Enquiry Concerning Human Understanding*, p. 84.
82. David Hume, *A Treatise of Human Nature*, ed. Selby-Bigge (Oxford: Oxford University Press, 1888), pp. xxii–xxiii.
83. Vico, *The New Science*, par. 347.
84. Vico, *The New Science*, par. 332–3, 360.
85. Vico, *The New Science*, par. 334–7.
86. Peter Winch, "Understanding a Primitive Society," *The American Philosophical Quarterly* 1 (1964), p. 322.
87. Vico, *The New Science*, par. 309. For a lucid elaboration of this notion, see James C. Morrison, "Vico's Doctrine of the Natural Law of the Gentes," *Journal of the History of Philosophy* 16 (1978), pp. 47–60.
88. Vico, *The New Science*, par. 161–2.
89. Berlin, "The Pursuit of the Ideal," in *The Crooked Timber of Humanity*, p. 18.
90. See the discussions in Berlin's *Concepts and Categories*: "The Purpose of Philosophy," pp. 7–8; "The Concept of Scientific History," pp. 129–30; "Does Political Theory Still Exist?," pp. 162–6.
91. Berlin, "Does Political Theory Still Exist?," p. 166.

5 The Case for the Enlightenment: A Comparative Approach

John Robertson

I.

To the historical scholar of the Enlightenment, Isaiah Berlin's legacy has been, at the least, double-edged. That he was more interested in a Counter-Enlightenment does not mean that he discounted the Enlightenment itself. On the contrary, his exploration of the idea of Counter-Enlightenment presupposed Enlightenment's existence and significance. He had a clear view of the nature of the Enlightenment: it was emphatically if not exclusively a movement of ideas, defined by its intellectual content. In its time, this was a view closest to what I shall call the philosophers' conception of the Enlightenment. But Berlin did not subscribe to the most rigorous, Kantian version of the philosophers' Enlightenment: as a movement of ideas which he associated principally with the French *philosophes*, Berlin's remained an Enlightenment which ordinary historians could recognize. Beyond that of the historians, moreover, Berlin's was an Enlightenment accessible to the educated lay reader—or, better still, to the interested audience hearing his remarkable lectures, whether in person or over the wireless. Even though his own interest in it was increasingly incidental to his desire to explore the Counter-Enlightenment, it was probably from Berlin more than anyone else that the postwar British derived their understanding of the Enlightenment, and learned to appreciate its ideals as vital bequests to modernity.

Yet there is no doubt that Berlin's presentation of its ideas was in the long run deeply damaging to the Enlightenment's reputation. Repeatedly—for reiteration was crucial to the rhetorical force of his lectures—Berlin identified the Enlightenment with a small number of simple doctrines: the uniformity of human nature, the timeless universality of natural law as a code of human moral behaviour, the conviction that a single perfect end for human society could be discovered and should be sought. Against these doctrines he played off the objections of the Counter-Enlightenment: that the varieties of human nature were more obvious and valuable; that human moral customs and codes differed across time and space; and above all, that the attempt to identify, and then dictate, a single perfect outcome for human society was both mistaken and profoundly dangerous.[1] Berlin was careful not to "take sides"; he did not hide the darker aspect of leading proponents of Counter-Enlightenment, Joseph de Maistre in particular. Nevertheless, the attention which he devoted to the Counter-Enlightenment cast a shadow over the Enlightenment whose ideas, by contrast, he summarized so ruthlessly. Whether or not he intended it, Berlin's way with the Enlightenment offered encouragement to those who wished to believe that its ideals of universalism and human perfectibility lay behind some of the modern world's greatest evils.

As a result, it is not impossible to trace a line from Berlin's account of the Enlightenment to the conclusion that if this is where Enlightenment has led us, it is time to repudiate it, and establish new, postmodern intellectual foundations for our thinking. In place of what it takes to be the Enlightenment conviction that the lot of humanity can be bettered by the power of reason and the adoption of certain universal values, postmodernity would leave different cultures to determine their own ends, refusing to discriminate morally or politically between them.

Historians of the Enlightenment have tended not to engage directly with this critique; but they could not escape the prevailing unease about the significance and value of their subject. While the volume of scholarship devoted to the Enlightenment continued to grow, the subject of study became increasingly fragmented. This was especially marked in English-language scholarship. The last major synthesis in English was Peter Gay's two-volume *The Enlightenment: An Interpretation*, published at the end of the 1960s. Despite its attempt to develop a social as well as intellectual history of the Enlightenment, the work was almost immediately judged inadequate by Robert Darnton.[2] Very soon Gay's insistence on the unities of the Enlightenment had come to seem either irrelevant or untenable in the face of a new emphasis on its diversity. As specialist studies on parts of the subject proliferated, many scholars began to question whether it was helpful to continue to think in terms of a single Enlightenment. If the tendency was to divide the Enlightenment into as many parts as scholars could study, without regard to their compatibility, it became easier to think of there having been "Enlightenments" in the plural. Even when the definite article remained, to satisfy the demands of textbook publishing, it was used to characterize the Enlightenment in a loose and inclusive way, as a series of debates and concerns, rather than as a unified intellectual movement.[3] Such characterization might be an effective response to those—they were rarely historians—who equated the Enlightenment with a single doctrinaire "project."[4] But it was a negative response, whose success depended on denying the Enlightenment a coherent historical identity. The monolithic edifice held responsible for modernity was simply abandoned, as historical scholars refashioned Enlightenment in the pluralist image of postmodernity. "The" Enlightenment, it was conceded, was dead; but "Enlightenments" might flourish.

Certainly, we can do better, and still make a case for the Enlightenment in the singular. In so doing, we could restore to the Enlightenment a definite intellectual content (though not that ascribed to it by Berlin). This is necessary, in the face of both the doubts of intellectual historians and the claims of the social or "cultural" historians, for whom ideas are the arbitrary "representations" of constructed social relations. Only if we insist on the original intellectual content of the Enlightenment will we be able to do justice to the question of its relation to the social contexts within which it has developed.[5] In what follows I shall make my own "case for the Enlightenment" in three stages. First, I will review the process by which Enlightenment studies fragmented after 1970, and identify what seem to have been the three principal tendencies to this effect. Next, I will outline how the Enlightenment might be reconstituted, according primacy to its intellectual originality. Finally, I shall illustrate my argument by sketching a comparative approach to the Enlightenment in two far-removed parts of Europe, Scotland and Naples, with two very different social and intellectual settings, but one Enlightenment in both.

II.

Before 1970 the Enlightenment owed its reputation, if not its existence, primarily to two types of historical scholarship, literary and philosophical. Though others have now joined them, both these approaches are still very much alive. The literary historians identified the Enlightenment, or *les lumières*, almost exclusively with a small circle of *philosophes* and those who associated with or visited them in France, which usually meant Paris. The *philosophes'* publications defined both the intellectual content of the Enlightenment and its chronology: it began with the works of Montesquieu and Voltaire in the 1720s and 1730s, and ended with the Revolution and the death of Condorcet.[6] Without denying the centrality of the *philosophes*, the historians of philosophy added a second dimension. The best-known and most compelling version of this approach was that of Ernst Cassirer, who believed that Kant's philosophy provided a systematic summation of the intellectual project of the entire Enlightenment, and could thus be used as a framework in which to place and assess the contributions of other thinkers across a range of fields, including metaphysics, aesthetics, morals, and politics.[7] Together, and indeed separately, the literary and philosophical approaches offered what most historians accepted were plausible accounts of the Enlightenment as an intellectual movement, composed of a relatively small number of men of letters, committed to certain leading ideas.[8]

After 1970, however, Enlightenment studies moved rapidly in several new directions. Although the divisions between them are not hard and fast, the new directions can be grouped under three headings: intellectual, national, and social. Each of these has enormously deepened our understanding of the Enlightenment; but they have also been taken to lengths which make it very difficult to maintain a coherent view of the Enlightenment as a whole.

The first new direction was towards a much more complex appreciation of Enlightenment thought. The old shibboleth that the Enlightenment was the "Age of Reason" has long since been abandoned by historians of philosophy. It is the strength of skepticism and the preoccupation with the passions as the strongest force in human nature which now command attention. The shift is especially clear in moral philosophy, where "the passions and the interests," in Albert Hirschman's phrase, have become the starting-point for enquiries in this and the related fields of political economy and historical theory.[9] More generally, however, the loosening of the philosophical definition of the Enlightenment created an unprecedented uncertainty over what should count as Enlightenment thinking. Claims began to be advanced on behalf of subjects hitherto regarded as marginal to its interests, notably by historians of science. If no single philosophy characterized the Enlightenment, it was asked, why should any area of intellectual activity at the time be excluded from it? As a result, it has come to seem difficult to exclude any not obviously reactionary form of thought from the Enlightenment's liberal embrace. But there is a price to pay: an Enlightenment so inclusive is in danger of losing any coherent, distinctive intellectual identity.

The second new direction in Enlightenment studies has been towards writing its history in national contexts. The assumption that the Enlightenment belonged exclusively to France and Germany was originally questioned by the great Italian historian Franco Venturi. Venturi's point was that the established account of the Enlightenment, which treated Italians such as Galiani and Beccaria effectively as "visiting members" by virtue of their stays in Paris and reception in the *salons*, had overlooked the extent of their activities and connections in their own country. In the Milan of Beccaria and the Naples of Galiani, as indeed in Piedmont, Tuscany, and even Venice and the Papal States, there existed self-conscious groups of *illuministi*, who did indeed look to Paris for inspiration, but who were also keen to apply Enlightenment ideas to the problems of their own societies.[10] A comparable view could be taken of the situation in Germany. In a similarly fragmented political context, the *Aufklärer* had exploited the opportunities of service in princely administrations to discuss and advance their ideas, even if they tended to be less actively critical of the existing order than their Italian counterparts.

But the most whole-hearted in their adoption of the national approach to Enlightenment have been English-speaking scholars. American, Scottish, and even English Enlightenments have emerged as subjects of study in this perspective. In the 1970s scholars began to take an interest in the Enlightenment in North America; but it has, for obvious reasons, proved difficult to keep this subject distinct from the development of the Revolution and the making of the constitution.[11] By contrast, the growth of interest in the Scottish Enlightenment since 1960, when it was scarcely recognized at all, has been spectacular. Initially, the emphasis explaining the Enlightenment was on the renewal of Scottish connections with Continental European thinking.[12] But in the 1980s Nicholas Phillipson led the way in setting it in national context, the better to facilitate writing a social history of its ideas.[13] By 1990, Scottish historians with a national, even a "nationalist," axe to grind were explicit in giving priority to the supposedly distinctive Scottish origins of the Enlightenment.[14]

By 2000, however, the Scots were in some danger of being eclipsed by a surge of interest in the Enlightenment in England. The case for an English Enlightenment is not quite as new as recent publicity might suggest. For some time the most likely candidates for association with the wider Enlightenment seemed to be the rational Dissenters. But over the past fifteen years a powerful alternative case has been mounted by John Pocock, now reinforced by Brian Young, for the existence of a distinctively Anglican Enlightenment. This Pocock would treat as the English variant of the Protestant Enlightenment, comparable with Enlightenments in Scotland, North Germany, and Switzerland; in his most recent formulation, in *The Enlightenments of Edward Gibbon*, it has become a specifically Socinian Enlightenment.[15] The late Roy Porter also provided a full-length statement of the case he first announced in 1981, which was reflected in its final form in the title of his last book: *Enlightenment. Britain and the Creation of the Modern World*. The argument appears to be that since England, and by extension Britain, created the modern world, it must have had an Enlightenment. On the strength of this conviction, Porter was able to include in a British Enlightenment virtually anything which took his fancy.[16]

That the national turn in Enlightenment studies has been enormously fruitful is beyond doubt. It has enlarged our understanding of the extent of Enlightenment activity across Europe, burying forever the assumption that it was simply a movement of French *philosophes*, afforced by the occasional foreign visitor to Paris and by the distant genius of Kant. But the consolidation of the approach under the rubric of "the Enlightenment in national context" has also clarified its dangers. Its natural tendency has been to fragment the Enlightenment into a series of more or less distinct Enlightenments, each defined as best suits national historiography. Just as almost any area of intellectual activity may be associated with Enlightenment, so it has come to seem equally reasonable to suppose that any nation (even England) must have had its Enlightenment.

The third new direction in Enlightenment scholarship has been the study of the movement's social settings, and of the publishing and dissemination of its ideas. Exploration of these goes back to Daniel Mornet's pioneering work in the 1930s; since the 1960s it has been taken much further by Daniel Roche, Roger Chartier, and Robert Darnton. The work of Chartier and Darnton continues to be marked, however, by a preoccupation with the question of the Enlightenment's relation to the Revolution; as a result, study of the former tends to be subordinated to explanation of the latter.[17] In reaction, younger American critics of Darnton have adapted the ideas of Habermas to suggest that the Enlightenment be characterized by association with the new culture of "sociability."

Two phenomena often associated with the Enlightenment seem particularly amenable to explanation in terms of a culture of sociability. One is Freemasonry, which had many adherents among those identified with Enlightenment in France, the German-speaking lands, and Naples. Quite why such a secretive, ritualistic creed should have appealed to men (and a few women) who were otherwise committed to the free, public discussion of ideas remains a puzzle; but it is at least plausible to suggest that its internal egalitarianism was in accord with the new ideals of sociability.[18] The second phenomenon is the *salon*. On Dena Goodman's account, the *salonnières* of Paris were not mere hostesses but rather also the directors and arbiters of a distinctive Enlightenment culture, enforcing the rules of polite conversation and mediating epistolary exchange. Here sociability was female-centered, the Enlightenment gendered as feminine. So arguing, Goodman can distinguish the "culture of the Enlightenment" from the Revolutionary culture which followed: the forms of political association characteristic of the latter were incompatible with those of Enlightenment sociability.[19]

But a defense of the Enlightenment's identity on these terms comes at a price. In setting out to write a "cultural" rather than an "intellectual" history of the Enlightenment, Goodman directs attention away from ideas as such, to the "discourse" of society at large. Again the effect (if not necessarily the intention) is deconstructive. If ideas are no longer the focus of attention, it is much harder to define and defend the Enlightenment's distinctive identity. It was as a movement of ideas that the Enlightenment acquired its historical significance, for good and ill; to marginalize its intellectual content, as the social and cultural historians tend to do, is to make "Enlightenment" into a label of convenience, with little or no substantive significance.

The volume and richness of new scholarship on the Enlightenment plainly make any return to the traditional account of it impossible. But if the implications of such work are to deprive the Enlightenment of an intellectual identity, to fragment it into separate national units, and to render it primarily a social and cultural phenomenon, can any new, uniform account of the Enlightenment be put in its place?

III.

If a case for the Enlightenment is to be made at all, it must begin with ideas. It is clear that the traditional equation of Enlightenment thought with the contents of the *philosophes'* books—with optional reinforcement from Kantian philosophy—is unsustainable. But the intellectual coherence of the Enlightenment may still be found in the commitment to understanding, and hence to advancing, the causes and conditions of human betterment in this world. The first part of this formula is as important as the second. The Enlightenment was committed to understanding, that is to analysis on the basis of good arguments leading to reasoned conclusions. There was a core of original thinking to the Enlightenment: it was not simply a matter of common aspirations and values. Within that core the understanding of human betterment was pursued across a number of interdependent lines of enquiry.

For many, the starting-point was human nature itself—the connected study of the understanding, the passions, and the process of moral judgment which David Hume christened "the science of man." In their systematic study of the understanding and the passions, as, still more, in their skeptical subordination of reason to the passions, eighteenth-century philosophers were of course the heirs of several seventeenth-century predecessors.[20] The Enlightenment philosophers were original, however, in the deliberate attempt to join mental and moral philosophy in a single science, in which the framework for the investigation of individual behavior was provided by human society rather than divine authority.

A second line of enquiry was into the conditions specifically of material betterment, the subject matter of political economy. Sophisticated writing on economic affairs of course predated the Enlightenment, being increasingly widespread from the later seventeenth century. But from the 1740s there can be seen a conscious attempt on the part of French, Italian, German, and Scottish thinkers to render political economy a distinct, systematic field of investigation. No longer concerned with the aggrandizement of governments at each other's expense, this was a political economy the goals of which were the wealth of nations (in the plural) and the improvement of the condition of all of society's members. Understood in these terms, political economy was the key to what the Enlightenment explicitly thought of as "the progress of society."

But the progress of society was not simply a matter of material improvement. Accompanying the enquiry into political economy was a third, more general concern to investigate the structure and manners of societies at the various stages of their development, to trace and explain the historical process from "barbarism" to "refinement" or "civilization." The scope of this line of enquiry was potentially wide, ranging across manners in all their variety, the rise and refinement of the arts and sciences, moral relations, including those between the sexes, and forms of property-holding; in turn the last of these was closely related to the question of the forms of government associated with different stages of development. Given the capacity of humanity to "polish" or even (as many followed Rousseau in supposing) to "perfect" its nature, it was widely believed that the progress of society should culminate in the achievement of a new state of civilization. But given the instability of history, few thought they had good reason to suppose the progress would end in a state of perfection; many continued to be troubled by doubt as to whether civilization could ever be made fully secure against "corruption."

My case for the Enlightenment's intellectual originality obviously needs qualification. To identify the science of man, political economy, and the progress of society as the connecting threads of the Enlightenment's commitment to understanding human betterment is not to suggest that they constituted a single, seamless intellectual project, pursued by all the Enlightenment's adherents. Few thinkers were equally interested, let alone competent, in each of the fields of enquiry. At the same time, few confined their interests to these fields. Many Enlightenment thinkers were also students of the natural world; others were passionately interested in music. It was a matter of priorities, and what characterized the Enlightenment was the new primacy accorded to human betterment, to the possibility—not the inevitability—of progress in the present world. Even then there remained wide scope for disagreement over the means to achieve progress, as well as over the definition and compatibility of its ends. Enlightenment enquiries, moreover, adapted and developed in response to fresh stimuli: the debates of the 1770s and 1780s were often markedly different from those of the 1750s.

It is also important to emphasize that the intellectual coherence of the Enlightenment was not predicated upon an explicit denial of the possibility of revealed religion. Here I differ from Jonathan Israel.[21] The boldness with which Spinoza, Toland, and Giannone had criticized the authority of Scripture continued to be an inspiration to many well after 1750. But Spinoza's materialism did not exhaust the philosophical resources available to Enlightenment thinkers, while the notorious fate of Giannone, kidnapped, imprisoned, and suffering confiscation of his writings, was a clear warning that open irreligion would not be tolerated in Catholic Europe. Criticism of the Church as an institution in this world was permissible, and indeed stronger in Catholic than in Protestant countries. But revelation itself was not automatically threatened: a focus on betterment in this world carried no necessary implication about the existence of the next. What the Enlightenment did proclaim was the inadequacy, indeed inhumanity, of the doctrine which held out the pleasures of the next world as consolation for the hardships of the present. Whatever might be awaiting the redeemed in the world to come, improvement of the human lot was possible in this world, here and now.

This conviction did not entail a uniformly benevolent conception of human nature. If anything, the contrary was true. In a striking observation, Berlin once declared that "what the entire Enlightenment has in common is a denial of the central Christian doctrine of original sin, believing that man is born either innocent or good, or morally neutral and malleable by education and environment, or, at worst, deeply defective but capable of radical and indefinite improvement by rational education in favourable circumstances, or by a revolutionary reorganisation of society as demanded, for example, by Rousseau."²² But the Enlightenment was deeply indebted to a group of thinkers to whom original sin had mattered very much—the Augustinian thinkers Pascal, Malebranche, and Bayle; more precisely, it was indebted to the encounter between Augustinian rigorism and the revived, supposedly Christianized Epicureanism championed by Gassendi and his followers. For it was from this encounter that there developed the realization that a society of purely self-interested men, driven by their passions rather than their reason, could nevertheless survive and meet its needs, with little or even no external assistance from Divine Providence and only limited intervention by government. The possibilities of such thinking were particularly displayed by two works published in the 1720s, Mandeville's *Fable of the Bees* (1723) and Vico's *Scienza nuova* (1725). If the second of these was the book the Enlightenment did not read, the first would be among the books most read and discussed by Enlightenment thinkers, precisely for its alarming demonstration that a society driven by men's and women's "vices" could work for the general benefit.²³ The significance of these two works for the Enlightenment in Naples and Scotland will be discussed in the last part of this paper.

In addition to re-establishing its intellectual coherence, a case for the Enlightenment as one intellectual movement must also show that ideas, books, and men of letters were able to travel across Europe, and did not simply stop in Paris. Enlightenment needed to transcend its national (and other) contexts, if it was to be—as Kant proclaimed—"cosmopolitan." In fact, as a growing body of scholarship confirms, the channels of literary and epistolary communication were already open within the European "Republic of Letters." Well before Paris and its *salons* had established their leading position in Enlightenment exchanges, the cities of the Netherlands had become the fulcrum of literary Europe: the periodical press, the encyclopaedia, and the translation were all aids to the international circulation of ideas whose viability had been established in the United Provinces in the later seventeenth century.²⁴ None of these aids could override all differences of inherited intellectual culture. The process of translation in particular was always liable to modify meaning, sometimes substantially.²⁵ Nevertheless, Enlightenment men of letters were able to adapt and refine these instruments of communication for their own use, generating and participating in a single, connected discussion, the better to redirect the intellectual agenda towards the new issues of human betterment.

A renewed emphasis on the intellectual and international character of the Enlightenment does not mean that the questions raised by its social historians can simply be set aside. Its adherents had to live in the world as well as think about it, and needed careers and recognition, along with outlets for their writings. Outside France there is still much to be learned about the material and cultural infrastructure of the Enlightenment.²⁶ But the social history of the Enlightenment cannot simply be left to its "social historians." A case for the Enlightenment which reemphasizes the primacy of its intellectual contribution also needs to reconsider the perspective in which its social history is written. I have already suggested that the vogue for social or cultural history tends to devalue ideas. Enlightenment thinkers themselves were not automatically hostage to their careers and institutional backgrounds, and their ideas should not be reduced to cultural discourses. On the contrary, it may be argued, their distinguishing social characteristic was their claim to an independent status in society, by virtue of their intellectual leadership.

This was the claim which Kant formulated, very precisely, in *Was ist Aufklärung?* in 1784. In their "private" capacities, as clergymen or professors, men of letters were bound to accept the restrictions on their freedom to speak, which the institutions for which they worked might impose. But in their "public" capacity, as members of society at large, they should expect and actively seek to advance the goals of Enlightenment.[27] They were to do this, it was generally agreed, by shaping "public opinion." Exactly what "public opinion" was may not have been clear at the time, and has been disputed by historians since. In some contexts it was perhaps little more than a figment of writers' imaginations. But even in such cases a point was made by appealing to it. Enlightenment men of letters deliberately broke with the traditional humanist model of the philosopher as the private counsellor of kings, whose advice was a secret. By choosing instead to address an educated "public," they retained for themselves the intellectual initiative, setting the terms on which they engaged with their readers.

This was not simply self-promotion: the Enlightenment thinkers had good intellectual reason to value public opinion above direct political influence. For implicit in their commitment to the study of the laws of political economy and of the progress of society was a recognition of the limits which they set upon politics. In a world in which commerce was becoming ever more widespread and important, decisions which affected the lives and well-being of many were being taken by individual economic agents out of a prevailing motive of self-interest, with little or no regard for what rulers wished to happen.[28] When the Enlightenment thinkers set themselves to identify the regularities in the patterns of men's commercial activities, and in the historically observable relations between forms of property-holding and stages of social organization, they were explaining why the powers of politicians and statesmen over society were effectively limited. In failing to appreciate this, moreover, the politicians were far more likely to obstruct than to facilitate the workings of society. These conclusions did not lead Enlightenment thinkers to discount the possibility of reform; I do not suggest that Enlightenment was apolitical. Even the most skeptical of Enlightenment philosophers left room at least for remedial political action. But the purpose of reform should be the removal of obstacles to the optimal course of development, not the imposition of ambitious schemes of the politician's own devising. Enlightenment thinking thus ran counter to the traditional doctrine of "reason of state," by which rulers had claimed to know what was good for their subjects, and had presumed to manipulate their affairs accordingly; instead, the point of appealing to "public opinion" was to exert an external, constraining influence on governments. By invoking "the public" as their tribunal, the Enlightenment thinkers could hope simultaneously to establish their own credentials as an independent source of intellectual authority, and to educate government and society at large in the forces which were shaping the modern world.[29] By the 1780s, writers in several parts of the continent were once again addressing governments directly; but now it was with the confidence that they spoke for "the public."

An Enlightenment reconstituted on the terms I have suggested does not include everything which many recent scholars have wished to associate with it. The Enlightenment *was* exclusive, both intellectually and geographically. The focus of its enquiries, and the subject of its most original contributions, was human society and the physical and moral well-being of individuals in this world. It was also confined to the European world (including colonial America). If historians find it convenient to speak of "Enlightenments" in other civilizations, they were not extensions of the European original. Even within Europe, the reach of the Enlightenment was uneven. There were areas in which individuals bravely pursued its intellectual commitments but were too isolated to be active participants in the wider movement.[30] Above all, the Enlightenment was exclusive in being a movement of an intellectual elite. Its adherents were indeed committed to the wider dissemination of their ideas (and as authors were of course delighted to benefit from sales of their works). They were also keen to engage a larger public in discussion. But their priorities remained intellectual, and they looked to public opinion to confirm their intellectual authority. As an intellectual movement, in short, the Enlightenment was not equivalent to a general culture of sociability, however it may have encouraged one to develop.

To insist that the Enlightenment was not all-inclusive is to set aside much that recent scholarship has suggested is of great interest. (It is not, of course, to suggest that what is set aside should not be studied in its own right.) But it is equally the case that the unrestricted definition of Enlightenment, or its alternative, the admission that there were multiple Enlightenments, has rendered the subject so blurred and indeterminate that it is impossible to reach any assessment of its historical significance. The Enlightenment for which I have made a case here is one, I suggest, which existed as an historical phenomenon rather than as an artificial philosophical construct. It is not an Enlightenment which can be held directly responsible for the horrors, any more than for the advances, of the twentieth century: far too much history lies in between. But as a specific intellectual movement of the eighteenth century, it is an Enlightenment which can be matched against the conditions which faced it in its own time. Its significance may then be assessed according to the extent to which it understood the developments in society which it observed and identified ways to improve the human condition as it found it.

IV.

The case for the Enlightenment as an historical phenomenon can be enhanced not by further study of its traditional heartlands, but by a comparison of its development in two of its most distant settings: Scotland and Naples (the kingdom as well as the city). Any historical comparison presupposes both differences and similarities, and focuses, for the purposes of its argument, upon one or the other. In this case, Scotland and Naples present two very different contexts, which may well be understood as "national contexts"; nevertheless, I want to argue that they shared a common engagement with the Enlightenment. What follows is a sketch of this argument, which I intend to develop at greater length in future.

There is no denying that the differences of context between Scotland and Naples were many and important. Not only were there obvious differences in terms of geography and respective economic, political, and religious histories, but there was also a marked discrepancy in the intellectual resources available to each as bases from which to engage with the Enlightenment. Naples might be the second city of the Counter-Reformation; yet it had also fostered strong dissident traditions within its Catholic intellectual culture. By the end of the seventeenth century, the writings of the French exponents of Cartesianism, Augustinianism, and Epicureanism were more or less freely available to Neapolitan philosophers.[31] The Scots, by contrast, ignored the new French philosophy in favor of an irenic but not very profound Stoicism.[32] At the beginning of the eighteenth century leading Scottish academics such as Gershom Carmichael did engage with the ideas of Malebranche; but Carmichael made no effort to introduce his students to the sceptical, Augustinian-Epicurean thinking of the Protestant Pierre Bayle.[33]

Yet by 1700 common preoccupations were beginning to emerge, and from these it is possible to see how the Scots and the Neapolitans were to become participants in the same movement of Enlightenment. The first such preoccupation was the result of the two countries' similarity of situation. Both were dependent kingdoms within greater composite monarchies, Naples within the Spanish, Scotland within the Stewart monarchy of Britain and Ireland. And in 1700 both found that what remained of their ancient autonomy was threatened by political circumstance: that of Naples by the Spanish Succession crisis, Scotland's by the British equivalent, the continuing problem of Jacobitism. Responding to these predicaments, publicists in the two countries debated their causes and possible outcomes in strikingly similar terms. Paolo Mattia Doria analyzed the condition of Naples as that of a "regno governato in provincia"; Andrew Fletcher warned that Scotland was sinking to the status of a "conquered province."[34] At the same time, Doria and Fletcher both attempted to chart a way forward for their countries by adapting Machiavellian concepts to a world in which commerce and great capital cities were making it very difficult for small nations to preserve their autonomy.

A second common preoccupation was more immediately intellectual: the challenge of the Augustinian-Epicurean account of man's self-interested sociability. In Naples Vico had been exposed to this from the 1680s, but it was in the 1720s that he decided to reckon with the challenge, making his response central to the *Scienza nuova*. Vico's "rational"—or reasoned—"civil theology of divine providence" was explicitly constructed to explain why men who "because of their corrupted nature, are under the tyranny of *amor proprio*, which compels them to make private *utilità* their chief guide," nevertheless settle in societies.[35] Vico's account of his isolation in his autobiography, as well as the apparent eccentricity of his interests in early Greek and Roman history and mythology, have encouraged his readers, Berlin at their head, to regard him as an original genius, born before his time, and presciently hostile to principles associated with the Enlightenment.[36] What should be emphasized, nevertheless, is the modernity of Vico's engagement with Augustinian-Epicurean thinking, and of his insight that human sociability and its history should be the subject of a "new science." This is not to make of Vico a participant in the Enlightenment, a movement of which he knew virtually nothing. His commitment to vindicating the role of Divine Providence in human history, in repeated, explicit rejection of the arguments of Hobbes, Spinoza, and Bayle was, I think, genuine; and his account of "the course of nations" in history discounted the idea of a progressive improvement in human affairs. But he was in no doubt that the Augustinian-Epicurean account of the human condition was where the new science must begin.

In Scotland, by contrast, the challenge of the Augustinian-Epicurean philosophy arrived late and abruptly, in the form of the 1723 edition of Mandeville's

Fable of the Bees. Fresh from studying under Carmichael in Glasgow, Francis Hutcheson immediately recognized the danger, and attempted to meet it by strengthening the philosophy of Shaftesbury. But this came late: when the young David Hume was struggling to work out the "new scene of thought" he had discovered in 1729, he got no help from Shaftesbury and Stoic morals, but did find "diversion and improvement" in reading Bayle.[37] The outcome of his struggle, ten years later (three of them spent in France) was of course *A Treatise of Human Nature* (1739–40). Rigorously skeptical, the *Treatise* was, among other things, a philosophical rendering of the Epicurean or Mandevillian account of society as the outcome of the selfish passions.[38] Unlike Vico, however, Hume left no room for the workings of Providence, and he agreed with Mandeville that man's self-interest included the desire to "meliorate" or improve his condition. Through Hume, in short, Epicureanism opened the door to Enlightenment.

The *Treatise* may have fallen, as Hume lamented at the end of his life, "dead-born from the press," but it was never as inaccessible as the *Scienza nuova*. Within five years its notoriety had cost Hume his chance of a university chair in Scotland; yet in a further six he was established in Edinburgh as his country's leading man of letters, whose *Essays*, philosophical, political, and economic, shortly followed by his *History*, set the agenda for others' enquiries. Hume's skepticism, his insistence that the greater part of our knowledge of this world is a matter of degrees of probability, while we have no grounds to claim knowledge of the divine, led him to be suspected, rightly, of irreligion. But until his death, and the posthumous publication of the *Dialogues of Natural Religion* (1779), he seldom indulged in open expression of his views on religion; rather, he avoided controversy and put his efforts into encouraging his fellow Scots men of letters to assume the responsibilities of intellectual leadership. By personal as well as intellectual example, Hume thus made possible Scotland's full participation in the Enlightenment.

A similar individual initiative brought the Enlightenment to Naples. In 1753 Antonio Genovesi issued his *Discorso sopra il vero fine delle lettere e delle scienze*, a call to the *studiosa gioventù* of the kingdom to commit themselves to its enlightenment and economic improvement. As Hume had done in his *Political Discourses* of 1752, Genovesi focused upon political economy. In this his avowed inspiration was the French economic writer Jean-François Melon, who had been one of the first outside Britain to recognize Mandeville's significance. If Vico had opened, and then blocked, the Epicurean door to Enlightenment, Genovesi found another way through it. Over the next twelve years, culminating in his anguished response to the famine of 1764, Genovesi was tireless in his endeavors to translate, publicize, and assess the works of the best French and British economic writers.[39] Hume was followed by Sir James Steuart and Adam Smith; after Genovesi came Giuseppe Palmieri, who made repeated attempts to assess the relevance to Naples of physiocratic doctrines. As the interest in physiocracy implies, the Neapolitan political economists differed from their Scottish counterparts on important issues. But they shared the underlying conviction, which made political economy a—perhaps *the*—central intellectual discipline of the Enlightenment, namely, that material betterment in this world was possible through the development of agriculture and commerce, to the benefit of all society's members, poor as well as rich.

Accompanying the interest in political economy was the broader enquiry into the historical progress of society. The same enquiry of the historical narratives of

Hume and William Robertson—and of the conjectural histories of Adam Ferguson, Adam Smith, and John Millar—was pursued in Naples by Genovesi, by Giuseppe Maria Galanti, by Gaetano Filangieri, and by Francesco Mario Pagano (who freely acknowledged his debts to, as well as differences from, "il nostro Vico"). Among both sets of philosophers we find optimism about the prospects for human betterment tempered by skepticism. Hume and Smith clearly did not believe in a perfect outcome to the progress of society, but nor did Filangieri or Pagano, both of whom were exercised by the near inevitability of corruption. The similarities between the Scots and the Neapolitans are not limited to their common intellectual interests. Despite the very different contexts provided by eighteenth-century Scotland and Naples, there are further similarities in the positions assumed by the two sets of thinkers within their societies, and in their attitudes to "public opinion." It is often observed that the Scottish thinkers appear to have been comfortably integrated into the established institutions of the universities, the Church and the law. But many of them also chafed at the restrictions which such institutions imposed and sought to imitate Hume's career as an independent man of letters. In Naples, Genovesi did hold university chairs, but the one from which he committed himself to the Enlightenment, the chair of Commerce and Mechanics, had to be specially created for him, and he used it to free himself of the constraints which the university and ecclesiastical authorities had previously imposed. Most of his successors were self-consciously independent, using legal careers, publishing, and independent means to give themselves the freedom to write, and associating with each other in the voluntary, if only semipublic, society of the masonic lodges.

In both countries, moreover, the men of letters consciously sought to address a "public" which was not restricted to the governing elite. Within Scotland they took advantage of the removal of government to Westminster to generate debate over specific issues of "improvement," such as the continued relevance of a national militia. At the same time, following the lead of Hume, they used their distance from the partisan world of London journalism to try to moderate English opinion, encouraging it to recognize its insularity, and to set party-political prejudices in a more accurate historical perspective. In Naples, Genovesi had made his educational purpose clear in his manifesto of 1753. Though it is doubtful whether he had a very definite idea of how large a "public" his teaching and publishing might reach, he was clear that philosophers should no longer confine themselves to counselling ministers in the traditional manner, especially ministers as narrowly legalistic as Bernardo Tanucci. The ambitions of the leader of the second generation of Neapolitan *illuministi*, Gaetano Filangieri, were even more radical. If philosophy was to be brought "to the aid of governments"—*la filosofia in soccorso de' governi*—it must be by subordinating the latter to the "invisible tribunal" of "public opinion." The only legitimate government, Filangieri argued, was one which in this way was "representative" of "the will of the people."[40]

When Filangieri wrote this, in the 1780s, the settings in which the Enlightenment was being pursued in the two countries were rapidly diverging. Under its independent Bourbon monarchy, and despite the reforming initiatives of several ministers in the 1770s and 1780s, the kingdom of Naples remained very definitely an *ancien régime* society. Scotland, by contrast, was fast becoming a modern one, catching up on and assimilating to the modern society of its southern neighbor, England. Nevertheless, it is what the Neapolitan thinkers continued to share with the Scots, even as their countries began to diverge, which made them both participants in the enterprise of Enlightenment. What they shared was the intellectual commitment to understanding how the progress of society occurred, in the past and in the present—and how, therefore, to modernize their own societies.

It can be shown, therefore, that the same Enlightenment existed in both Scotland and Naples, notwithstanding the difference of the contexts and their distance from Paris. Thus, a case for the Enlightenment as a single, coherent intellectual movement can be made. It may be objected that I have demonstrated no more than its existence as a historical fact, and have offered no new assessment of its enduring significance. The historian's answer must be that the significance of the Enlightenment is a subject for further historical investigation, through exploration of the impact of its ideas and example on later European thought and the public role of intellectuals. Assessment of its significance, however, will be on a surer footing if we are once again confident that there was a common Enlightenment.

The case of Scotland and Naples may even make it possible to go a little further. For the divergence in the fortunes of the two societies after 1790 raises a final question. Should the comparison of Scotland and Naples end in a judgment of the success or failure of Enlightenment in the two countries? More precisely, should we conclude that the ideas which apparently worked in Scotland were inadequate in the face of the obstacles they encountered in the kingdom of Naples? It is not a question I am in a position to answer yet; it is probably not a question which a historian can ever expect to answer at all definitely. But if the Enlightenment is to be judged, it should be on the basis of the challenges it set itself, not by events two centuries later.

Notes

* Following the Tel Aviv conference to which this paper was first contributed, versions of it have been given to the History of Political Thought Seminar, Institute of Historical Research, London; the History Seminar at the University of Leicester; the Trinity College, Dublin History Society; and the Central European University, Budapest. I am grateful to the organizers and participants at all these occasions for stimulating discussion.

1. Isaiah Berlin, "The Counter-Enlightenment," in *Against the Current: Essays in the History of Ideas*, ed. and with a bibliography by Henry Hardy, with an introduction by Roger Hausheer (Oxford: Oxford University Press, 1981).
2. Peter Gay, *The Enlightenment: An Interpretation* (New York: Knopf, 1966–1969); R. Darnton, "In search of the Enlightenment: recent attempts to create a social history of ideas," *Journal of Modern History*, 43 (1971), pp. 113–32.
3. Dorinda Outram, *The Enlightenment* (Cambridge, U.K.: Cambridge University Press, 1995), p. 3; cf. Thomas Munck, *The Enlightenment. A Comparative Social History 1721–1794* (New York: Oxford University Press, 2000), p. 7, where the Enlightenment is defined as "an attitude of mind, rather than a coherent system of beliefs." But as his subtitle indicates, Munck is not attempting an account of the Enlightenment as a whole; in its comparative approach to the social basis of

Enlightenment, his book represents a welcome attempt to restore a recognizable unity to the movement.
4. An example of such a response is James Schmidt, "What Enlightenment project?", *Political Theory* 28 (2000), pp. 734–57, quoting Outram with approval on p. 737; with the ensuing exchange between Christian Delacampagne and Schmidt in *Political Theory* 29 (2001), pp. 80–90.
5. An even more defiant, and substantially longer, "case for the Enlightenment" in predominantly intellectual terms has recently been argued by Jonathan Israel, in *Radical Enlightenment: Philosophy and the Making of Modernity 1650–1750* (Oxford: Oxford University Press, 2001). Israel identifies "Enlightenment," however, with the philosophy of Benedict Spinoza and his radical followers, John Toland, Pietro Giannone, and many others, thinkers of the late seventeenth and early eighteenth centuries. As his dates indicate, this Enlightenment was over by 1750: by implication, whatever occurred after 1750, if it was Enlightenment at all, was an epilogue. By contrast, I would like to make the case for the Enlightenment in the period with which it is usually associated, from the mid-eighteenth century to the 1790s. This is not to discount the interest or importance of the "early" or "pre"-Enlightenment, an understanding of which is essential to understanding the Enlightenment as a whole. But the two were not simply continuous: because it was explicitly irreligious, Israel's "radical Enlightenment" was never able to be the public intellectual movement which the Enlightenment became after 1750.
6. This account of the Enlightenment as *les lumières* continues to have proponents: for a late instance (though based on lectures given some 40 years earlier), Alphonse Dupront, *Qu'est que les lumières?* (Paris: Gallimard, 1996).
7. Ernst Cassirer, *The Philosophy of the Enlightenment* (originally published in German in 1932), trans. Ralph Manheim, (Princeton, N.J.: Princeton University Press, 1951).
8. Gay's *The Enlightenment: An Interpretation* can be regarded as a summation of the traditional understanding of the Enlightenment, with an acknowledged debt to Cassirer, even as it also anticipated several of the lines of enquiry which the social historians of the Enlightenment were later to champion.
9. Albert O. Hirschman, *The Passions and the Interests: Political Arguments for Capitalism Before its Triumph* (Princeton, N.J.: Princeton University Press, 1977).
10. Venturi first made the point in 1953, in a paper published as "La circolazione delle idee," *Rassegna storica del Risorgimento* 41 (1954), pp. 203–22. There followed three edited volumes of *Illuministi italiani*, iii, *Riformatori lombardi, piemontesi e toscani* (Milan & Naples: R. Ricciardi, 1958), v, *Riformatori napoletani* (Milan & Naples: R. Ricciardi, 1962), and (with Giuseppe Giarrizzo and Gianfranco Torcellan), vii, *Riformatori delle antiche repubbliche, dei ducati, dello Stato Pontificio e delle isole* (Milan & Naples; R. Ricciardi, 1965). The individual threads were then woven together in the five volumes of *Settecento riformatore* (Turin: G. Einaudi, 1963–1990); the work was still unfinished when Venturi died in 1994. For a general review, John Robertson, "Franco Venturi's Enlightenment," *Past and Present* 137 (1992), pp.183–206. Venturi was a friend of Berlin, who arranged for the translation into English of his book on Russian Populism. But their conceptions of the Enlightenment remained very different.

11. Henry F. May, *The Enlightenment in America* (New York: Oxford University Press, 1976); Donald H. Meyer, *The Democratic Enlightenment* (New York: Putnam, 1976).
12. Hugh Trevor-Roper, "The Scottish Enlightenment," *Studies on Voltaire and the Eighteenth Century* lxviii (1967), pp. 1635–58.
13. Nicholas Phillipson, "The Scottish Enlightenment," in Roy Porter and Mikulas Teich, eds., *The Enlightenment in National Context* (Cambridge, U.K.: Cambridge University Press, 1981).
14. Alexander Broadie, *The Tradition of Scottish Philosophy* (Edinburgh: Polygon, 1990); David Allan, *Virtue, Learning and the Scottish Enlightenment* (Edinburgh: Edinburgh University Press, 1993).
15. The Dissenting Enlightenment is approached from various points of view in Knud Haakonssen, ed., *Enlightenment and Religion: Rational Dissent in Eighteenth-century Britain* (Cambridge, U.K.: Cambridge University Press, 1996). For the Anglican alternative, J. G. A. Pocock, "Clergy and commerce. The conservative Enlightenment in England," in R. Ajello, ed., *L'età dei lumi. Studi storici sul settecento europeo in onore di Franco Venturi*, 2 vols., (Naples: Jovene, 1985), I, pp. 523–62; and now *The Enlightenments of Edward Gibbon 1737–1764*, Volume I of *Barbarism and Religion* (Cambridge, U.K.: Cambridge University Press, 1999). Also, Brian Young, *Religion and Enlightenment in Eighteenth-century England* (Oxford: Oxford University Press, 1997).
16. Roy Porter, *Enlightenment: Britain and the Creation of the Modern World* (London: Allan Lane, 2000). The title is the argument. See pp. xvii–xviii for his endorsement of Pocock's typically shrewd suggestion that we should drop the definite article and capital letter; this and other professions of agreement with Pocock might mislead the unwary reader into thinking that Porter's case for an English Enlightenment is the same as Pocock's.
17. Daniel Mornet, *Les origines intellectuelles de la Révolution française* (Paris: A. Colin, 1933); Robert Darnton, "The High Enlightenment and the low-life of literature in pre-Revolutionary France," *Past and Present* 51 (1971), pp. 81–115; and *The Forbidden Best-Sellers of Pre-Revolutionary France* (New York: Norton, 1996), esp. ch 3 "Philosophical pornography," and Part III "Do books cause Revolutions?"; Roger Chartier, *The Cultural Origins of the French Revolution* (Durham and London: Duke University Press, 1991), chs 4: "Do Books Make Revolutions?," and 8: "Do revolutions have Cultural Origins?" Daniel Roche, by contrast, has sought to distance his work from this preoccupation.
18. Margaret Jacob, *Living the Enlightenment: Freemasonry and Politics in Eighteenth-century Europe* (Oxford: Oxford University Press, 1991); Giuseppe Giarrizzo, *Massoneria e illuminismo nell'Europa del Settecento* (Venice: Marsilio, 1994).
19. Dena Goodman, *The Republic of Letters. A Cultural History of the French Enlightenment* (Ithaca and London: Cornell University Press, 1994).
20. Susan James, *Passion and Action: The Emotions in Seventeenth-century Philosophy* (Oxford: Oxford University Press, 1997).
21. Israel, *Radical Enlightenment*; see note 6, above.
22. Berlin, "The Counter-Enlightenment," p. 20.
23. E. J. Hundert, *The Enlightenment's Fable: Bernard Mandeville and the Discovery of Society* (Cambridge: Cambridge University Press, 1994).

24. Lorraine Daston, "The Ideal and Reality of the Republic of Letters in the Enlightenment," *Science in Context* 4 (1991), pp. 367–86; Anne Goldgar, *Impolite Learning: Conduct and Community in the Republic of Letters, 1680–1750* (New Haven and London: Yale University Press, 1995).
25. Fania Oz-Salzberger, *Translating the Enlightenment: Scottish Civic Discourse in Eighteenth-century Germany* (Oxford: Oxford University Press, 1995); László Kontler, "William Robertson and his German Audience on European and non-European Civilisations," *Scottish Historical Review* LXXX (2001), pp. 63–89. Both develop a more sympathetic, less manipulative understanding of the process of translation than that offered by Isaiah Berlin in "Hume and the sources of German anti-rationalism," in *Against the Current*; see Oz-Salzberger, *Translating the Enlightenment*, p. 80.
26. But Munck's *The Enlightenment: A Comparative Social History* provides an up-to-date conspectus of what is known, especially for northern Europe.
27. James Schmidt, ed., *What Is Enlightenment? Eighteenth-Century Answers and Twentieth-Century Questions* (Berkeley and Los Angeles: University of California Press, 1996), pp. 58–64: Immanuel Kant, "An answer to the question: What is Enlightenment?" (1784), with an excellent commentary on pp. 253–69 by John Christian Laursen, "The Subversive Kant: The Vocabulary of Apublic and Apublicity."
28. On this fundamental theme, Istvan Hont, "Free Trade and the Economic Limits to National Politics: Neo-Machiavellian Political Economy Reconsidered," in John Dunn, ed., *The Economic Limits to Modern Politics* (Cambridge, U.K.: Cambridge University Press, 1990), pp. 41–120.
29. See Daniel Gordon, *Citizens without Sovereignty: Equality and Sociability in French Thought 1670–1789* (Princeton, N.J.: Princeton University Press, 1994), esp. pp. 199–208, on the relation between *sociabilité* and public opinion as constraints on absolute monarchy in the thought of the *philosophes*, and of Morellet in particular.
30. For example, Greece and the Balkans, studied by Paschalis Kitromilides, *The Enlightenment as Social Criticism: Iosipos Moisiodax and Greek Culture in the Eighteenth Century* (Princeton, N.J.: Princeton University Press, 1992).
31. On which see Vittor Ivo Comparato, *Giuseppe Valletta. Un intellettuale napoletano della fine del seicento* (Naples, 1970); this aspect of Neapolitan intellectual culture is overlooked in H. S. Stone, *Vico's Cultural History: The Publication and Transmission of Ideas in Naples 1685–1750* (Leiden: E. J. Brill, 1997), to the detriment of its understanding of its principal subject.
32. J. C. L. Jackson, *Royalist Politics, Religion and Ideas in Restoration Scotland 1660–1689*, Cambridge University Ph.D. thesis (1998); David Allan, "In the Bosome of a Shaddowie Grove: Sir George Mackenzie and the Consolations of Retirement," *History of European Ideas* 25 (1999), pp. 251–73.
33. James Moore and Michael Silverthorne, eds., *Natural Rights on the Threshold of the Scottish Enlightenment: The Writings of Gershom Carmichael* (Indianapolis: Liberty Fund, 2002).
34. Paolo Mattia Doria, *Massime del governo spagnolo a Napoli* (1709–10), eds. G. Galasso and V. Conti (Naples: Guida, 1973), pp. 21–43; John Robertson, ed., *Andrew Fletcher: Political Works* (Cambridge, U.K.: Cambridge University Press, 1997), specifically "Speeches" (1703), p. 133.

35. Giambattista Vico, *La Scienza nuova* (1744), paragraph 341, in the translation by T. G. Bergin and M. H. Fisch, *The New Science of Giambattista Vico*, revised edition (Ithaca, N.Y.: Cornell University Press, 1984).
36. Isaiah Berlin, "The Philosophical Ideas of Giambattista Vico," in *Vico and Herder: Two Studies in the History of Ideas* (London: Hogarth Press, 1976), pp. 1–142, preceded by "One of the Boldest Innovators in the History of Human Thought" (1969), reprinted in *The Power of Ideas*, ed. Henry Hardy, (Princeton, N.J.: Princeton University Press, 2000), pp. 53–67.
37 *The Letters of David Hume*, ed. J. Y. T. Greig (Oxford: The Clarendon Press, 1969), vol. I, p. 12: Hume to Michael Ramsay, March 1732; and p. 13: "Letter to a Physician," [March 1734].
38. James Moore, "Hume and Hutcheson," in M. A. Stewart and John P. Wright (eds), *Hume and Hume's Connexions* (Edinburgh: Edinburgh University Press, 1994), pp. 23–57.
39. John Robertson, "The Enlightenment above National Context: Political Economy in Eighteenth-Century Scotland and Naples," *The Historical Journal* 40 (1997), pp. 667–697.
40. Antonio Genovesi, *Discorso dopra il vero fine delle lettere e delle scienze* (Naples 1753), in *Scritti economici*, ed M.L. Perna, 2 vols, (Naples: Jovene, 1984), pp. 47–50. Gaetano Filangieri, *La scienza della legislazione* (Naples 1780–1791), Bk. IV, Part iii, ch. 43.

6 | The Real Counter-Enlightenment: The Case of France

Darrin M. McMahon

To pose the question "What is Counter-Enlightenment?" is necessarily to ask "What is Enlightenment?" The question is an old one, debated famously by Kant, Mendelssohn, and others in the pages of the *Berlinische Monatsschrift* in the 1780s, but in fact also posed repeatedly by a great number of educated men and women throughout the century.[1] Both as a process and a movement, as well as a characterization of an age, enlightenment—*the Enlightenment*—generated from the start a tremendous variety of reflection on the meaning of the term and the time. Arresting the gaze of contemporaries, thus has the century of lights captivated the attention of posterity, serving until the present day as a set piece for rumination on the meaning of modernity, a field upon which to project the fears and hopes of humanity. Little surprise, then, that the Enlightenment continues to generate a perplexing array of definitions and interpretations. *Siècle des lumières, Aufklärung, illuminismo, illustración*, Enlightenments low and high, radical and conservative, Scottish and Jewish, Protestant and Catholic—the very number of terms begs the question as to whether it is even possible to speak of the Enlightenment as a single entity, as a unified movement, a reified whole.

Scholars of the eighteenth century disagree over this question, and probably always will, for it is to a large extent a problem of definition—one, clearly, that presents itself to anyone seeking to understand the corollary question, "What is *Counter*-Enlightenment?" Indeed, Sir Isaiah Berlin constructed his definition of the Counter-Enlightenment on the basis of what he took to be the principal doctrines of the Enlightenment itself—doctrines that he formulated in slightly different ways at different times, but that can be reduced (and this is simplifying the case somewhat) to the following general propositions: that human nature was fundamentally the same in all times and all places; that local and historical variations in human culture and society were of relative unimportance; and that there existed universal human goals and universal human ends, on the basis of which—and following the scientific methods of Newtonian physics—one could establish a logically connected structure of laws and generalizations that would replace the dark chaos of ignorance, prejudice, dogma, fanaticism and "interested error" that for so long had prevented the cultivation of virtue, truth, and human happiness. In turn, it was over and against these common Enlightenment propositions that Berlin looked for competing, Counter-Enlightenment currents, finding them, of course, in the irrational, vitalist, relativist, organic, and historicist strains present in the thought of Vico, Hamann, Herder, Jacobi, Möser, and a handful of others. Primarily a movement in the history of ideas (in the history of philosophy), Berlin's Counter-Enlightenment was also primarily a German phenomenon, constructed in opposition to a largely French *siècle des lumières* (although it is true that in the definitional essay, "The Counter-Enlightenment," Berlin does mention two post-Revolutionary French writers, Bonald and Maistre).

It would be redundant here to emphasize the importance of Berlin's definition both in terms of its explanatory power, and in terms of the influence it has exerted on subsequent discussions of the Counter-Enlightenment. This being said, and with all due respect to the memory of a great thinker and a great man, it should be noted that Berlin's definition has its drawbacks. First, it tends to *limit* discussion of the Counter-Enlightenment to a relative handful of great thinkers—a perfectly legitimate exercise, to be sure, but one that, nonetheless, fails to do justice to the contexts in which the Enlightenment and Enlightenment thought were opposed. Second, Berlin's definition has tended to limit research and discussion of the Counter-Enlightenment overwhelmingly to Germany. It is true that his idealist definition of, if you will, *Gegen-Aufklärung*, certainly provides scope for discussing other, non-German thinkers (and of course Vico here is the obvious exception), but it remains the case in practice, that Berlin's set of criteria for defining the Counter-Enlightenment was overwhelmingly suited to the German example—a fact that may well have something to do with the shadow under which Berlin's own thought was formed—in other words, the experience of Nazi Germany and the Second World War. Third, and somewhat paradoxically given what I have said so far, Berlin's definition seems potentially to broaden the Counter-Enlightenment beyond any clearly demarcated historical boundaries. In other words, if the Counter-Enlightenment is primarily defined in contrast to a set of philosophical principles, then it becomes possible to locate *counter*-enlightenment principles well beyond, and indeed, well before the eighteenth century. Berlin himself, it is true, for the most part avoids this trap, confining his discussion of the Counter-Enlightenment by and large to the long eighteenth century (thereby giving it a firm historical context), although in general it seems clear that there is a teleological thrust to much of his writing on Counter-Enlightenment figures. In contrast, a number of those studying the Counter-Enlightenment in this vein have been less cautious. To cite but one example, Jochen Schmidt's edited volume, *Aufklärung und Gegenaufklärung in der europäischen Literatur, Philosophie und Politik von der Antike bis zur Gegenwart* (Darmstadt, 1989), contains, as the title indicates, articles spanning the whole of Western history, from Epicurus to the Weimar Republic, with forays into the Middle Ages, the Italian Renaissance, Baroque literature, the thought of Freud, Hegel, Hamann, and the painting of Hieronymus Bosch, to name only a few. Whatever the individual interest of a number of these essays, the collective result is to obliterate completely the historicity of the concepts Enlightenment and Counter-Enlightenment.

A more fruitful approach to the question of Counter-Enlightenment would be to adopt a less philosophical, and more historical, perspective, on the movement and to apply to it some of the methods and tools that have been used over the last twenty-five years by such cultural and intellectual historians as Robert Darnton, John Pocock, Quentin Skinner, and Keith Baker. In this regard, the case of France is suggestive. For it was here, after all, that the Enlightenment was in many ways centered and based, it was here that it was born, and so it should not surprise us that in France, no less than in Germany, the Enlightenment had enemies: militant clergy, members of the *parti dévot*, unenlightened aristocrats, traditionalist *bourgeois*, Sorbonne censors, conservative *parlementaires*, recalcitrant journalists, unfashionable salon hostesses, and sundry others, the so-called "fanatics" of the Enlightenment catechism, men and women I call anti-*philosophes*—not an arbitrary term, for they used it themselves, as did the *philosophes*, adding it to a host of far less flattering terms.

The term anti-*philosophe* appeared at roughly the same time that the Encyclopedists began to claim the mantle *"philosophe"* for themselves. One finds it in such works as Diderot's *Pensées philosophiques* of 1747, the abbé Allamand's *Pensées anti-philosophiques* of 1751, Voltaire's *Dictionnaire philosophique* of 1764, and Louis Mayeul Chaudon's *Dictionnaire anti-philosophique* of 1767. Indeed, the very same years that witnessed the first major onslaught of the Enlightenment in the form of the publication of the initial volumes of the *Encyclopédie*, also witnessed the first stirrings of a self-conscious opposition. As early as 1755, in fact, the General Assembly of the Clergy was warning the crown of the "contagion" being spread "throughout the realm" by the poisonous writings of "so-called *philosophes"*—men who disdained established opinions, spread immorality and vice, rejected sovereign power, mocked the saintly truths of religion, and everywhere fostered a spirit of "independence and revolt."[2] They repeated these accusations at each of their national assemblies down through the century, stressing, as well, in countless pastoral letters, *mandements*, and pulpit sermons that the spirit of "blasphemy" and "sedition" fostered by the "coryphaeuses" of the new learning would lead to "bloodied thrones" and the "horrors of anarchy" if not contained.[3]

In the secular republic of letters, too, anti-*philosophe* journalists and Grub-Street hacks joined forces to combat the *philosophes* on their own terrain. The abbé Gabriel Gauchat, for example, devoted thousands of pages of his monthly journal, the *Lettres critiques, ou Analyse et refutation de divers écrits modernes contre la réligion* (1755–1763) explicitly to refuting the works of men who "combined against truth ... the salt of irony, the bitterness of criticism, the equivocations of sophism, and the blackness of calumny."[4] Decrying both the scale and the intensity of the *philosophes'* attacks as unprecedented in the history of "the religion of Jesus Christ," Gauchat lashed out at their "fanaticism," "intolerance," and the eagerness with which the public "devoured their productions of malice and error."[5] Likewise, the *avocat* Jean Soret and the *père* Jean-Nicolas-Hubert Hayer sought early on to refute impious *philosophes* in the pages of their twenty-one volume periodical, *La Religion vengée, ou Réfutation des auteurs impies* (1757–1763).[6] Their efforts were sustained by many in a lively anti-*philosophe* press.[7]

Finally, in French courts of law, and the French court itself, devout magistrates and ministers such as Antoine-Louis Séguier and Jean-Omer Joly de Fleury made war on what these men saw as a concerted effort to destroy France.[8] As early as 1759, Fleury was warning his colleagues in detail of a "conceived plan" to "sustain materialism and destroy religion."[9] Eleven years later, this seemed more evident still. "It is no longer possible to cover up the fact," Séguier admonished in an *arrêt* of 1770, that a "criminal league," an "impious and audacious sect ... decorating its false wisdom with the name of *Philosophie*" has risen up. "With one hand, [it] seeks to shake the throne, and with the other, to overthrow altars." And unless authorities took proper measures, Séguier emphasized, the "civil order as well as the spiritual" would be destroyed.[10]

Needless to say, these apocalyptic warnings—with their invocation of blood and anarchy, toppled thrones and altars—were grossly overstated. Moreover, the picture they painted of an incendiary, even revolutionary *philosophie* is radically at odds with what we have come to think of as the sober, if mildly progressive, "High Enlightenment." How to account for this disjuncture? In part it stems from the firm conviction of many eighteenth-century figures (and in particular, many eighteenth-century Catholics) that their age was one of unparalleled religious decline, precipitated, as Gauchat commented above, by the single most concerted attack on the faith in the history of Christianity. His was by no means an isolated viewpoint. It was one, furthermore, that only grew in credence as the leading *philosophes* established themselves in the 1760s and 1770s as an important force, conquering the salons and literary academies, the drawing rooms and sinecures of the *beau monde*, while insinuating their anticlerical invective into the mainstream of French culture. From the perspective of men like Gauchat, then, *philosophie* was a potent force, one that flowed like a poison, outward and downward from the pens of a few leading *philosophes* to encompass all those who claimed to carry the torch of *lumières*, and from there, to French society as a whole. As the esteemed court preacher, the abbé de Cambacérès observed in his noted *Sermon sur les incrédules* of the late 1760s:

> Without doubt, unbelief has produced a revolution, and to speak only of France, it has made enormous changes in the morals and character of the nation. ... What were we? What have we since become? Incredulity has affected all classes, respecting neither rank, nor age, nor sex. ... Crime itself has ceased to be a crime, and in the middle of this general decadence and the shock of all the passions, Religion is filled with consternation, threatened, tottering on a precipice.[11]

Incredulity, in short, was a force ravaging society from top to bottom. Neither simply the result of long-term shifts in social mores, nor the gradual "secularization" of society, it was, rather, the outcome of conscious, willful manipulation.[12] As the National Assembly of the Clergy observed in a pastoral letter circulated in every parish in France in 1775, "In previous centuries there were impious persons here and there, but without party and without results. There were books that taught impiety, but [they were] obscure and little read. Today, by contrast, the unbelievers form a sect, divided as it should be, over the objects of its belief; but united in the revolt against the authority of divine revelation."[13]

A united front with common ends, if uncommon means, modern incredulity—modern philosophy—attacked religion on a scale and with an intensity unprecedented in human history. In these respects, its assault was without parallel. Yet, in the opinion of enemies of the Enlightenment, there were, nonetheless, bases for historical comparison. Above all, the cultural memory of the Reformation and the Religious Wars of the sixteenth century provided French Catholics with what Amos Hofman has called a "paradigm of civil disorder," a terrible test case of the consequences that could be wrought by a systematic attack on the Church.[14] For here was a graphic illustration of how religious heresy led to political upheaval, of how dissent from the one truth faith could unravel into the tangled web of internecine conflict and bloody civil war. By unleashing the tight rein of Catholic tradition, dogma, and ecclesiastical authority, the Reformation had turned men and women over to the frenzy of the unbridled human intellect, seducing them to believe that they could arrive at truth independently—through private study of scripture and the private sounding of one's heart and mind to the exclusion of all else. This was pride of the most extreme sort, and the results were all too predictable: limitless, subjective speculation, continual conflict over scripture, the dissolution of the original *protestants* into an endless babble of conflicting sects and heretical factions, and ultimately the long series of religious wars that had bathed Europe in blood.

This memory, then, provided many in the eighteenth century with a specter of the perils of religious dissent. It likewise offered a ready-made vocabulary that could be easily transferred to the *philosophes* and their fellow travelers. From the vantage point of many Catholic enemies of the *philosophes*, in fact, there was something dangerously Protestant about the Enlightenment as a whole.[15] Did not the *philosophes* adopt as their spiritual heirs a range of Protestant thinkers, from Tindal and Collins to Locke and Newton? Was not the Protestant demand of "tolerance" the central battle cry of the *philosophes*, for whom the heretic Calas was a Voltairean martyr and saint? And like their Protestant forefathers, did the *philosophes* not continually attack the authority of the Church, placing their trust in the subjective prompting of individual reason alone? From this perspective— skewed to be sure—it was fairly easy to view *philosophie* as yet another of the deviations wrought by the Reformation, another aberration spawned by the original rupture with Catholic orthodoxy. Indeed, Catholic apologists of the eighteenth century employed much of the very same language to combat *philosophes* as their Counter-Reformation predecessors had used against Lutherans and Calvinists.[16] The term *prétendu philosophe*, for example, mirrored that of the *prétendu réformé* favored by French Counter-Reformation writers, while the continual references to the *philosophes* as a "sect" or "cabal" of "fanatics" also recalled earlier writings. When, towards the end of the century, Louis XVI relented to long-standing pressure to grant limited civil status to French Huguenots in the 1787 Edict of Toleration, many orthodox Catholics saw this as the direct result of the machinations of a joint Protestant-*philosophe* plot.[17] The two—*protéstantisme* and *philosophisme*—were one in their minds.

Future fears of religious upheaval, and worries of the Protestant past—these were the forces giving shape, and consistency, to the rhetoric of the Catholic Counter-Enlightenment in the second half of the eighteenth century. There were, however, other central themes that surfaced and resurfaced continually in the language of Catholic militants. Linking together the disparate religious apologists and journalists, pulpit preachers and civil magistrates alluded to above, this language crystallized in the final decades of the *ancien régime* into a clearly demarcated linguistic strand, a consistent, reified portrait of the *siècle des lumières* and of the bright lights who gave it its name—what I call an "anti-*philosophe* discourse."[18] In other words, it became a construction of what the Enlightenment was. And here a number of the most important points warrant mention.

First, the anti-*philosophes* of the last decades of the *ancien régime* reduced the varied and variegated opinions of the French Enlightenment to a single whole, or *philosophie*, which they charged collectively with engendering atheism. For in their countless anticlerical tirades, their questioning of the authenticity of scripture, and their arrogant confidence in the power of the human mind, the *philosophes*, so their enemies charged, "made pretensions to doubt all," bidding men and women to set foot on the slippery slope that led ultimately to disbelief.[19] Releasing the individual from the mitigating yolk of Catholic certainty—revelation and the tradition and authority of the Church—the *philosophes* turned him over, naked and unbound, to the speculation of the unchained human intellect. Error and aberration of every sort was the necessary consequence. As a journalist of the anti-*philosophe* *Année littéraire* challenged in 1783, "I defy you to cite for me an error, however absurd ... that the *philosophes* have not adopted," guided solely "by the torch of reason, of *philosophie*."[20] Or as the Abbé Augustin Barruel affirmed in his widely selling anti-*philosophe* novel of the 1780s, *Les Helviennes*, "It is always necessary to come back to this truth ... that the *philosophie* of my century is nothing but the true chaos of all possible contradictions."[21] Rather than question the wisdom of seeing the diversity of the *philosophes'* religious opinions as part of a single movement, their enemies insisted instead on depicting this very heterogeneity as evidence of common perversity and common intent. As the abbé Lamourette observed typically, "the unity of the end brings together atheists, materialists, theists, and all manner of unbelievers into a single class of men, rendering them all in equal measure the plague of virtue and the destroyers of society."[22]

While enemies of the Enlightenment thus portrayed atheism as the necessary outcome of eighteenth-century philosophy—one that French society was achieving on an alarming scale—they viewed this result as at once the cause and effect of another of *philosophie*'s pernicious qualities, moral depravity. For the men and women in question were moved by the conviction that morality without religion was a contradiction in terms; that secular ethics, practically speaking, was an impossibility; that the "modern paganism" of the *philosophes* was a sham. By eliminating the fear of God and an afterlife, breaching the ramparts of Christian morality, and destroying respect for religious authority, the *philosophes* had removed all impediments to man's basest tendencies. Bereft of the restraining bourne of religion and the self-controlling impulse of conscience, men and women would engage in all manner of depravity.

There was, of course, nothing particularly new about this emphasis on the inherent depravity of man. It was, after all, a straightforward Christian reading of the Fall, central to the teaching of Augustine, and with a long tradition in Catholic thought. Yet *philosophie* did more than simply remove the Christian yoke and turn men and women over to their naturally depraved appetites. It actively encouraged them as well. The *philosophes'* apologies for the delights of this world—principal among them being sex—became, in their enemies' reading, a lusty summons to indulge the most frightful passions. "Under the pretext that there are natural and necessary human penchants, a false and dangerous *philosophie* eulogizes the most unbridled passions," emphasized the abbé Gérard, a leading and widely read anti-*philosophe* polemicist."[23] The *philosophes* "flatter the passions," asserted his comrade in arms, the abbé de Crillon, and urge their followers to seek happiness in their gratification alone.[24] The general utilitarian calculus of so much Enlightenment thought, moreover—particularly evident in the writings of Helvétius—seemed to enjoin men and women to base their actions entirely on calculations of pleasure and pain, equating the good with what was pleasurable in the here and now, and the bad with what denied it. The result, anti-*philosophes* maintained, was an ethics of utility that sanctioned horrible egotism and made personal interest the overriding criterion of morality. As the abbé Liger commented in a typical refrain, "All the duties of men are reduced to personal interest and pleasure."[25] "According to the *philosophes*," the Grub-Street anti-*philosophe* Jean-Marie Bernard Clément echoed, "everything is arbitrary and so personal interest becomes the sole motive for our actions."[26]

The natural effect of this indulgence, in turn, was the severing of all the ties of obligation, duty, and responsibility that bound men and women together in society, which led to subject turning against king, son against father, and wife against husband. The *philosophes* encouraged a "universal disgust for ... domestic duties," pointed out the abbé Lamourette.[27] They "eroded, at once, all the ties that bound together and gave happiness to fathers, husbands, wives, and children."[28] "Oh discord of families!," the "horrible monster" created by the *philosophes*, lamented another typical observer, bemoaning the ease with which husbands and wives alike cast aside their oaths of fidelity to pursue their own selfish pleasure, and the facility with which children disavowed their parents' strictures. Once a refuge from the evils of the world, the family was now a germinating source of its corruption. For inasmuch as "society as a whole" was nothing but an "imitation" of the order of families, the horrors within spread abundantly without. "It is the domestic virtues," the author continued, "that prepare the social virtues. And he who does not know how to be a husband, a father, a son, a friend, or a neighbor, will not know how to be a citizen."[29]

It was but a small step from this latter charge to the assertion that the *philosophes* were rapidly undermining the political foundations of France. For again, despite the range of political views they espoused, the collective effect of their doctrine, in their enemies' minds, was to cut the restraints that for centuries had kept subjects in check. By killing God, they removed the spiritual basis for divine-right monarchy; by founding human relations on self-interest, they dissolved the social nexus that underlay duty, hierarchy, deference, and respect; by weakening the family, they introduced license and revolt into the very heart of civil society; and finally, by continually mocking the wisdom of history, custom, and tradition—what Burke would later call the collected reason of the ages—the *philosophes* unchained man from all that made him decent. Just as the end result of the *philosophes'* attack on religion was atheism, so would their assault on society end in anarchy. It was a point that enemies of the Enlightenment were prepared to make with exceptional clarity. As the prolific religious apologist, the Dominican Charles-Louis Richard, emphasized in a small primer intended to warn ordinary men and women of the dangers of *philosophie*:

> Everywhere *philosophie* lights the torch of discord and of war, prepares poisons, sharpens swords, lays fires, orders murder, massacre, and carnage, sacrifices fathers by the hands of sons, and sons by the hands of fathers. It directs lances and swords at the heads and the breasts of sovereigns, placing them on scaffolds, which it yearns to see flowing with sovereign's blood—blood that it will drink in deep draughts as it feasts its eyes on the horrible specter of their torn, mutilated, and bloody members.[30]

Richard's text was singular in its graphic imagery but not in its general point. For when, in the final decade of the Old Regime, *philosophie* appeared to flood all levels of society in what became a sort of fashionable kitsch or "modish lifestyle," anti-*philosophes* could only recoil in horror, decrying what they saw as the coming apocalypse.[31] As the provincial academician, and anti-*philosophe littérateur*, Rigoley de Juvigny, bemoaned in 1787, "the destructive spirit that dominates today no longer has anything to stop it. *Philosophisme* has penetrated everywhere, has corrupted everything."[32] The future, to these observers, looked dark indeed.

One result of this apocalyptic expectation and apocalyptic rhetoric—at least in France—was that many of these very same figures greeted 1789 as the horrible fulfillment of their worst fears, a fact that, as I elaborate elsewhere, has important things to teach us about the early dynamics of the French Revolution. Here, though, I want to emphasize another point—one made explicit by the title of Richard's work cited above: *La Doctrine des philosophes modernes*. Here, we note the occlusion, the reification, implying that there was, in fact, a single philosophical doctrine, that *philosophie* was a thing, a unified whole. And indeed, neither Richard nor his colleagues had any doubts about this. *Philosophie*, *philosophisme*, the so-called *siècle des lumières* was a coherent entity comprising common assumptions, common aspirations, and most importantly, common consequences.

It is important to stress this point, because what one clearly discerns in this collective, anti-*philosophe* discourse is the first creation, the first construction of the Enlightenment, of *philosophie*, or the *doctrine philosophique*. The reigning argument, made by Roger Chartier, Thomas Schleich, Rolf Reichhardt, and Hans-Dietrich Gumbrecht, among others, is that the Enlightenment was only constructed after the fact—during the Revolution—in an attempt to confer paternity and legitimation on the break with the past. As Chartier comments: "Should we not consider ... that it was the Revolution that invented the Enlightenment by attempting to root its legitimacy in a corpus of texts and founding authors, reconciled and united, beyond their extreme differences, by their preparation of a rupture with the old world. When they brought together (not without debate) a pantheon of ancestors including Voltaire, Rousseau, Mably, and Raynal, when they assigned a radically critical function to philosophy (if not to all the Philosophes), the revolutionaries constructed a continuity that was primarily a process of justification and search for paternity."[33] I do not disagree that this process took place, but I believe Chartier overlooks the fact that this same process occurred first among the Enlightenment's opponents. Well before Kant had even posed the question, "What is Enlightenment?," its enemies had answered, "Darkness masquerading as light." *Philosophie*, in their view, was an abomination, a plague, an infectious virus that spread in epidemic proportion, eating away at everything in its path.

It is in this respect, then, that it makes sense and is useful to consider these men and women as part of a *Counter*-Enlightenment movement. For it was *not* over and against some retrospective assemblage of philosophical principles, a retrospective interpretation of what the Enlightenment entailed that these authors combated, but rather against their own understanding, their own construction of what the Enlightenment was. And by tendentiously posing, and then answering, the question, "What was the Century of Lights?" these polemicists of course were at the same time making both implicit and explicit counter-claims. Their

Enlightenment, in other words, was largely a foil against which to work out competing counter-positions.

Now this side of things, the more positive ideological program of what I am presenting here as a French, Catholic, Counter-Enlightenment is, of course, a discussion unto itself. I shall just highlight some of the more salient points—which follow naturally from what has been said so far. The mechanism, in effect, was straightforward, based upon simple, if rhetorically effective, oppositions. Thus, whereas the *philosophes* allegedly undermined religion, tilling the soil of atheism, the anti-*philosophes* put forth religion's necessity to human happiness and social security. Whereas the *philosophes* urged the satisfaction of personal pleasures, the sanctity of individual rights, the anti-*philosophes* stressed the incumbency of duty, the priority of the social whole. Whereas the *philosophes* spoke in ungrounded abstractions, opposing history, custom, and prejudice with the speculations of reason, anti-*philosophes* emphasized the rootedness of the past, the primacy of constancy over change, of tradition over innovation. Whereas the *philosophes* deemed the individual the basic constituent element of society, the anti-*philosophes* gave prominence to the family, regarding it as both the model and the guardian of all social organization. Whereas the *philosophes* advocated the free circulation of ideas, the tolerance of opinion and belief, the anti-*philosophes* alleged the hypocrisy of these claims, the danger of giving free rein to error. And whereas the *philosophes* spoke of the natural goodness of men and women, the anti-*philosophes* emphasized their capacity for evil.

Certainly, one should not overemphasize the coherence of these countervailing positions. This was not a clearly worked out political platform or slate, but rather a loose, though identifiable, set of ideological propositions articulated with increasing consistency by this rather broad cross-section of enemies of the Enlightenment I refer to as anti-*philosophes*. As I have argued in my book *Enemies of the Enlightenment*, it was before this common, negative symbol of the *siècle des lumières* took shape that diverse, and in certain respects otherwise conflicting, forces began to come together in the final years of the Old Regime—and in the process, shaped what was an inchoate, but nonetheless fairly consistent, ideological position of the right. Unlike the great majority of French historians who trace the right in France (or a spectrum of right-wing positions) solely to the Revolution, I try to argue that it was before the Enlightenment first and foremost that the right in France took shape—a position held by other scholars such as Klaus Epstein, James Sack, and Javier Herrero who have traced similar phenomena in Germany, England, and Spain.

From the perspective of the above, however, the most interesting aspect of the discussion on the meanings and implications of the Counter-Enlightenment is the negative one—the negative portrait or construction of the Enlightenment spread by this anti-*philosophe* discourse. It was, to be sure, a far cry from the much more sophisticated critiques of the Enlightenment presented by Isaiah Berlin's, principally German, *Gegen-Aufklärer*. Shaped above all by a militant defense of the orthodox Catholic faith, this French Counter-Enlightenment produced few if any thinkers who could today be considered great, or timeless, in the way that Berlin surely considered Hamann or Herder. Moreover, the anti-*philosophe* construction of the Enlightenment itself was, to say the least, overstated, reductive, superficial, and grossly unfair—a fact that has led the great majority of students of the eighteenth century over the past two hundred years to dismiss it as so much fanaticism, writing off such polemic and the men who made it as unworthy of serious attention—a tendency, evident I should add, even among scholars more or less sympathetic to the study of religion. The great French scholar of Catholic theological apologetics of the eighteenth century, Albert Monod, for example, in speaking of the more virulent opponents of the *philosophes*, commented simply, "they deserve to be forgotten."[34] Even the undoubtedly more sensitive Robert Palmer, in his admirable and groundbreaking study, *Catholics and Unbelievers in Eighteenth-Century France*, purposefully set aside what he called "the more absurd productions of the orthodox," excluding "writings that were only cries of horror, wild assertions and promiscuous calling of names." He acknowledged, however, that this process "may well give a false view of the real ideas of the time."[35]

I wholeheartedly agree with this assertion, for in the literally hundreds and hundreds of books, pamphlets, sermons, and journals from the end of the Old Regime I have consulted, the *philosophes*, and more generally the Enlightenment, are treated in precisely the terms spelled out above. In short, if we are to get at the "real ideas" of the time, we need to take these "wild assertions" seriously—if for no other reason than that they were disseminated in such volume.

One must add, moreover, that this Catholic Counter-Enlightenment was by no means confined to France, but rather had parallel movements throughout Western and Eastern Europe, and even in the New World (Brazil, Mexico, Montréal). Clearly, one has to be careful in making such global claims—sensitive to regional variations, national inflections, and circumstances, as well as to the fact, of course, that Catholicism itself was by no means an uncomplicated whole. Nevertheless, within the complex web of tense, and even discordant, traditions, one can identify closely gathered strands spun of the same intellectual fiber, making it possible to speak of a Catholic Counter-Enlightenment international, given consistency not just by the universal church but by the tremendous prestige and currency of French religious apologists in the eighteenth century. Ironically, a century that is usually considered a dark moment in the history of the Christian religion nonetheless produced a startlingly large amount of religious apology and defense. And whatever the judgment of posterity, in the eyes of eighteenth-century Catholics, French religious apologetics was the state of the art—the most sophisticated and the most battle-hardened, forged as it was, on the very field where the first attacks on the Enlightenment were waged. As a consequence, and due in part also to the international currency of the French language in the eighteenth century, French religious apologists were continually cited by their Catholic brethren in other countries who repeated, borrowed from, and recycled these arguments against the Enlightenment, and in fact, they were often translated in their entirety. In fact, when one begins to read through, for example, Italian or Spanish religious apologists, or to look at such international publications as the *Journal historique et littéraire*, published in Luxembourg by a group of Jesuit exiles in the 1770s and 1780s, it is striking, how consistent are their portrayals of the Enlightenment, of the *philosophes* who, after all, were considered the principal enemies both within France and without.

With the advent and radical turn of the French Revolution, moreover, the anti-*philosophe* discourse of the Old Regime grew immensely in persuasive power and cultural resonance. And this is tremendously important. For as the Revolution took on an increasingly radical character—persecuting priests, assailing monarchies, and consuming Europe in international conflagration—yesterday's fanatics began to look more and more prescient.[36] No longer could one dismiss out of hand the men and women who had warned, prior to 1789, of the dangers of *philosophie*. Had they not *predicted* the terrible anarchy and religious apostasy that would issue from Europe's obsession with "enlightened" ideas? Had they not *foretold* the consequences of straying from the path of God? Particularly in the aftermath of the Terror—when tales circulated through Europe and the New World of the blood-curdling violence carried out in a country that had placed Voltaire and Rousseau in the Panthéon, openly proclaiming the *philosophes* as their spiritual forefathers—such logic was compelling.

For many men and women it remained so. The right, from this perspective, was right, always had been, always would be—its analysis of the dangerous consequences of Enlightenment confirmed, not simply created, by the Revolutionary experience. The Revolution provided bloody corroboration of what the Enlightenment could do—what the Enlightenment *would* do—and so it followed that its resurgence need be fought at all cost—a conclusion spread in great abundance by Catholic polemicists and European heads of state in the first third of the nineteenth century; a conclusion further confirmed (or at least so it seemed) by the Revolutions of 1830 and 1848, and by the gradual progress of what was deemed *philosophie*'s bastard child, liberalism; a conclusion lurking in the background of the Syllabus of Errors, and a conclusion, finally, stated and restated in literally thousands of histories, newspaper articles, political engravings, and pulpit sermons, in which conservative Catholics spread throughout Western and Eastern Europe, and throughout the Catholic world the image of the *philosophes* first created in the eighteenth century. In Latin America, francophone Canada, the Philippines, the West Indies, and elsewhere, one finds these same anti-*philosophe* constructions trotted out again and again well into the twentieth century. When one comes to terms with this fact, it becomes easier to understand, I think, why so many for so long could have seen in the Enlightenment a constellation of values of insidious and malignant power, a source, not of reason and light, but of darkness and despair. At the very least, such prodigious output suggests the importance of broadening our conceptions of the Counter-Enlightenment—or Counter-Enlightenments—to include the pedestrian as well as the philosophically profound.

Notes

1. On this debate, see Norbert Hinske and Michael Albrecht, *Was ist Aufklärung? Beiträge aus der Berlinischen Monatsschrift* (Darmstadt: Wissenschaftliche Buchgesellschaft, 1973), and the fine English translations and commentary provided in James Schmidt, ed., *What is Enlightenment? Eighteenth-Century Answers and Twentieth-Century Questions* (Berkeley and Los Angeles: University of California Press, 1996).
2. "Mémoire au roi," *Procès-verbal de l'assemblée générale du clergé de France, tenue à Paris, au couvent des grands-augustins, en l'année mil sept cent cinquante-cinq* (Paris, 1764), pp. 327–9.

3. *Procès-verbal de l'assemblée générale du clergé de France, tenue à Paris, au couvent des grands-augustins, en l'année mil sept cent soixante-cinq et continuée en l'année mil sept cent soixante-six* (Paris, 1773), pp. 200–2, and *Procès-verbal de l'assemblée générale du clergé de France, tenue à Paris, au couvent des grands-augustins, en l'année mil sept cent soixante-dix* (Paris, 1776), p. 124.
4. [Gabriel Gauchat], *Lettres critiques, ou Analyse et réfutation de divers écrits modernes contre la réligion*, 19 vols. (Paris, 1755–1763), i, "Preface," p. 7.
5. Ibid.
6. [Jean G. Soret and Jean-Nicolas-Hubert Hayer], *La Religion vengée, ou Réfutation des auteurs impies ... par une Société de Gens de Lettres*, 21 vols. (Paris, 1757–1763).
7. For further reflections on this anti-*philosophe* world of letters, see Darrin M. McMahon, "The Counter-Enlightenment and the Low-Life of Literature in Pre-Revolutionary France," *Past & Present* 159 (1998), pp. 77–112. A somewhat dated, though still useful, account is also provided in Kurt Wais, *Das antiphilosophische Weltbild des französischen Sturm und Drang 1760–1789* (Berlin: Junker und Dünnhaupt, 1934).
8. Fleury, a scion of a distinguished parliamentary family, served as *avocat général* at the Paris *Parlement* beginning in 1746, *premier avocat général* in 1756, and *président à mortier* from 1774–1790. He took an instrumental role in pursuing the persecutions of many of the *philosophes* in the 1750s and 1760s. Séguier, likewise an *avocat général*, was also a member of the *Académie française* (1757), and an equally dogged opponent of the *philosophes*.
9. Bibliothèque nationale. MS Nouv. acq (*Collection Joly de Fleury*), Vol. 352, 3807–19, folio 6. *Arrêsts de la cour de Parlement, portant condamnation de plusieurs livres et autres ouvrages imprimés ... Extrait des registres de parlement du 23 Janvier 1759* (Paris, 1759), pp. 2–4.
10. [Antoine-Louis Séguier], *Réquisitoire sur lequel est intervenu l'arrêt du Parlement du 18 août 1770, qui condamne à être brûlées différents livres ou Brochures, intitulés, etc., etc., imprimé par ordre exprès du Roi* (Paris, 1770), pp. 1–4.
11. J. P. Migne, *Collection intégrale et universelle des orateurs sacrés*, 99 vols. (Paris, 1844–46), Vol. 65, *Oeuvres complètes de Cambacérès*, Sermon III, "Sur les incrédules," pp. 1047–8.
12. This critique frequently led to charges of a formal *philosophe* conspiracy. On the *ancien-régime* prevalence of such conspiratorial accusations, see Amos Hofman, "The Origins of the Theory of the *Philosophe* Conspiracy," *French History* 2 (1988), pp. 152–72, and Darrin McMahon, *Enemies of the Enlightenment: The French Counter-Enlightenment and the Making of Modernity* (New York: Oxford University Press, 2001), esp. pp. 56–65.
13. [Jean-George Le Franc de Pompignan], *Avertissement de l'assemblée-générale du Clergé de France aux fideles de ce royaume sur les avantages de la religion chrétienne et les effets pernicieux de l'incrédulité* (Paris, 1775), p. 5.
14. Hofman, "The Origins of the Theory of the *Philosophe* Conspiracy," p. 168.
15. This, of course, would later prove a central assertion of Hegel, who argued at length in the *Phenomenology of Sprit* that the French Enlightenment was merely the "Lutheran Reformation in a different form." It is noteworthy that this assertion had been put forth in considerable detail by orthodox Catholics in the eighteenth century. On Hegel's understanding of the Enlightenment,

see Lewis Hinchman, *Hegel's Critique of the Enlightenment* (Gainesville, Fla.: University Presses of Florida, 1984).
16. See Hofman's analysis in "Origins of the Theory of the *Philosophe* Conspiracy," pp. 163–9, as well as the insightful reflections of J. M. Roberts in his "The Origins of a Mythology: Freemasons, Protestants and The French Revolution," *Bulletin of the Institute of Historical Research*, xliv, No. 109 (1971), pp. 80–93.
17. On the significant anti-*philosophe* and anti-Protestant reaction generated by the Edict, see McMahon, *Enemies of the Enlightenment*, Ch. 1.
18. See ibid.
19. [Stéphanie-Félicité Ducrest de Saint-Aubin de Genlis], *La Religion considérée comme l'unique base du bonheur & de la véritable philosophie* (Paris, 1787), p. 222.
20. *Année littéraire*, 1783, vi, p. 5.
21. [Augustin Barruel], *Les Helviennes, ou Lettres provinciales philosophiques*, 5 vols. (Paris, 1781–88), iv, pp. 156–7. Barruel, of later conspiracy theory fame, worked on the *Année littéraire* in the late 1770s and early 1780s, and from 1788–1792 served as editor of the *Journal ecclésiastique*, the leading professional publication of the clergy. *Les Helviennes*, went through at least five augmented editions between 1781 and 1788.
22. Antoine-Adrien Lamourette, *Pensées sur la philosophie de l'incredulité, ou Réflexions sur l'esprit et le dessein des philosophes irréligieux de ce siècle* (Paris, 1785), p. 59. Élie Harel noted similarly that "the [the *philosophes*'] principles are so inconsistent that they lead directly to atheism." [Maximilien-Marie Harel, called le P. Élie], *La Vraie philosophie* (Strasbourg and Paris, 1783), p. 13.
23. [Abbé Philippe-Louis Gérard], *Le Comte de Valmont, ou Les égarements de la raison*, 6 vols. (Paris, 1826), i, p. 212. First published in 1774, the *Comte de Valmont* was considerably augmented and republished in at least seven editions by 1784, making it one of the anti-*philosophe* "best-sellers" of the end of the Old Régime.
24. [Louis Athanase des Balbes de Berton de Crillon], *Mémoires philosophiques du Baron De****, 2nd ed., 2 vols. (1779), i, p. 135.
25. René Liger, *Triomphe de la religion chrétienne, sur toutes les sectes philosophiques* (Paris, 1785), p. ix. See also pp. 187 ff.
26. [Jean-Marie-Bernard Clément], *Satires, par M. C**** (Amsterdam, 1786), p. 165. On Clément and his carrière, see McMahon, "The Counter-Enlightenment and the Low-Life of Literature," pp. 94–8.
27. Lamourette, *Pensées sur la philosophie*, p. 191.
28. Barruel, *Les Helviennes*, iv, pp. 173–4.
29. *Journal ecclésiastique*, xcviii, Part 2, February, 1785, p. 163.
30. Charles-Louis Richard, *Exposition de la doctrine des philosophes modernes* (Malnes, 1785), pp. 52–3. It is worth stressing that the *philosophes modernes*, to whom Richard refers here, included the standard figures of the High Enlightenment pantheon: Voltaire, d'Alembert, Diderot, Raynal, Helvétius, Holbach, Robinet, and others.
31. Hans Ulrich Gumbrecht and Rolf Reichardt, "*Philosophe, Philosophie*," in Rolf Reichardt and Eberhard Schmitt, eds., *Handbuch politisch-sozialer Grundbegriffe in Frankreich 1680–1820*, 10 vols. (Munich: R. Oldenbourg, 1985–), pp. 59–61.
32. Jean-Antoine Rigoley de Juvigny, *De la décadence des lettres et des moeurs, depuis les grecs et les romains jusqu'à nos jours* (Paris, 1787), p. 452–3. Rigoley was a

conseiller honoraire of the *Parlement* of Metz and a member of the *Académie des Sciences, Arts & Belles-Lettres de Dijon.*

33. Roger Chartier, *The Cultural Origins of the French Revolution*, trans. Lydia G. Cochrane (Durham and London: Duke University Press, 1991), p. 5.
34. Albert Monod, *De Pascal à Chateaubriand: Les défenseurs français du Christianisme de 1670 à 1802* (Paris: n.p., 1916), p. 472.
35. Robert Palmer, *Catholics and Unbelievers in Eighteenth-Century France* (Princeton: Princeton University Press, 1939), p. 21.
36. On the way in which French Counter-Enlightenment and Counter-Revolutionary observers interpreted the Revolution, from its onset, as the realization of *philosophie*, see McMahon, *Enemies of the Enlightenment*, ch. 2.

7 Berlin and the German Counter-Enlightenment

Frederick Beiser

I. The Basic Equation

Since the beginning of the nineteenth century in Germany, there has been one very popular formula for the interpretation of many issues of social and political authority. This formula can be found among those on both the left and the right, and even in the moderate center. According to this formula, liberal equals rational; in other words, fundamental liberal values—such as freedom of conscience, toleration, liberty of press, and equality before the law—rest upon the authority of reason. Hence it is often thought that to question or criticize this authority in any manner whatsoever is to impugn these liberal values themselves. Whether by intention or implication, it is to support such nonliberal values as the sanctity of tradition and the unity of state and Church.

The source of this equation goes back to the 1790s and the advent of the French Revolution, those heady days when the French *philosophes* attempted to defend their grand ideals of liberty, equality, and fraternity in the name of reason. Some conservative critics of the Revolution, such as Justus Möser, A. W. Rehberg, and Friedrich Gentz, criticized these ideals by questioning the authority of reason itself. The disputes between left and right in Germany then became enmired in epistemological issues concerning the powers of reason. Can reason determine the fundamental principles of the state? And, if so, does it have the power to motivate people to act on these principles? The battle lines between left and right were drawn according to their conflicting answers to these questions. The left defended its liberal principles by stressing the *powers* of reason, while the right criticized these principles by emphasizing the *limits* of reason.

The debates of the 1790s set a powerful and lasting precedent. For in the 1830s the dispute between the liberals and the conservatives was couched in essentially the same terms. While the liberals continued to defend their ideals in the name of reason, their romantic opponents would appeal to the authority of tradition to justify a return to monarchy, the unity of Church and state, and the preservation of the old class-distinctions (*Stände*). The equation persisted well into the 1930s, and beyond. Marxists saw themselves as the heirs of the Enlightenment, and have attacked the right for its relapse into irrationalism. Ironically, some Nazi ideologues accepted the charge, but only to insist that reason is not the solution but the problem. In order to uphold the German values of community, nation, and tradition, they attacked the legacy of Enlightenment rationalism.

But is it necessarily the case that the "liberal" is the "rational"? Is there some logical connection between these concepts? Or is this equation simply accidental and historical, the result of generalizing some historical debates as if they held for all epochs? That there is no necessary connection between them—or at least that the connection is much more complex than many would admit—becomes clear from the Counter-Enlightenment, that group of late eighteenth-century thinkers opposed to the *Aufklärung*, which is best represented by J. G. Hamann, J. G. Herder, and F. H. Jacobi.[1] These thinkers were sharp critics of the claims of reason made by the *Aufklärung*; yet they also made these criticisms *to defend* liberal values. They argued that the excessive claims of reason made by the *Aufklärer* not only undermined toleration and religious freedom, but that they also supported the oppression of ethnic identities and cultural traditions. Of course, the *Aufklärer* responded to these criticisms in kind: *they* were the true protectors of freedom, and it was the irrationalism of the *Schwärmer* that was undermining liberal values.[2] Yet the mere fact that there is debate here should forewarn us that the liberal-rational equation is problematic. We cannot make it without abstracting from historical contexts and begging philosophical questions.

While the problematic status of the liberal-rational equation has been little recognized in discussions of the Counter-Enlightenment, the equation itself has not been without its critics. One of the most persuasive and powerful of these has been Isaiah Berlin. Influenced by Romanticism and the Counter-Enlightenment, Berlin questioned the Enlightenment rationalism that has been the traditional support of liberalism.[3] More specifically, he rejected the Enlightenment doctrine of natural law, according to which there is a single universal system of values holding for mankind as such. Nevertheless, Berlin remained a liberal, insisting that fundamental liberal principles have to be based upon an acceptance of a variety of incommensurable and competing values. For Berlin, the fundamental problem for liberalism in the postmodern world was how to justify its central values without the problematic assumptions of Enlightenment rationalism.

It is to Berlin's great credit, I believe, not only that he questioned the dogma of the liberal-rational equation, but that he also recognized the challenge posed by the Counter-Enlightenment to the Enlightenment faith in reason. For Berlin, thinkers like Hamann, Herder, and Jacobi were not simple relics from that old curiosity shop known as the history of philosophy: they were innovative and powerful critics of rationalism in all its forms who have questioned the belief—still so common to philosophers today—that the basic social and political problems are resolvable by reason. The German Counter-Enlightenment is indeed still very much with us today in the form of "postmodernism." The criticisms of Enlightenment rationalism in the work of Richard Rorty and Alasdair MacIntyre were, in almost all fundamental respects, anticipated by Hamann, Herder, and Jacobi. While their pietistic faith is now a relic of history, their criticism of reason still resonates.

Yet, despite all his sympathy with Hamann, Herder, and Jacobi, and despite his being so deeply influenced by them, Berlin still remained a harsh critic of the

German Counter-Enlightenment. He especially disapproved of what he regarded as its extreme anti-intellectualism, thus censuring it for its "obscurantism," its defense of prejudice and myth, and its hatred of science. Though Hamann, Jacobi, and Herder themselves protested against the label, Berlin did not hesitate to characterize their philosophy as "anti-rationalism" and "irrationalism."[4] More importantly, however, Berlin was suspicious of the political intentions and consequences behind the Counter-Enlightenment critique of reason. Time and again in his *The Magus of the North*, Berlin labels Hamann "a reactionary" for his opposition to the reforms of Friedrich II, and persistently maintains that Hamann was a bitter opponent of liberal culture.[5] The irony is that while Berlin himself had doubts about the liberal-rational equation thanks to the Counter-Enlightenment, he sometimes wrote of Hamann, Herder, and Jacobi as if *their* thought was still stuck in this formula. It is as if their critique of reason were still antiliberal, both by intention and by implication.

My purpose here is not to examine the liberal-rational equation itself—obviously, a gargantuan task—and still less to tackle Berlin's question about the foundations of liberalism. My task is a much more modest historical one: I wish to examine Berlin's interpretation of the German Counter-Enlightenment, and more specifically whether it is accurate to describe it as "reactionary" and "irrational." Although it is tempting to dismiss these terms as mere "slurs" or *Schimpfwörter*, there are complex interpretive assumptions behind them, which need to be examined and exposed. Unfortunately, these labels have stuck, contributing to some very widespread misunderstandings about the Counter-Enlightenment.

My main argument here is that, in regarding the Counter-Enlightenment as reactionary and irrational, Berlin's interpretation is not only anachronistic but also tendentious. Simply to label it as "reactionary" is to ignore Hamann's, Herder's, and Jacobi's deep commitment to basic liberal values. And to brand it as "irrationalism" or "antirationalism" is to ride roughshod over their own strident protests against these labels. Even worse, it is to beg the question about the limits of reason and the nature of freedom, and involves the taking of sides in some complicated disputes thereon. It is important to see that, for all their criticisms of the *Aufklärung*, Hamann, Herder, and Jacobi never questioned the *value* and *necessity* of reason itself; for them the only question in dispute concerned its *limits*. But, of course, just how we draw these limits is a very difficult and delicate dialectical task. Since there are different, even incompatible, ways of defining these limits, one person's rationalism becomes another's irrationalism.

My argument, however, is that the fundamental weakness of Berlin's interpretation is that it fails to see the *liberal* inspiration behind the Counter-Enlightenment critique of reason.[6] If we place Hamann's, Herder's, and Jacobi's criticism of the *Aufklärung* in its proper historical context, we can see that its purpose was not to undermine, but rather to support basic liberal values, especially toleration and freedom of conscience. Hamann, Herder, and Jacobi believed that the *Aufklärer* had betrayed their own liberal values of toleration and of freedom of speech and press by identifying their religious and political beliefs with the standards of reason itself. The *Aufklärer* saw their own form of rationalized Protestantism as the *only* legitimate form of faith, and they saw modern European values as the *universal* values of mankind as such. Worst of all, however, they sanctioned the autocratic policies of absolutist governments that oppressed traditional liberties and ethnic identities. In short, the *Aufklärer* were guilty of "the tyranny of reason" (*Alleinherrschaft der Vernunft*), of oppressing different religions and cultures in the name of reason. That phrase summarizes perfectly the Counter-Enlightenment critique of the *Aufklärung* and at the same time captures the Counter-Enlightenment's essentially liberal spirit.

II. The Politics of the Counter-Enlightenment

To clarify this contention, I proceed to examine the first of Berlin's labels, his claim that the Counter-Enlightenment was "reactionary." There are two senses in which Berlin uses this phrase that are perfectly accurate. First, Berlin refers to the Counter-Enlightenment as reactionary "in the strict sense" because Hamann, Herder, and Jacobi "wished to return to the older tradition of the ages of faith," which consisted in a way of thinking that emphasized quality over quantity, the simple over the analyzable, and the concrete over the abstract.[7] There is some truth to this point; but it has no political significance. In another sense Berlin states that the Counter-Enlightenment was reactionary because Hamann, Herder and Jacobi were opponents of the reforms of Friedrich II of Prussia and of Joseph II of Austria.[8] This point too is indisputable. It is well known that Hamann, Herder, and Jacobi despised the increasing centralization and bureaucratization of the Frederician and Josephine reforms, which put more power in the hands of the central government at the expense of ancient liberties, traditions, and identities.

Neither of these points entail, however, what the term "reactionary" so often suggests: namely, *antiliberalism*, a belief in the need for traditional forms of authority and a suspicion of all new forms of human freedom. Berlin attempts to secure this added conclusion, however, by implying that the Frederician and Josephine reforms were liberal, modernizing, and progressive, in a way that makes it seem as if all opposition to them had to be reactionary.[9] But it is simply bad history to assume that these reforms were liberal in spirit. Their purpose was not to guarantee the rights of man, or liberty, equality, and fraternity, but to consolidate the control and power of the central monarchy.

To understand Hamann's, Herder's, and Jacobi's critique of the *Aufklärung*, it is of the first importance that we place it in the context of their opposition to absolutism. They were such sharp critics of the rationalism of the *Aufklärung* chiefly because, perfectly justifiably, they associated it with Friedrich's and Joseph's absolutism. The *Aufklärer* were indeed in the vanguard of Friedrich's and Joseph's reforms, which they defended in the name of reason. Such *Aufklärer* as Carl G. Svarez, E. F. Klein, and J. A. Eberhard in Prussia, and Josef von Sonnenfels, J. H. G. von Justi, and C. A. Beck in Austria, would appeal time and again to the principles of natural law to defend the reforms. These principles were supposed to be self-evident, universally valid, and true of mankind as such, so that those who dared to protest against them had to be acting according to their private interests rather than the public good. But, to Hamann, Herder, and Jacobi, the imposition of these laws was leading to increasing uniformity, bureaucracy, and centralization, and ultimately to a brutally efficient state where every citizen became a cog in a machine. They protested against these reforms because, in their view, they were leading to the loss of local liberties, ethnic identities, and cultural traditions.

To be sure, theirs was not a defense of the rights of man against tyrannical oppression; but neither was it the conservative critique of enlightened rationalism found among the "Hannoverian Whigs" (writers like Justus Möser, Ernst Brandes, and A. W. Rehberg), whose main interest was to defend the old *Ständesstaat*; and still less was it a critique like that of those reactionary writers of the 1790s, the *Eudemonisten*, who attacked absolutist reforms in the name of the traditional prerogatives of the church and the rights of the aristocracy.[10] Rather, Hamann's, Herder's, and Jacobi's main concern was much more "postmodern," namely, to defend cultural pluralism against absolutist centralization and bureaucratic uniformity. They advocated the rights of the Latvians, Poles, and Saxons to maintain their old ways of life, and the unique values of their own languages and cultural traditions.

It was because of the *Aufklärer* alliance with absolutism that Hamann, Herder, and Jacobi accused them of "the tyranny of reason." This phrase was given a very definite meaning by Jacobi.[11] The tyranny of reason arose, he explained, from the *Sektengeist*, which claims that one sect or party alone represents *the* principles of reason. This was a dangerous error because if the views of only one party or sect were rational, there would be no point in listening to, or tolerating anyone else, whose views would be by definition irrational and so beneath discussion. Jacobi contended, very plausibly, that this view was not only politically undesirable but also philosophically fallacious. Reason, he contended, is only a *formal* power, which determines nothing more than the inferential relations between propositions; it is not a *substantive* power which consists in specific principles or standards. As just such a formal power, reason is neutral with regard to all parties, and is a tool to which everyone has a claim simply as a partner in a discussion; it is therefore intolerant—not to mention absurd—for anyone to claim that *their* standpoint alone is rational. According to Jacobi, it was Lessing who first defended this broad formal concept of reason, which permitted toleration between opposing views. This explains how Jacobi, despite his critique of the *Aufklärung*, could still identify so strongly with that most radical of *Aufklärer*.

That the critique of absolutism was an important motivation for the Counter-Enlightenment critique of reason becomes clear from several sources, not least from Hamann's diatribes against Friedrich II, and from Herder's tirade against the machine state in his *Auch eine Philosophie der Geschichte der Menschheit*. Nowhere is it more evident, however, than from a neglected early essay by Jacobi, his 1780 "Etwas, daβ Lessing gesagt hat."[12] This essay is important since it marks the start of Jacobi's campaign against the Berlin *Aufklärung*, a struggle that eventually culminated in his famous controversy with Mendelssohn in 1786, the so-called *Pantheismusstreit*. The impetus behind Jacobi's essay was his indignation over the religious reforms of Joseph II, which had swept away traditional Catholic institutions in Austria. Monasteries not engaged in education were closed, new posts were filled with candidates schooled in rationalist theology, and the many rituals and holidays of the Church were reduced or abolished. In Joseph's Austria, the Church had a merely secular and social function: its sole purpose was to educate the people, to teach them the basic precepts and the rewards of good conduct. While Jacobi was not himself a Catholic, still less a theocrat, he felt that these reforms were a threat to religious freedom, and indeed to the very existence of religion itself.

Jacobi's later attack upon the Berlin *Aufklärer* in 1786 was essentially an extension of his critique of the Josephine reforms in 1782. Jacobi was suspicious of the Berliners—Friedrich Gedike, J. J. Engel, Friedrich Nicolai, and J. E. Biester—not least because they were in league with Friedrich II and all too happy to enlist his support in enforcing their own narrow rationalized version of Protestantism. His suspicions were especially reinforced by the so-called "Crypto-Catholicism" controversy, which began in 1784 when two leading *Aufklärer*, Biester and Gedike, wrote articles in the *Berlinische Monatsschrift* criticizing the Protestant practice of allowing Catholics to worship in Protestant churches.[13] Biester and Gedike feared that this practice was the product of "false tolerance," for the Catholics were only using the churches as a foothold for their reconquest of lost Protestant lands. They warned the public that the Catholics had never renounced their claim to be the only saving faith, and that they had never abandoned their ideal of reuniting Christendom under one banner. Hence, in their view, Protestants who tolerated Catholics were naive, allowing themselves to be reconquered in the name of freedom of conscience. Although Biester and Gedike continued to profess their belief in toleration, they argued that it has very clear limits, so that force should be used against those who proselytize and conspire for Catholicism. There followed in the pages of the *Berlinische Monatsschrift* a very lively debate about the meaning of toleration itself.

Jacobi's later dispute with Mendelssohn arose from this earlier debate. According to Jacobi, the *Aufklärer* had again committed their cardinal sin of the tyranny of reason, mistaking the views of their own party for those of reason in general. They failed to see that reason could not lie in the principles of any particular party but only in the reasoning common to all parties. They also had a false view about the basis of toleration: its foundation lies not in the mistaken belief that all people are the same, sharing in some universal human nature, but in the recognition that people are inherently different and that difference itself is valuable.

III. The Religion of the Counter-Enlightenment

Of course, the hatred of absolutism was not the only motive for the Counter-Enlightenment critique of the *Aufklärung*. There was another motive that played an even more important role: the defense of faith and religious values. It is necessary here to discuss briefly Hamann's, Herder's, and Jacobi's religious beliefs because they are crucial for an understanding of their liberalism, and for their critique of absolutism. Once their religious sympathies are pinned down, there cannot be any doubt about their liberal intentions.

The common interpretation of Counter-Enlightenment piety, which Berlin follows, stresses its origins in pietism. Berlin characterizes pietism as "one of the most introspective, austere and self-absorbed of all the inner currents of Lutheranism," as "that wing of German Lutheranism which ... laid stress on the depth and sincerity of personal faith and direct union with God, achieved by scrupulous self-examination, passionate, intensely introspective religious feeling, and concentrated self-absorbtion and prayer."[14] This is a fine general description of pietism, but it does not really help to explain the religious origins of the Counter-Enlightenment. The problem is that pietism, like so many "isms," is an umbrella term that covers all kinds of groups. One still needs to know the *specific form* of pietism characteristic of the Counter-Enlightenment. Only then is it possible to understand the depth of its liberalism.

Hamann, Herder, and Jacobi were all influenced by one extreme strand of pietism, whose origins lay in the Radical Reformation of the sixteenth century.[15] Though its ideas persisted well into the eighteenth century, the Radical Reformation antedates pietism itself, going back to the early days of the Reformation. Some of its chief exponents were Sebastian Franck, Caspar Schwenkfeld, Valentin Weigel, Jakob Boehme, Gottfried Arnold, Christian Edelmann, and, last but not least, Lessing. The radical reformers differed from the main stream of pietism founded by Spener and Francke in at least one fundamental respect: their aim was not simply to reform the Church from within, so that it could play a better role in the state, but rather to cut the bond between state and Church. As radical champions of religious liberty, they opposed the very idea of a state Church and advocated instead the idea of toleration. The radical reformers clung to Luther's grand ideals—the liberty of the Christian, the priesthood of all believers—but they believed that Luther had compromised his ideals before the princes. The fundamental principle of the Peace of Augsburg—*cuis regio, eius religio*—meant that the prince was sovereign in all religious matters; this destroyed any hope for the separation of Church and state and thus any prospect for true freedom of conscience. According to these radical reformers, the essential spirit of the Reformation entails that all true faith must spring from the heart of the believer, and that means that any attempt to enforce faith destroys it. Any kind of state interference in matters of religious faith is therefore not only counterproductive but also impious.

Now it was this spirit of the Radical Reformation that was so central to the social and political values of the Counter-Enlightenment. Hamann, Herder, and Jacobi did not merely want to reform the Church, and so to accept the unity of state and Church of orthodox Lutheranism; they were also perfectly happy with the idea of toleration, and ready to recognize Jews, Catholics, and freethinkers within the state. Like the radical reformers, they too insisted that freedom of conscience is sacrosanct, and that no official religion should ever impinge on its domain. This was indeed the chief source of their opposition to absolutism. They argued that not only piety but also all happiness and virtue must stem from the inner heart of the individual. It was no more possible to compel a person to be happy or virtuous than it was to force them to be pious.

Given Hamann's, Herder's, and Jacobi's adherence to the radical form of Luther's principle of Christian liberty, it is not surprising to find them endorsing one of the fundamental principles of the *Aufklärung*: what Kant called "the right of self-thought" (*Selbstdenken*), the right of the individual to examine all beliefs according to his own reason and conscience. But, in their view, it was the *Aufklärer* who had betrayed this principle. Nowhere is this critique of the *Aufklärung* more apparent than in Hamann's letter to C. J. Kraus of December 18, 1784, where he attacks Kant's famous essay "Was ist Aufklärung?"[16] Kant's distinction between the private and public use of reason, Hamann complains, means that one really has freedom only when writing an article for the *Berlinische Monatsschrift*, while in one's vocation and daily life one remains a hypocrite and a slave. In the end, Kant's ideal of the *Aufklärung* amounts to nothing more than a paraphrase of Friedrich's dictum: "Say what you want but obey!" To Hamann, it was all too obvious why in Prussia the common man does not have the power to think for himself: Friedrich had a huge disciplined army enforcing his every command.

Although Hamann, Herder, and Jacobi all endorse the principle of self-thought, it is important to see that they do not give it the same meaning as that of the *Aufklärer*. They do not equate self-thought with rational criticism alone, that is, the power of assessing beliefs according to the evidence. Rather, they see it in terms of the individual's need to test all beliefs through inner experience. It is not that they deny that we must have sufficient reasons for our beliefs, but that they interpret these reasons in different terms from those of the rationalists. Their terms are not only discursive, and so can be formulated in propositions, but they are also intuitive, resting upon inarticulable feelings or sensations. In either case, no matter how we interpret the principle of self-thought, it should be clear that Hamann, Herder, and Jacobi embrace it as much as the *Aufklärer* did. For this reason alone, we have to recognize their profound commitment to liberal values.

IV. The Issue of Irrationalism

There remains the question of the accuracy of Berlin's other epithet: "irrationalism." There are three very plausible reasons for applying this term to Hamann, Herder, and Jacobi, and each of them deserves careful consideration.

First, one might charge these thinkers with irrationalism because they limit the sphere of rational criticism and extend the realm of faith. It is one of their favorite arguments that reason cannot demonstrate or refute even the most ordinary beliefs—one's beliefs in the existence of tables and chairs, in the existence of other minds, and even in the existence of one's own self—and that all such beliefs ultimately rest upon faith alone. What makes these beliefs true is simply some special feeling or sensation, and it is no more possible to criticize such feelings or sensations than it is to question tastes, sounds, colors. Either one has had the experience or one has not, in the same way that one cannot know whether oranges have a tangy taste or whether red is brighter than blue unless I taste oranges and see red and blue. In thus limiting the powers of rational criticism, and in thus conflating religious beliefs with ordinary ones, Hamann, Herder, and Jacobi seem to be violating the principle—so dear to the Enlightenment—that *all* beliefs, no matter how sacred, must submit to criticism.

The underlying assumption behind this argument is that it would be irrational to limit the rights of reason *in any manner*, or that the right of criticism has to be *unrestricted* if reason is not to be undermined. But that this assumption is deeply problematic was one of the central insights of the greatest *Aufklärer* of them all, Immanuel Kant. It was one of the basic teachings of the first *Kritik* that the authority of reason depends upon its own self-constraint, and that reason must restrict itself if it is not to turn into its very opposite, unreason. If reason transcends its own limits, then it becomes unreason because it naturally and necessarily lapses into all kinds of fallacies, such as the paralogisms, amphiboles, and antinomies. Hamann's, Herder's, and Jacobi's critique of reason begins with Kant's demand for the *self*-critique of reason—hence their critique is entirely immanent—but they take it a step further and make it into the *meta*-critique of reason. They insist that if reason is to follow its own demand for radical criticism, then it must criticize criticism itself, for the practice of criticism too has its presuppositions.

Another problem with this argument is that it plays fast and loose with the term "irrationalism." Strictly speaking, it applies only to that doctrine which enjoins us to hold beliefs *contrary* to the evidence. In this precise sense, the paradigm case of irrationalism would be Tertullian's adage *"Credo quia absurdam."* This is not, however, the position of Hamann, Herder, and Jacobi. They contend that those beliefs we hold as a matter of faith have no evidence against them at all, so that reason can neither support nor refute them. Applying the old medieval distinction of beliefs according to reason, those contrary to reason and those above reason, they are in effect arguing that most of our beliefs are above reason and not contrary to it. This might be called "supra-rationalism" but hardly "anti-rationalism."

The second reason for thinking Hamann, Herder, and Jacobi are irrationalist is that they elevate the intuitive component of knowledge and denigrate its discursive or rational component. They elevate the intuitive component when they claim that the main source of all our knowledge is the senses. It is only our senses that give us a direct knowledge of reality itself, they argue, because (a) reality is particular and existence is determinate, and (b) only the senses perceive a particular as a particular. They denigrate the discursive source of our knowledge when they maintain that all concepts are abstract and hence removed from particular and determinate reality. On these grounds, Hamann and Jacobi would often dismiss discursive knowledge as artificial and arbitrary, as resting upon a mere manipulation of signs. To think that discursive knowledge gives us insight into reality itself, they claim, is to lapse into the oldest and worst of all fallacies: hypostasis. It is this belief in the reality of abstractions, they contend, that characterizes the *Aufklärung*'s faith in reason.

To call this doctrine "irrationalist" is, however, to beg the question, and at the very least it is to fail to appreciate its sources. True to their Protestant roots, Hamann, Herder, and Jacobi were all the heirs of the nominalism of Ockham and the *via moderna*, a tradition that forms the cornerstone of Protestant spiritualism and of Luther's and Calvin's theology.[17] According to the nominalist tradition, universal terms do not designate any special kind of entity—whether an eternal archetype in a Platonic heaven or a substantial form inherent in things—but rather refer indifferently to any of a class of particulars. Since the general terms give us no insight into an intelligible world, reason is limited to the sphere of sense experience alone. It is this nominalism that provides the basis of so much of the Counter-Enlightenment critique of reason, as Berlin rightly appreciates. The notion that reason suffers the illusion of hypostasis, that it grasps only the inferential relationships between signs, that a concept is indistinguishable from its linguistic embodiment, that only the senses grasp reality itself, and that reasoning is only a manipulation of symbols—all these themes of the Counter-Enlightenment grew out of the nominalist tradition. Because of the limitations it imposes upon reason, the nominalist tradition has been accused of irrationalism down through the ages. And yet to establish the validity of this charge, it is necessary to meet the challenges posed by one of the most subtle and sophisticated logicians of the Middle Ages—the *Venerabilist inceptor*, Ockham himself. It is necessary, in other words, to show that nominalism unduly restricts the powers of reason. Nothing less justifies the use of the irrationalist label.

The third and final reason for thinking that Hamann and Jacobi are guilty of irrationalism is that they seem to think that there is a *conflict* between reason and faith, and that one should choose one's faith contrary to reason. If this were so, then they would indeed be irrationalists in the strict sense because they would champion faith even if it were contrary to the evidence of reason. In this respect, Berlin points out that Hamann and Jacobi did not hold the classical Protestant doctrine that reason and faith are valid in distinct domains, as if reason is valid for the earthly and natural realm whereas faith is legitimate for the heavenly and supernatural realm.[18] Rather than separating and balancing the claims of reason and faith, they seem to oppose them insofar as they present us with a dramatic dilemma: either we accept a rational atheism and fatalism or we take an irrational leap of faith. Indeed, this is precisely what Jacobi appears to argue during the pantheism controversy when he tells us that all rationalism leads to the atheism and fatalism of Spinozism, and that the only way to escape such an abyss is through a *salto mortale*.

The problem with this objection is that it confuses some of Hamann's and Jacobi's rhetoric with their final position. While they do sometimes write as if there were a conflict between reason and faith, they also think that there is a means of resolving that conflict to the satisfaction of both sides in the dispute. They maintain that if reason does lead to atheism and fatalism, then it has gone beyond its legitimate boundary, which consists only in determining the inferential relationships between propositions. Their final position is not that reason leads to atheism and fatalism but that it ends in complete skepticism, to a suspension of all claims pro and con about any claims to existence. In this case, any leap of faith will not be *contrary* to reason because there will be no evidence either for or against it; rather, it will simply be *above* and *beyond* reason. While it is perhaps true that Hamann, Herder, and Jacobi do not accept the classic Protestant theory of two worlds, or *Zweiweltentheorie*, it is noteworthy that they also establish a kind of dualism all of their own, which assigns reason and faith to their respective domains. Thus they maintain that all faith deals with existence, and that it alone reveals facts—whether natural or supernatural—while reason determines only the inferential relationship between propositions about these facts. For them, the great fallacy is to think that reason reveals, or somehow discloses facts, when all that it really can do is determine the relationships between propositions. In more modern terms, they are saying that all reasoning is hypothetical: it determines only that *if* P, then Q but never *that* P.

The difficulties in applying the term "irrationalism" to the Counter-Enlightenment are compounded when we consider that Hamann and Jacobi themselves protested vigorously against this label. Even if they are ultimately guilty as charged, their protests alone show that we have entered into philosophically treacherous waters. Hamann stated explicitly that reason is one of the greatest gifts of humanity, but that we misuse it by extending it beyond its proper limits.[19] Reason is the source of all truth and illusion, the tree of our knowledge of good and evil, he told Jacobi, so that both those who curse it and those who praise it are right and wrong.[20] For his part, Jacobi protested that he was not advocating "blind faith"—that is, refusing to examine beliefs that we *can* evaluate according to reason—but simply pointing out that we hold many beliefs we *cannot* evaluate according to reason.[21] In "Etwas, daß Lessing gesagt hat," before his campaign against the *Aufklärung* in the *Pantheismusstreit*, he had already explained his attitude toward reason. As if to forestall the charges of irrationalism that he knew would be raised against him, Jacobi wrote in some remarkable lines:

> Obviously, reason is the proper, true life of our nature, the soul of the spirit, the bond of all our powers, an image of the eternal unchangeable cause of all truth ... Without reason we cannot possibly do anything but act against ourselves ... With it we are immovably at one with ourselves ... The desire for happiness is based on nothing more than the conviction that it can be found along the path of reason alone...[22]

We might conclude with these lines: for they serve as a fitting epitaph for the irrationalist interpretation.

Notes

1. There is some debate, of course, as to whether Herder should be considered an opponent of the *Aufklärung*, given that so much of his thinking is indebted to it. Some scholars have stressed Herder's allegiance to the Enlightenment tradition; see, for example, Robert Norton, *Herder's Aesthetics and the European Enlightenment* (Ithaca, N.Y.: Cornell University Press, 1991). Others have emphasized his distance from the Enlightenment, especially during the Bückeberg period; see, for example, Robert Clark, *Herder, His Life and Thought* (Berkeley and Los Angeles: University of California Press, 1969), pp. 179–214. In his "Herder and the Enlightenment," *Three Critics of the Enlightenment*, ed. Henry Hardy, (London: Pimlico, 2000), pp. 168–242, Berlin brilliantly captures Herder's very ambivalent relationship to the Enlightenment. While fully recognizing Herder's ambivalence on this issue, in this essay I have placed him within the Counter-Enlightenment tradition. I have done so because (a) there can be no doubt that Herder was also a passionate critic of the Enlightenment, (b) his criticisms are very similar to those of Hamann and Jacobi, and (c) the similarity is not accidental because of Herder's profound debt to Hamann.
2. This argument was made most notably by Kant. See the close of his essay "Was heißt: Sich im Denken orientiren?", in Kant, *Gesammelte Schriften*, ed. Wilhelm Dilthey et. al. (Berlin: de Gruyter, 1902–), VIII, p. 144.
3. On Berlin's criticism of traditional rationalism, see John Gray, *Isaiah Berlin* (Princeton, N.J.: Princeton University Press, 1993), pp. 5–10.
4. Isaiah Berlin, *The Magus of the North: J. G. Hamann and the Origins of Modern Irrationalism* (London: Murray, 1993), pp. 4, 23, 121. See also his *The Roots of Romanticism*, the A. W. Mellon Lectures in the Fine Arts, 1965, ed. Henry Hardy (Princeton: Princeton University Press, 1999), pp. 48, 55, 61, 67.
5. Berlin, *The Roots of Romanticism*, pp. 4, 30, 46, 52, 56, 68, 108.
6. Needless to say, the term "liberal" here is anachronistic. In its modern political sense it did not come into common use in Germany until the 1820s. On the early use of the term in Germany, see Fritz Valjavec, *Die Entstehung der politischen Strömungen in Deutschland* (Munich: Oldenbourg, 1952), pp. 426–9. On the formation of the word "*Liberalismus*" in a political sense see the article "Liberalismus" by U. Dierse, R. K. Hoevar, and H. Dräger in the *Historisches Wörterbuch der Philosophie*, ed. K. Gründer et. al. (Darmstadt: Wissenschaftliche Buchgesellschaft, 1980), V, 256–71.

7. Isaiah Berlin, "Hume and German Anti-Rationalism," in *Against the Current: Essays in the History of Ideas*, ed. and with a bibliography by Henry Hardy, with an introduction by Roger Hausheer (New York: Viking, 1980), p. 170.
8. Isaiah Berlin, *The Magus of the North*, pp. 125–6. Cf. "Hume and German Anti-Rationalism," p. 165.
9. Berlin, *The Magus of the North*, p. 125. Berlin writes of the ideals of the Prussian regime as "reason, progress, liberty or equality."
10. On the Hannoverian Whigs and the Eudemonists, see my *Enlightenment, Revolution and Romanticism* (Cambridge, Mass.: Harvard University Press, 1992), pp. 288–309, 326–34.
11. For Jacobi's reflections on this theme, see Jacobi to La Harpe, May 5, 1790, in Jacobi, *Werke* (Leipzig: Fleischer, 1812), II, 516–9, 529–30, and his "Über den frommen Betrug," *Werke* II, 485, 486, 488–90, 491–3.
12. Jacobi, *Werke*, II, 327–88.
13. Some of the main articles of this dispute are collected in *Was ist Aufklärung?*, ed. Norbert Hinske (Darmstadt: Wissenschaftliche Buchgesellschaft, 1981), pp. 139–369.
14. Cf. "Hume and German Anti-Rationalism," p. 165 and *The Magus of the North*, p. 5.
15. For some good introductory accounts of the Radical Reformation, see A. Koyré, *Mystiques, spirituels, alchimistes du XVIe Siecle Allemand* (Saint Amand: Gallimard, 1971); G. H. Williams, *The Radical Reformation* (London: Weidenfeld & Nicholson, 1962); and R. M. Jones, *Spiritual Reformers in the 16th and 17th Centuries* (London: Macmillan, 1914).
16. Hamann, *Briefwechsel*, ed. Arthur Henkel (Frankfurt: Insel, 1955–79), V, 289–92. The letter has been translated and reprinted in *What is Enlightenment?*, ed. James Schmidt (Berkeley: University of California Press, 1996), pp. 145–53.
17. On the significance of the *via moderna* for the Protestant tradition, see my *The Sovereignty of Reason* (Princeton: Princeton University Press, 1996), pp. 33–45.
18. Berlin, *The Magus of the North*, p. 68.
19. Hamann to J. F. Hartknoch, *Briefwechsel*, September 25, 1786. Cf. *Wolken*, in Hamann, *Werke*, ed. Josef Nadler (Vienna: Herder, 1949–57) II, 108.
20. Hamann to Jacobi, April 29–30 to May 1, 1787.
21. Jacobi, *David Hume*, in *Werke* II, 147ff.
22. Jacobi, *Werke*, II, 343–4.

8 | Isaiah Berlin's Joseph de Maistre

Graeme Garrard

I. Introduction

The publication of Isaiah Berlin's essay "Joseph de Maistre and the Origins of Fascism" in 1990 was one of the most important—and certainly most controversial—events in the normally quiet world of Maistre scholarship. Berlin may have done more to attract attention to Maistre with this one essay than did everything else written about him in the last 100 years put together, for better or worse. This essay, a somewhat modified version of part of a BBC radio series on "Freedom and Its Betrayal" first broadcast four decades earlier, sparked a surprising amount of interest in Maistre when it appeared in print in three successive issues of the *New York Review of Books* and as a chapter of Berlin's *The Crooked Timber of Humanity*.[1] In Italy a major newspaper (supposedly inspired by Berlin's essay) printed a piece which was illustrated by pictures of Joseph de Maistre and Hitler side by side. Those who believe that Maistre has been an unjustly neglected figure in the history of ideas must now be wondering if bad publicity is really preferable to no publicity at all.

The principal claim of Berlin's essay is that something dark and sinister lurks beneath the classical, conservative façade of Maistre's writings, something "approaching the worlds of the German ultra-nationalists, of the enemies of the Enlightenment, of Nietzsche, Sorel and Pareto, D. H. Lawrence and Knut Hamsun, Maurras, d'Annunzio, of *Blut und Boden* ... Maistre's deeply pessimistic vision is the heart of the totalitarianisms, of both left and right, of our terrible century."[2] It is this provocative claim—that the thought of an ultramontane Catholic has "an affinity with the paranoic world of modern Fascism"—that has stirred up attention and controversy.[3] Recent revelations about the views and actions (and inactions) of the Vatican during the Second World War may have played some part in stimulating interest in Berlin's thesis, given Maistre's ultramontanism.[4]

But this bold claim and the debate that it has aroused have eclipsed an even more striking aspect of Berlin's essay: that a twentieth-century Jewish liberal would credit a notorious eighteenth-century Catholic reactionary like Maistre with a "genius" for "the depth and accuracy of his insight into the darker, less regarded, but decisive factors in social and political behaviour."[5] Nor is this an isolated remark. Berlin's comments on Maistre are liberally spiced with words such as "bold," "uncannily penetrating," "original," "brilliant," "sharp-eyed," "deep," "effective," "lucid," "exceedingly pungent," "sharp[ly] realistic," "insightful," and "acute." This positive dimension of Berlin's view of Maistre has been obscured amid the controversy over his assertion of Maistre's link with Fascism. Yet Berlin's interest in Maistre is hardly surprising given his general fascination with the *Panthéon inconnu* of marginal figures like Hamann and Fichte, who lurk largely unnoticed in the dark corners of the history of ideas.

It is true that Berlin thought that Maistre was playing with very dangerous ideas that took him beyond orthodox Catholicism and traditional conservatism in the direction of a sinister "ultra-modernism" with Fascist "affinities."[6] But he also perceived what he believed were some important, if unpalatable, truths in Maistre's thought, mixed in with a great deal that is hyperbolic, polemical and frequently repulsive. This is particularly true of Maistre's political psychology, which Berlin described as very often "astute" and "penetrating," if at times grotesquely overblown. The pessimistic, "realist" liberalism that Berlin propounded shares *some* (only some) of the dark assumptions of Maistre's reactionary outlook while utterly rejecting its illiberal prescriptions.[7] Although most forms of liberalism trace their origins back to the Enlightenment, Berlin's has roots in soil that nurtured many of the opponents of the Enlightenment, such as Maistre.[8] Whereas these pessimistic assumptions led Maistre to reactionary conclusions, for Berlin they pointed in the opposite direction, towards a liberal politics of pluralism, tolerance and self-restraint designed to secure as tolerable a life as possible in the tragic circumstances in which human beings unavoidably find themselves.

The present essay assesses Berlin's controversial depiction of Joseph de Maistre, concluding that, on the one hand, it is not as negative as its title suggests and, on the other, that it fails to do justice to some of the conflicting tendencies within Maistre's thought. One of the most intriguing features of Maistre's work is its mixture of traditionalism and modernism, orthodoxy and scandal, realism and mysticism, pragmatism and extremism. Berlin's account understates the first of each of these, resulting in a misleadingly one-sided portrait of him that tends to overlook his more conventional side. Yet Berlin's emphasis on the dark modernism of Maistre's vision is entirely appropriate, something that his more orthodox interpreters tend to downplay.

II. The Apostle of Darkness

For Berlin, Joseph de Maistre is first and foremost a great "apostle of darkness" whose appreciation of "the dark, nocturnal side of things" lies at the core of his thought. For Maistre, he argues, there is an "impenetrably dark" mystery at the heart of man that the weak "flickering light" of human reason can never hope to penetrate. In his essay "The Hedgehog and the Fox," Berlin claims that Maistre had, "[m]ore clearly and boldly than anyone before him," depicted reason as nothing more than "a feeble instrument when pitted against the power of natural forces; that rational explanations of human conduct seldom explained anything. He maintained that only the irrational, precisely because it defied explanation and could therefore not be undermined by the critical activities of reason, was able to persist and be strong."⁹ Berlin's Maistre is distinctive by dint of his acute sense of the almost mystical subterranean forces that influence human behaviour from "below the level of consciousness."¹⁰

Berlin believed that Maistre's terrifyingly dark and vivid depiction of man and nature, while grotesquely exaggerated, was not without an important kernel of truth often denied by thinkers in the Enlightenment tradition that Maistre opposed. Berlin clearly appreciated what he regarded as Maistre's psychological realism in particular, which he compared favorably with that of the *philosophes* who, he thought, tended to overestimate the power of reason. He did not merely *describe* Maistre's psychological "realism"; to a surprising extent he *subscribed* to it as well. This can best be seen in the following, revealing passage, which deserves to be quoted in full:

> While all around him there was talk of the human pursuit of happiness, he [Maistre] underlined, again with much exaggeration and perverse delight, but *with some truth*, that the desire to immolate oneself, to suffer, to prostrate oneself before authority, indeed before superior power, no matter whence it comes, and the desire to dominate, to exert authority, to pursue power for its own sake—that these were forces historically at least as strong as the desire for peace, prosperity, liberty, justice, happiness, equality. His realism takes violent, rabid, obsessed, savagely limited forms, but *it is realism nevertheless* ... Blindly dogmatic in matters of theology (and theory generally), in practice he was a clear-eyed pragmatist ... No one who has lived through the first half of the twentieth century, and, indeed, after that, can doubt that Maistre's political psychology, for all its paradoxes and the occasional descents into sheer counter-revolutionary absurdity, has proved, if only by revealing, and stressing, destructive tendencies—what the German romantics called the dark, nocturnal side of things—which humane and optimistic persons tend not to want to see, at times a better guide to human conduct than the faith of believers in reason; or at any rate *can provide a sharp, by no means useless, antidote to their often over-simple, superficial and, more than once, disastrous remedies* [my emphasis].¹¹

As this passage reveals, even when Berlin credited him with insight into some dark truth about the human condition, he believed that Maistre had a dangerous tendency to exaggerate, to "push things too far with his ultra-verités."¹² For Berlin, Maistre's was what might be called an "exaggerated realism," from which we can draw *something* useful. This ambivalence is encapsulated in Berlin's claim that Maistre "revealed (and violently exaggerated) central truths, unpalatable to his contemporaries, indignantly denied by his successors, and recognised only in our own day."¹³

Not surprisingly, Maistre's fascination with violence features prominently in Berlin's account. It was above all his "grimly unconventional and misanthropic view about the nature of individuals and societies" that was the most distinctive and captivating aspect of his thought for Berlin.¹⁴ He believed that Maistre's mature writings, with their notorious descriptions of constant blood-letting as natural, inescapable and, up to a point, even beneficial, were among the most powerful and pessimistic accounts of the ruthlessness and violence of nature to be found anywhere. Berlin unequivocally rejects the common view that reduces this preoccupation with blood and death to a psychological defect; Maistre's fascination with these dark themes, Berlin writes, was "not a mere sadistic meditation about crime and punishment, but the expression of a genuine conviction."¹⁵

Berlin's surprisingly positive response to Maistre's thought was probably influenced by his reading of Tolstoy. The great Russian novelist was much impressed by Maistre, whose work he read while writing *War and Peace*. This is apparent throughout the book, particularly in the battle scenes, and Maistre is even mentioned by name in it.[16] Berlin's essay on "Leo Tolstoy's Historical Scepticism," first published in 1951, devotes considerable attention to a comparison of the ideas of Tolstoy and Maistre, and is Berlin's first significant engagement with the latter's thought. He describes both as "sharp-eyed foxes" and "acute observers of the varieties of experience."[17] The essay that eventually became "Joseph de Maistre and the Origins of Fascism" was first broadcast as part of a radio series around the same time that Berlin wrote his essay on Tolstoy. It is hard to imagine that Tolstoy's interest in and generally favorable view of Maistre did not significantly influence Berlin's reception of him, particularly given that Berlin speaks appreciatively of those very aspects of Maistre's outlook that seem to have made the greatest impression on Tolstoy, such as his account of war.

Berlin has been criticized for claiming that Maistre not only *described* this "universal law" of violence, but actually *subscribed* to it. This is the view of Owen Bradley, who argues in *A Modern Maistre: The Social and Political Thought of Joseph de Maistre*, that Maistre's "deep lifelong interest in violence and irrationality, which might indeed be called an obsession, does not at all necessarily imply he praised them. The step from the one to the other, which Berlin nowhere doubts, is in Maistre's case quite precarious."[18] For Bradley, Maistre's disturbing accounts of violence and the dark forces that dominate both human and nonhuman nature are *purely* descriptive. He therefore concludes that "the reader should remain skeptical when Berlin concludes that 'these gloomy doctrines ... inspired nationalism, imperialism, and finally, in their most violent and pathological form, Fascist and totalitarian doctrines.' On the contrary, we shall see that Maistre's dark vision encouraged him instead to defend every limit against the spread of that darkness."[19]

It is true that *most* of what Maistre says on the subject of violence is descriptive. But Berlin is right when he claims that Maistre occasionally went further. This is nowhere more apparent than in his *Considerations on France* (1797). After a shockingly brutal account of the "universal law" of violence—as a consequence of which "the effusion of human blood has never ceased in the world"—Maistre adds that "there is room to doubt whether this violent destruction is, in general, such a great evil as is believed." He argues that, under *some* circumstances—when, for example, the human soul "has lost its strength through laziness, incredulity, and the gangrenous vices that follow an excess of civilisation"—individuals and groups can be "retempered by blood." He then draws an analogy between mankind and a tree, in which "an invisible hand is continually pruning and which often *profits* from the operation [my emphasis]." A "skilful gardener" will carefully avoid pruning the fruits of the tree. "Now the real *fruits* of human nature—the arts, sciences, great enterprises, lofty conceptions, manly virtues—are due especially to the state of war. We know that nations have never achieved the highest point of the greatness of which they are capable except after long and bloody war."[20] The gardener in this analogy is God who, like any good horticulturalist, knows that to cultivate the fruit of mankind it is sometimes necessary to undertake a "terrible purification" of the human tree. This view is repeated in

Maistre's "masterpiece," the *St. Petersburg Dialogues*, published in the year of his death (1821). In it, he writes through the character of the Senator that, "in the vast domain of living things, there reigns a manifest violence ... [F]rom the maggot up to man, the universal law of violent destruction of living things is unceasingly fulfilled. The entire earth, continually steeped in blood, is only an immense altar on which every living thing must be immolated without end, without restraint, without respite until the consummation of the world, until the extinction of evil, until the death of death."[21] Although it may be objected that the Senator does not speak for Maistre here, everything that he says on this subject is consistent with views expressed elsewhere by Maistre, who was himself a senator.

For Maistre, violent destruction is not only healthy (sometimes); it is also moral. God is both a gardener with a blood-red thumb who uses violence to combat sickness and a moral judge who employs violent means such as war and revolution to punish the guilty (and occasionally the innocent too). Maistre held that human affairs can only be properly understood in the larger context of a divine plan, complete knowledge of which is forever beyond human understanding. It is precisely this larger context that was missing from the prevalent interpretations of contemporary revolutionary events, according to Maistre. One of the fundamental objectives of his *Considerations on France* was to fill in this missing "big picture," thereby explaining the violent circumstances of the 1790s in providential terms, in which the crimes of the modern age are punished by an "invisible hand" operating through French Revolutionaries, who are mere "instruments of God." Maistre thereby goes beyond mere description and *legitimizes* (in his own Christian mind) the violence and bloodshed of the French Revolution as a form of divine punishment meted out on Europe for the crimes of the eighteenth century. It is because "Europe is guilty" that "she suffers." This is moral because, according to Maistre, "punishment can have no other end than the removal of evil."[22] He confessed that during the French Revolution it was "gratifying amid the general upheaval to have a presentiment of the plans of Divinity."[23] This providential interpretation of the Revolution is closer to the position of Maistre's German contemporary Hegel than it is to Edmund Burke, with whom he is often associated. Like Hegel, Maistre was seeking to interpret the epochal events of his times as a theodicy, a perspective that led them both to affirm *everything*, even violent revolution, to the degree of being a consequence of God's will. Hence his view of the Revolution as a reflection more of God's intentions than those of men, a perspective quite unlike that of Burke, for whom it had more to do with human folly than divine wisdom. Burke was much more of a counter-revolutionary than Maistre in this sense.[24]

Maistre did not deviate from this line in his *St. Petersburg Dialogues*, which he subtitled "Conversations on the Temporal Government of Providence." In this work, he seeks to account for "the ensemble of ways of Providence in the governance of the moral world."[25] One of these ways is war which, like violent revolution, Maistre defines as a "department ... whose direction Providence has reserved to itself."[26] The "moral" dimension of war, according to Maistre, is in its function as an instrument of divine justice. In the *Dialogues*, the Senator explains that war is divine "in the mysterious glory that surrounds it" and "in its results, which absolutely escape the speculations of human reason."[27] Although Maistre was fascinated by war, it was less a morbid fascination than a religious fascination that comes from witnessing (as he genuinely thought he was) the hand of a divine judge working through human affairs. Berlin's claim that Maistre "glorifies war, and declares it to be mysterious and divine" is therefore substantially correct.[28] While he did not explicitly glorify war as something *inherently* good, he did stress its divine power and acknowledge both its beneficial effects and its moral function within a scheme of Christian providence. Violence and bloodshed are in some sense sanctified for Maistre by their incorporation within a plan designed and executed by God.

III. Maistre the Modernist?

Berlin perceived something not only disturbingly dark at the heart of Joseph de Maistre's thought, but something "terrifyingly modern" as well. It is this that distinguished him decisively from more traditional conservatives and apologists of religious orthodoxy such as Bossuet and his supposed "twin" Louis de Bonald.[29] For Berlin, Maistre's "modernism" resides principally in a "violent preoccupation with blood and death," a trait that was absent from the "rich and tranquil England of Burke's imagination."[30] This "doctrine of violence at the heart of things" is, he claims, far removed from the "frozen reactionaries who immured themselves against the champions of freedom or revolution within the thick walls of medieval dogma."[31] Maistre is "our contemporary" because he criticised the impotence of abstractions and scholastic methods which predominated among pious Catholic apologists.[32] His intense anti-intellectualism and "violent hatred of free traffic in ideas" were, Berlin tells us, "not mere conservatism, not the orthodoxy and loyalty to the church and state in which he [Maistre] was brought up, but something at once much older and much newer."[33] On this view, Maistre has moved far beyond traditional authoritarianism, leaving the "symmetrical Aristotelian constructions of Thomas Aquinas or Suarez" far behind.[34] According to Berlin, the virulent pessimism of Maistre's outlook not only distinguishes him from traditional conservatives but, more controversially, gives him "an affinity with the paranoic world of modern Fascism."[35]

Berlin characterized Maistre's link with Fascism in a variety of different ways. In its most positive formulation, his account credits Maistre with having prophetically "visualised" twentieth century totalitarianism, the advent of which "has vindicated the depth and brilliance" of Maistre as "a remarkable and terrifying, prophet of our day."[36] Berlin's most negative formulation of the link has Maistre exercising a "dominant influence" on "reactionary, obscurantist and, in the end, Fascist ideas."[37] A version of this claim also appears in his essay on "The Counter-Enlightenment," in which it is argued that Maistre's "gloomy doctrines" actually "inspired nationalism, imperialism, and finally, in their most violent and pathological form, Fascist and totalitarian doctrines in the twentieth century."[38]

Berlin offers no real evidence to support the more critical of these two formulations. Maistre certainly had little (if any) direct influence on any prominent Fascists beyond the *Action française* (least of all in Germany), and I am not aware of any evidence of an indirect influence that was anything more than negligible. However extensive his influence may have been in such circles, it was certainly far from "dominant." His posthumous influence peaked in the second half of the nineteenth century among some Catholics, and was inspired principally by his defense of ultramontanism in *Du Pape* (1819), a conservative work in which Maistre's "modernism" and fascination with violence are *least* in evidence. He also made a strong impression on many thinkers who could not reasonably be classified as Fascist, protofascist or even straightforwardly conservative.

More typical of Berlin's comments on Maistre's link to Fascism are those that lie somewhere between these two extremes, and stress the "unmistakable" ideological resonance between them that falls short of a direct causal connection yet goes beyond mere foresight.[39] Berlin depicts Maistre as standing near the beginning of a broad current of thought, the "richest flowering and the most ruthless application" of which did not come until the twentieth century, rather than in the mainstream of traditional conservatism with figures such as Aquinas, Bossuet, and Burke.[40] Maistre is therefore best understood, "not as the last voice of a dying culture, as the last of the Romans (as he saw himself)," but as "the first theorist in the great and powerful tradition which culminated in Charles Maurras, a precursor of Fascists, and of those Catholic anti-Dreyfusards and supporters of the Vichy regime who were sometimes described as being Catholics before they were Christians."[41] Standing in this stream with Maistre and Fascism are figures such as Carlyle, Fourier, Sorel, Cobbett, Proudhon, Bakunin, Nietzsche, Pareto, D. H. Lawrence, d'Annunzio, Drumont, Belloc, Maurras, Barrès, Drumont, and Deroulede, all of whom used a similar vocabulary and articulated themes that were strongly echoed in twentieth-century Fascism. For example, Maistre's violent anti-intellectualism is hyperbolically described as sounding "what is perhaps the earliest note of the militant anti-rational Fascism of modern times."[42] Elsewhere, Berlin argues that Maistre "assembles for the first time, and with precision, the list of the enemies of the great counter-revolutionary movement that culminated in Fascism,"[43] a list that includes Protestants, Jansenists, deists, atheists, Freemasons, Jews, scientists, democrats, Jacobins, liberals, utilitarians, anti-clericals, egalitarians, perfectibilians, materialists, idealists, lawyers, journalists, secular reformers, and intellectuals. Berlin also claims that Maistre's terrible vision of life, obsessed with "blood and death," has an unmistakable "affinity" with Fascism.[44]

Berlin's case here is as overstated as it is underdeveloped. The association of Maistre with Fascism has a distinctly sensationalistic ring to it, and it is not supported by much explanation of what is meant by "Fascism," the precise meaning of which is still highly contested. He sheds more light on this in *The Roots of Romanticism*, although even here Berlin stops short of a definition, and the connections that he makes between disparate ideas and movements are very loose and vague at best. In this work, Fascism is depicted as "an inheritor of romanticism," with which it shares

> the notion of the unpredictable will either of a man or of a group, which forges forward in some fashion that is impossible to organise, impossible to predict, impossible to rationalise. That is the whole heart of Fascism: what the leader will say tomorrow, how the spirit will move us, where we shall go, what we shall do—that cannot be foretold. The hysterical self-assertion and the nihilistic destruction of existing institutions because they confine the unlimited will, which is the only thing which counts for human beings; the superior person who crushes the inferior because his will is stronger: these are a direct inheritance—in an extremely distorted and garbled form, no doubt, but still an inheritance—from the romantic movement ... to

this extent romanticism in its full form, and even its offshoots in the form of both existentialism and Fascism, seems to me to be fallacious.[45]

This anthropocentric conception of Fascism is actually the *opposite* of Maistre's theistic providentialism, in which agency is a property more godly than human. What they do share is a belief that human affairs are dominated by a mysterious will that defies rational human understanding and control. But in Fascism that will is principally racial and ethnic, whereas in Maistre's writings it is fundamentally religious. Berlin's irreligious interpretation of Maistre is "theologically unmusical," as Weber once said of himself. Maistre's views cannot be fully and properly understood except in terms of his faith. The link between Maistre and Fascism that Berlin asserts is extremely weak at best, and probably would not have been made had Berlin had more of an ear for Maistre's religious convictions.

Given the association that Berlin posits between Maistre and Fascism, it comes as no surprise that he regarded Maistre as anti-Semitic. He writes that Maistre classed Jews among the ranks of "the sleepless enemy that never ceases to gnaw at the vitals of society."[46] This view is shared by E. M. Cioran, who writes that, while in St. Petersburg, "when Maistre realised that the Jews in Russia, faithless toward their own theocratic tradition, were echoing certain ideologies imported from France, he turned against them, calling them subversive spirits and—the depth of abomination in his eyes—comparing them to Protestants."[47]

To his discredit, Maistre does claim in his posthumously published *Letters on the Spanish Inquisition* (1822) that in the fifteenth century "Judaism deeply shot its roots into the soil of Spain, and threatened to kill the national plant ... The Jews were nearly masters of Spain ... An insurrection broke out in the year 1391, and a dreadful slaughter ensued ... it was indispensably necessary to establish the Inquisition, as best calculated to cure the political cancer which was rapidly corroding the heart of the nation."[48] However, this is, as far as I am aware, the only overtly anti-Semitic remark in Maistre's published writings, which run to over a dozen volumes. Also, these *Letters* boast that the capital of Catholicism was "the only part of Europe where the Jew feels himself neither maltreated nor humbled ... distinguished by the glorious title of *'the Jewish paradise.'* "[49] In fact, Maistre's attitude on this subject compares favorably with that of Voltaire, whose writings are peppered with anti-Semitic remarks.[50] Maistre professed his admiration for Moses—"a wonderful man"—as one of the few great legislators of antiquity.[51] Despite arguing that no constitution can be made or written *a priori*, Maistre granted just one "magnificent" exception, that of "the Divine mission of the great Hebrew Lawgiver."[52] There is even some truth to Cioran's characteristically exaggerated claim that Maistre's "affinities with the spirit of the Old Testament were so deep that his Catholicism seems, so to speak, Judaic, imbued with that prophetic frenzy of which he found but a faint trace in the gentle mediocrity of the Gospels."[53] Yet Cioran is finally unimpressed, dismissing this all as a "transient enthusiasm" on Maistre's part, adding that he "dares not imagine the invectives reserved for them [the Jews] had he [Maistre] foreseen the role they were later to play in the movements of social emancipation, as much in Russia as in Europe."[54] Unfortunately, Cioran offers no evidence to back up this claim, although it does not sound far-fetched.[55]

One problem with Berlin's portrait of Maistre as a "modernist" is that he does not define what he means by this notoriously slippery term. A strong case could be made that Maistre was at least as much an antimodernist as a modernist, or that his "modernism" was in the service of antimodernism. If he really was a man ahead of rather than behind his times, then this only served to strengthen his implacable opposition to many of the central features of modernity, such as secularization, pluralism, individual autonomy, democracy and equality, that he feared would play an ever greater part in Europe's future.

Even so, some of Berlin's critics have overstated their case against him in this regard. For example, Owen Bradley objects that to "blame Maistre for the dangers he perceived in our disenchanted world has been the error of almost every rejection of his thinking. Berlin repeats it when he tries to connect him more directly to twentieth-century cultural politics ... In turn, the existence of those evils that Berlin seeks to trace back to Maistre would themselves seem to imply that Maistre was all too correct that political order is irrationally maintained and underwritten by cultural discourses—by language, Maistre would say—and that the achievements of the Enlightenment have done little enough to change that so far."[56] But Berlin did not blame these dangers on Maistre, as Bradley claims. At most, as we have already seen, he claimed that Maistre's writings offered some inspiration to "nationalism, imperialism, and finally, in their most violent and pathological form, Fascist and totalitarian doctrines in the twentieth century."[57] To this Bradley replies that Maistre "offers trenchant criticisms of nascent nationalism and imperialism alike as consequences of democracy that destroy cultural traditions."[58] Although Bradley may well be right here, it does not mean that Berlin is wrong. Maistre's works contain contradictory elements, some of which would appeal to nationalists (if not imperialists), others of which would not. *Considerations on France*, for example, criticizes the universalist pretentions of the "Declaration of the Rights of Man and Citizen," arguing that the very idea of "mankind" is an abstract creation of the eighteenth-century imagination. "Now there is no such thing as *man* in the world," he wrote in one of his better-known passages. "I have seen in my lifetime Frenchmen, Italians, Russians and so on. Thanks to Montesquieu I even know that *one can be a Persian*. But as for *man*, I declare that I have never in my life met him; if he exists, he is unknown to me."[59] Maistre also claims in this work that religion and patriotism are "the two great thaumaturges of this world," the antidote to modern philosophy, which involves "the substitution of the individual mind for the national mind."

> Religious and political dogmas must be merged and mingled together to form a complete *common* or *national reason* strong enough to repress the aberrations of individual reason, which of its nature is the mortal enemy of any association whatever because it produces only divergent opinions. All known nations have been happy and powerful to the extent that they have very faithfully obeyed this national reason, which is nothing other than the annihilation of individual dogmas and the absolute and general reign of national dogmas, that is to say, of useful prejudices ... Man's first need is that his nascent reason be curbed under a double yoke, that it be abased and lose itself in the national reason, so that it changes its individual existence into another common existence, just as a river that flows into the ocean always continues to exist in the mass of water, but without a name and without a distinct reality. What is *patriotism*? It is this national reason of which I am speaking, it is individual *abnegation*.[60]

It is not at all difficult to imagine how such words, even when read in their proper context, could offer inspiration and support to nationalist thought. At most, Berlin is guilty here of failing to give a complete picture of Maistre, one that does justice to the internal development and complexity of his thought. Sometimes, by not going far enough, Berlin goes too far in his portrait of Maistre. But to deny that there is at least a strong (and quite potent) element of nationalism in Maistre's thought is inconsistent with his own declamations even if, in Maistre's later writings, particularly *Du Pape*, such sentiments are eclipsed by an emphasis on a pan-European Catholic civilization headed by the Pope.

To many of Maistre's more orthodox admirers this conclusion does not go nearly far enough. For them, Berlin's portrait of Maistre is simply a grotesque caricature. For example, Jean-Louis Darcel believes that Maistre is best understood within the context of his own time and of the Catholic tradition to which he adhered. When viewed from this perspective, Berlin's picture of Maistre as a "precursor of Fascism" represents a "disquieting turnaround" of his thought, making "a complete counter-sense of the philosophy and intentions of the author of the *Soirées*." Darcel's Maistre, in contrast to Berlin's, was "inspired by the constant theology of the Church, that of the Greek Fathers, that of St. Augustine."[61] Far from having an affinity with twentieth-century totalitarianism, Maistre "analysed and denounced, in the name of Christian values, the first version of state terrorism, the Jacobin dictatorship of Public Safety."[62] Darcel further objects that many of the most incriminating passages from Maistre invoked by Berlin—always the same notorious extracts on war and execution—have been unfairly taken out of their proper contexts, resulting in a distorted and anachronistic interpretation. These dark passages should "rather be interpreted within the framework of a Christian gnosis that is made up of orthodoxy and free intellectual speculation." Thus situated, Darcel asserts, it will be seen that, "without departing from a loyalty to the Church, intimately lived and many times proclaimed, he [Maistre] threw out bridges between the past and the present, Antiquity and Modernity."[63] Finally, Darcel complains that Berlin's over-reliance on one of Maistre's most uncompromisingly reactionary works, *Quatre chapitres sur la Russie* (posthumously published in 1859, although dated December 1811), obscures the fact that it was addressing a highly particular and, in Maistre's eyes, very volatile situation. Berlin's attempt to depict this piece as a general apology of state violence is "to betray on all points the intentions of the author for whom war is in all cases a scourge, even if it is 'a law of the world.' "[64]

By contrast, E. M. Cioran presents an image of Maistre that is remarkably similar to Berlin's. For Cioran, Maistre is "our contemporary" precisely *because* he is a "monster." We should be attracted to him not because of his reasonableness, moderation and humanity, but rather because of "his pride, his marvelous insolence, his lack of equity, of proportion, and occasionally of decency. If he did not constantly irritate us."[65] Cioran argues that Maistre's relevance for the modern age resides in his repulsiveness, excesses, and "outrages to common sense." "Every time he insults our principles or upbraids our superstitions in the name of his own," he writes, "we have occasion to rejoice: the writer then excels and outdoes himself. The darker his vision, the more he will enfold it in a light, transparent appearance."[66] Cioran's Maistre, like Berlin's, is far from the moderate conservatism of Darcel's Maistre. Rather, he is "the Machiavelli of theocracy" who was "Christian by persuasion rather than by sentiment, quite alien to the figures of the New Testament."[67]

One side in this debate over Maistre emphasizes his conservative orthodoxy (Darcel and Lebrun), while the other stresses his reactionary modernism (Berlin, Cioran, and Bradley). There is some truth in both of these positions because Maistre's thought contains elements of both: on the one hand a very hard-nosed (at times brutal) "realism" that he occasionally took to violent extremes that even Hobbes might have found shocking; on the other hand a more restrained Burkean traditionalism and a genuine Catholic faith. What Berlin manages to convey so effectively in his essay on Maistre is the former. After all, Maistre did write a defense of the Spanish Inquisition, offer a providential justification of the slaughter of the innocent and the "divinity" of war, claim that there is "nothing but violence in the universe" and that this is not an entirely bad thing, prescribe the deliberate retardation of enlightenment in Russia, and call for the integration of church and state. Darcel, by contrast, succeeds where Berlin and Cioran do not in recognizing the importance of Maistre's faith and the conventional conservatism of many of his views.

IV. Conclusion

Not all forms of liberalism derive either historically or logically from the Enlightenment. Indeed, I have argued elsewhere that there is a distinctive form that has its genesis in the reaction *against* the Enlightenment, and that Isaiah Berlin is one of the foremost representatives of this view.[68] Although the *philosophes* were, he thought, well-intentioned and on the whole admirable, they operated from naive assumptions about morality, human nature, and truth that were to prove quite disastrous when put into practice. One of the principal reasons for Berlin's criticism of the Enlightenment is his dissent from what he sees as its implausibly benign conception of human nature and its unwarranted optimism—beliefs to which Maistre was completely immune. Simplistic Enlightenment assumptions about human nature, on Berlin's view, have been rightly replaced in the nineteenth and twentieth centuries by "an increasingly complicated and unstable picture as new and disturbing hypotheses about the springs of action were advanced by psychologists and anthropologists."[69]

According to Berlin, many of the political disasters of the last two centuries, beginning with the "Reign of Terror," originated in the Enlightenment project to unbend "the crooked timber of humanity" to make it conform to a single, universal ideal. That is why he believed that "the great eighteenth-century philosophers were ultimately responsible for a lot of intellectual tyranny, ending in the Soviet Union, in the *gulag*; ... these good men, who were against superstition, falsification, authority, and were great legislators, had nevertheless preached doctrines which led, albeit in a somewhat perverted form, to tragic consequences."[70] Berlin's Counter-Enlightenment liberalism arose in opposition to this monistic project. Just as the *philosophes* unintentionally brought about consequences that undermined their own goals, many of the thinkers of the Counter-Enlightenment inadvertently promoted liberal, pluralistic ends in spite of their reactionary intentions. This idea features again and again in Berlin's work, and is one of the major themes of his thought. It is the law of unintended consequences applied to both the Enlightenment and Counter-Enlightenment and is one of his central insights.

Given this, it is not so surprising after all to find that Isaiah Berlin, the "patron sage of English liberalism,"[71] was not only interested in, but actually had some appreciation for, Joseph de Maistre, the "lion of antiliberalism."[72] In some of his basic assumptions he is remarkably close to the "realist" enemies of the Enlightenment such as Maistre, many of whose pessimistic views of history have been in his view tragically vindicated in his eyes, particularly in the twentieth century. Unlike most Counter-Enlightenment figures, however, Berlin believed that it is precisely *because* of these grim realities that we must cultivate the liberal virtues of self-restraint, tolerance, and mutual respect. Although he had a grudging respect for Maistre's willingness to articulate some of the unpalatable truths about human beings that many in his age preferred to deny, he also found Maistre's works instructive for what they tell us about the potential dangers that come from blowing such truths out of proportion. That, I believe, is the real reason that he insisted on stressing the link between Maistre and Fascism, as a warning to those who might be tempted to swallow Maistre whole.

Notes

1. Isaiah Berlin, "Joseph de Maistre and the Origins of Fascism," in *The Crooked Timber of Humanity*, ed. Henry Hardy (Princeton, New Jersey: Princeton University Press, 1990). A version of this essay was reprinted in the *New York Review of Books* on 27 September 1990, 11 October 1990, and 25 October 1990. Another version was published as the introduction to a translation of Maistre's *Considerations on France*, trans. R. A. Lebrun (Cambridge: Cambridge University Press, 1994). The edited radio broadcasts have been published as *Freedom and Its Betrayal: Six Enemies of Human Liberty*, ed. Henry Hardy (London: Chatto and Windus, 2002).
2. Berlin, "Joseph de Maistre and the Origins of Fascism," pp. 126–7.
3. Berlin, "Joseph de Maistre and the Origins of Fascism," pp. 112–3.
4. Recent examples of this literature are: Susan Zuccotti and Furio Colombo, *The Italians and the Holocaust: Persecution, Rescue and Survival* (Lincoln: University of Nebraska Press, 1996); John Cornwell's *Hitler's Pope: The Secret History of Pius XII* (London and New York: Viking, 1999); Randolph Braham, *The Vatican and the Holocaust* (New York: Columbia University Press, 2000); Ronald Rychlak, *Hitler, the War and the Pope* (Columbus, Missouri: Genesis Press, 2000); and Michael Phayer, *The Catholic Church and the Holocaust, 1930–1965* (Indiana: Indiana University Press, 2000); Garry Wills, *Papal Sin* (New York: Doubleday, 2000); Susan Zuccotti, *Under His Very Windows: The Vatican and the Holocaust in Italy* (New Haven: Yale University Press, 2001); James Carroll, *Constantine's Sword: The Church and the Jews: A History* (Boston: Houghton Mifflin, 2001); and Daniel Goldhagen, *A Moral Reckoning: The Role of the Catholic Church in the Holocaust and Its Unfulfilled Duty of Repair* (New York: Knopf, 2002).
5. Berlin, "Joseph de Maistre and the Origins of Fascism," p. 166.
6. Berlin, "Joseph de Maistre and the Origins of Fascism," p. 96.
7. This attitude is well expressed by E. M. Cioran: "His [Maistre's] observations seem to us exact; his theories and his value judgments, inhuman and erroneous" ("Joseph de Maistre: An Essay on Reactionary Thought," in *Anathemas*

and Admirations, trans. Richard Howard [New York: Little, Brown and Co., 1986], p. 38).
8. I develop this argument in detail in my "The Counter-Enlightenment Liberalism of Isaiah Berlin," *Journal of Political Ideologies*, 2 (1997), pp. 281–96.
9. Berlin, "The Hedgehog and the Fox," in *Russian Thinkers*, ed. Henry Hardy and Aileen Kelly (Harmondsworth: Penguin, 1994), p. 59.
10. I explore this theme in depth in my "Joseph de Maistre's Civilisation and Its Discontents," *Journal of the History of Ideas*, 57 (1996), pp. 429–46.
11. Berlin, "Joseph de Maistre and the Origins of Fascism," pp. 167–68.
12. Berlin, "Joseph de Maistre and the Origins of Fascism," p. 169.
13. Berlin, "The Counter-Enlightenment," in *Against the Current: Essays in the History of Ideas*, ed. Henry Hardy (Oxford: Oxford University Press, 1981), p. 174.
14. Berlin, "The Hedgehog and the Fox," pp. 57–8.
15. Berlin, "Joseph de Maistre and the Origins of Fascism," p. 118. The common view of Maistre's preoccupation with violence that Berlin rejects is typified by Stephen Holmes, for whom "Maistre's extreme, not to say macabre, theory of the executioner-priest discloses a strain of near-dementia in his works" (*The Anatomy of Antiliberalism* [Cambridge, Mass.: Harvard University Press, 1993], p. 31).
16. Berlin writes that, in November 1865, "in the middle of writing *War and Peace*, Tolstoy wrote down in his diary "I am reading Maistre," and on 7 September 1866 he wrote to the editor Bartenev, who acted as a kind of general assistant to him, asking him to send the "Maistre archive," i.e. his letters and notes ... Tolstoy possessed the *Soirées*, as well as Maistre's diplomatic correspondence and letters, and copies of them were to be found in the library at Yasnaya Polyana. It is in any case quite clear that Tolstoy used them extensively in *War and Peace*. Thus the celebrated description of Paulucci's intervention in the debate of the Russian General Staff at Drissa is reproduced almost verbatim from a letter by Maistre. Similarly Prince Vasily's conversation at Mme. Scherer's reception with the "homme de beaucoup de mérite" about Kutuzov, is obviously based on a letter by Maistre, in which all the French phrases with which this conversation is sprinkled are to be found. There is, moreover, a note in one of Tolstoy's early rough drafts, "at Anna Pavlovna's Maistre—Vicomte," which refers to the *raconteur* who tells the beautiful Hélène and an admiring circle of listeners the idiotic anecdote about the meeting of Napoleon with the Duc d'Enghien at supper with the celebrated actress Mlle, Georges. Again, old Prince Bolkonsky's habit of shifting his bed from one room to another is probably taken from a story which Maistre tells about the similar habit of Count Stroganov. Finally the name of Maistre occurs in the novel itself, as being among those who agree that it would be embarrassing and senseless to capture the more eminent princes and marshals of Napoleon's army, since this would merely create diplomatic difficulties" ("The Hedgehog and the Fox," pp. 57–9).
17. Berlin, "The Hedgehog and the Fox," pp. 80, 77.
18. Owen Bradley, *A Modern Maistre: The Social and Political Thought of Joseph de Maistre* (Lincoln and London: University of Nebraska Press, 1999), p. xvi.
19. Bradley, *A Modern Maistre*, p. xvi.

20. Maistre, *Considerations on France*, pp. 28–9.
21. Maistre, *St. Petersburg Dialogues*, trans. R. A. Lebrun (Montreal and Kingston: McGill-Queen's University Press, 1993), pp. 216–7.
22. Maistre, *St. Petersburg Dialogues*, quoted in Richard Lebrun, "Joseph de Maistre's 'Philosophic' View of War," in *Proceedings of the Annual Meeting of the Western Society for French History*, 7 (1979), p. 46.
23. Maistre, *Considerations on France*, p. 31.
24. For a particularly good comparison on this subject, see Richard A. Lebrun's "Joseph de Maistre and Edmund Burke: A Comparison," in *Joseph de Maistre's Life, Thought, and Influence: Selected Studies*, ed. R. A. Lebrun (Montreal and Kingston: McGill-Queen's University Press, 2001).
25. Maistre, *St. Petersburg Dialogues*, p. 7.
26. Maistre, *St. Petersburg Dialogues*, p. 220.
27. Maistre, *St. Petersburg Dialogues*, pp. 218–9.
28. Berlin, "The Hedgehog and the Fox," p. 66.
29. See W. J. Reedy, "Maistre's Twin? Louis de Bonald and the Enlightenment," in *Joseph de Maistre's Life, Thought and Influence*.
30. Berlin, "Joseph de Maistre and the Origins of Fascism," pp. 126–7.
31. Berlin, "Joseph de Maistre and the Origins of Fascism," pp. 126–7.
32. Berlin, "Joseph de Maistre and the Origins of Fascism," pp. 171–2.
33. Berlin, "Joseph de Maistre and the Origins of Fascism," p. 150.
34. Berlin, "Joseph de Maistre and the Origins of Fascism," pp. 126–7.
35. Berlin, "Joseph de Maistre and the Origins of Fascism," pp. 112–3.
36. Berlin, "Joseph de Maistre and the Origins of Fascism," p. 174.
37. Berlin, "Joseph de Maistre and the Origins of Fascism," pp. 134–5.
38. Berlin, "The Counter-Enlightenment," p. 24.
39. Berlin, "Joseph de Maistre and the Origins of Fascism," p. 158.
40. Berlin, "Joseph de Maistre and the Origins of Fascism," p. 155.
41. Berlin, "Joseph de Maistre and the Origins of Fascism," p. 170.
42. Berlin, "Joseph de Maistre and the Origins of Fascism," p. 150.
43. Berlin, "Joseph de Maistre and the Origins of Fascism," p. 119.
44. Berlin, "Joseph de Maistre and the Origins of Fascism," pp. 112–3.
45. Berlin, *The Roots of Romanticism*, ed. Henry Hardy (Princeton, NJ: Princeton University Press, 1999), pp. 145–6.
46. Berlin, "The Counter-Enlightenment," pp. 22–3. Berlin also attributes this view to Maistre in "Joseph de Maistre and the Origins of Fascism," p. 119.
47. Cioran, "Joseph de Maistre," pp. 47–8.
48. Maistre, *Letters on the Spanish Inquisition*, trans. Thomas J. O'Flaherty (Delmar, N.Y.: Scholars' Facsimiles and Reprints, 1970), pp. 22–3.
49. Maistre, *Letters on the Spanish Inquisition*, p. 33.
50. Peter Gay, "Voltaire's Anti-Semitism," in *The Party of Humanity: Studies in the French Enlightenment* (London: Weidenfeld and Nicolson, 1964), pp. 97–108.
51. Maistre, *Essay on the Generative Principle of Political Constitutions*, reprint of 1847 ed. (Delmas, NY: Scholars' Facsimiles, 1977), p. 93.
52. Maistre, *Essay on the Generative Principle of Political Constitutions*, p. 94.
53. Cioran, "Joseph de Maistre," p. 48.
54. Cioran, "Joseph de Maistre," pp. 47–8.

55. Owen Bradley eloquently and persuasively summarizes the "case for the defense": "This [the view that Maistre was anti-Semitic] is to ignore that Maistre himself was an émigré intellectual who showed an admiration of Judaism extremely rare within the Catholic tradition and wholly lacking, for example, from Burke. That 'the barbarism of the Hebrew people is one of the favourite theses of the 18th century' was for Maistre a sure sign of that century's nullity. Above all, these charges ignore his unrelenting hostility to right-wing revolutionaries" (*A Modern Maistre*, p. xvii).
56. Bradley, *A Modern Maistre*, pp. xvii–xviii.
57. Berlin, "The Counter-Enlightenment," p. 24.
58. Bradley, *A Modern Maistre*, p. xvi.
59. Maistre, *Considerations on France*, p. 53.
60. Maistre, "On the Sovereignty of the People," in *Against Rousseau*, trans. R. A. Lebrun (Montreal: McGill-Queen's University Press, 1996), pp. 87–8.
61. Jean-Louis Darcel, "The Roads of Exile, 1792–1817," in *Joseph de Maistre's Life, Thought and Influence*, p. 29.
62. Darcel, "The Roads of Exile, 1792–1817," p. 29.
63. Darcel, "The Roads of Exile, 1792–1817," p. 30.
64. Darcel, "The Roads of Exile, 1792–1817," p. 29. Darcel's reference here to the "scourge of war" is from Maistre's *Considerations on France*: "There is only one way of restraining the scourge of war, and that is by restraining the disorders that lead to this terrible purification" (p. 29).
65. Cioran, "Joseph de Maistre," p. 23.
66. Cioran, "Joseph de Maistre," p. 70.
67. Cioran, "Joseph de Maistre," p. 33.
68. See note 8 above.
69. Berlin, "Georges Sorel," in *Against the Current*, pp. 323–4.
70. Berlin, quoted in Henry Carpenter, *The Envy of the World* (London: Weidenfeld and Nicolson, 1996), p. 127.
71. Martin Bull, "God, creation and the genitals," review of *The Magus of the North* by Isaiah Berlin, *The Guardian*, 26 October 1993, p. 15.
72. Stephen Holmes, "The Lion of Antiliberalism," *The New Republic*, 30 October 1989, pp. 32–7.

9 | Benjamin Constant on Liberty and Love

Lionel Gossman

In memory of Jack Lively

I. Introduction

To the best of my knowledge, Isaiah Berlin never wrote directly on Benjamin Constant. This is the more surprising as there is general agreement among Berlin's interpreters that Constant was a decisive influence on his reflections on liberty. Besides scattered references throughout Berlin's essays—usually, it is true, in a list along with other figures such as Madame de Stael, Jeremy Bentham, James Mill, and Guizot—Constant is singled out on two occasions for his contribution to the articulation of modern liberal thought: first in the celebrated Oxford inaugural lecture on "Two Concepts of Liberty" of 1958 and again in the essay on "Liberty" drafted for a BBC program in 1962 (but published only in 1995). But it was in a letter to Conor Cruise O'Brien, dated 10 April 1991, that Berlin made the most explicit acknowledgment of his indebtedness to Constant. In an otherwise favorable review of Berlin's *The Crooked Timber of Humanity* in the *New York Review of Books*, O'Brien had taken Berlin to task for including Edmund Burke "in a list of 'reactionary' thinkers, along with Hamann, Möser, and Maistre." Berlin responded by confessing that he knew "virtually nothing about [Burke] except what most people know—the image handed down in history books and conversations," and therefore "really should not argue" with O'Brien about him. A postscript to the letter left no doubt that Constant, not Burke, had helped Berlin to articulate his ideas on liberty. "That cold, perceptive, independent, civilised Swiss wrote better about the destruction of individual liberty and the horrors of both the Terror and, to some degree, of Bonapartist rule, than anybody," he claimed. "I cannot deny that his famous essay on the difference between the conceptions of liberty in the ancient and modern worlds did have a pretty strong influence on me." He went so far as to suggest that "perhaps it was Benjamin Constant who showed the sharpest penetration into the French Revolution and its aftermath" and—hedged round by parentheses—that Constant's writings might be "in some ways more interesting than even Burke's."[1] As far as political ideas are concerned the affinity of Constant and Berlin thus seems to be beyond dispute.

Those who knew Berlin well will be able to judge whether there is any foundation in fact for my hunch that Constant may have appealed to Berlin more broadly, in the way that Alexander Herzen appealed to him, because of his almost debilitating capacity to understand and sympathize with conflicting points of view. Herzen, to whom Berlin did devote a couple of brilliant essays, is not even mentioned in C. J. Galipeau's *Isaiah Berlin's Liberalism* (Oxford, 1994). Yet the profound liberality of temper as well as conviction, the extraordinary intellectual honesty and openness, and the vast range of sympathies of the author of *My Past and Thoughts* surely had as great an impact on Berlin, steeped as he was in Russian literature and highly sensitive to literary values, as the more formal theories of liberal political philosophers. Constant, in my view, is Herzen in a different key— classical, somewhat "cold" as Berlin put it himself, rather than romantic, Swiss rather than Russian, but equally cosmopolitan and endowed with the same capacity for seeing the world through others' eyes. In one of the essays on Herzen ("A Revolutionary without Fanaticism") Berlin himself placed the two in the same category of "enlightened sceptics," along with Erasmus and Montaigne, Bayle and Fontenelle, Humboldt and the English Philosophical Radicals.

Like Berlin, Constant did not shrink from taking positions, but he did so, like Berlin, without the ease and assurance of the party man or dogmatist, and his choices were often tactical, favoring now one position or line of action, now another, as the situation and the occasion seemed to him to require, and never, therefore, enjoying the sense of being fully at one with himself that is the undeserved privilege of the dogmatic and self-righteous. While his aim was to achieve as much individual freedom as possible, he always acknowledged that there were other human needs and goods besides individual freedom and that these were not always compatible with it: love, heroism, security, solidarity. Constant's irony and ambivalence, as well as the discomfort they caused him, the sense of "not being a real person," as he put it, might well have struck an even deeper chord in Berlin than his political ideas as such. It is hard to imagine that Berlin was not as drawn to the Constant of *Adolphe*, the *Journaux intimes*, and the wonderful letters to his friends as he was to the author of the essay on "The Liberty of the Ancients Compared with that of the Moderns." There is, after all, some truth in Ortega y Gasset's potentially dangerous assertion that "liberalism is far more a general view of life than a question of politics."[2]

The two generically disparate texts by Constant that will be the focus of my attention—a political pamphlet (*De l'Esprit de conquête et de l'usurpation*) and a short novel (*Adolphe*) composed in the classical French syle of Mme. de Lafayette's *La Princesse de Clèves*—were written about the same time (1806–1807) and published within a couple of years of each other. The pamphlet appeared in 1814, in Hanover and London, and then in Paris, within two weeks of Napoleon's abdication; the novel in London and Paris in 1816. An English translation of the novel, by Alexander Walker, a friend of Constant's from his student days in Edinburgh, also appeared in 1816, only two months after the original French. I shall take up each text separately and then consider elements common to both.

First, a brief word about Constant himself. There is a copious literature on his extraordinarily active and varied public and private life and numerous love affairs—almost as exhausting to read about as they must have been for him to engage in. In particular, there are two excellent biographies—a truly elegant one by Harold Nicolson, and a much more detailed recent volume by Dennis Wood.[3] For our purposes, it will have to be sufficient to emphasize that Constant was a thorough cosmopolitan: French ancestry; Swiss birth (in 1767) and family connections (including several relatives who had distinguished themselves as writers); education in Germany (at the University of Erlangen, briefly) and in Scotland (at the University of Edinburgh, 1783-85—"the happiest years of my life"); close ties to and much travel and residence in Switzerland, Germany, England, Scotland, and Holland as well as France; two marriages (both to German women) and countless love affairs with German, French, English, Irish, and Swiss women, including a long-standing and notoriously stormy relationship with the redoubtable Mme. de Stael; and an active political career, as a pamphleteer, a member of the *Tribunat* at the time of the First Consulate, a member of Napoleon's *Conseil d'Etat* during the Hundred Days, and a parliamentary deputy and leading liberal under the Restoration (1818 until his death in 1829). With all that, the author of translations from the German, literary and political essays, a large treatise on political theory and another on religion, a couple of short novels, a tragedy, and various autobiographical writings, from the *Cahier Rouge* to the memorable *Journaux intimes*. Like Mme. de Stael, Constant belongs to European culture in the Age of Goethe far more than to French culture as such, and of course he was as much at home in English and German as in French. In particular, the influence of his two years at Edinburgh University, during which he participated actively in lively student discussion and debating societies, has been emphasized by a number of scholars. Adam Smith was alive at the time and Adam Ferguson was still teaching. A French translation of the latter's widely read *Essay on the History of Civil Society* of 1767 appeared the year Constant arrived in Edinburgh (1783) and, judging by its broad distribution in public libraries throughout France today, appears to have reached a large public. The impact of Smith and Ferguson on Constant has not been carefully investigated but there is every reason to believe that it was considerable.[4]

In lieu of a visual portrait of Constant, let me cite one particularly vivid verbal description. It comes from Harold Nicolson's introduction to a popular English-language edition of *Adolphe*, published just after the Second World War:

> Benjamin Constant at that date was twenty-seven years of age. His appearance was not prepossessing. His carroty hair hung over his forehead in wisps, his white face was blotched with yellow patches; his little eyes glinted within half-closed eyelids and behind green spectacles; his lips were mobile and slim. He had a weedy body, and white freckled hands which jerked nervously; his finger was constantly in his mouth. He had a thin, rather effeminate voice, and when he uttered his epigrams, the sibilants hissed and whistled.[5]

II. De l'Esprit de conquête et de l'usurpation

The material Constant drew on for this pamphlet was first set down around 1806 in a large manuscript outlining a liberal theory of politics, which Constant explains was simply not publishable under Napoleon. (It appeared in an abbreviated version as *Principes de politique*, in 1815, but was not available in its entirety until quite recently). By late 1813, however, Constant evidently thought the moment was opportune for giving some of his general reflections a topical turn and injecting them into the contemporary political and historical situation. "The author has cut out all the purely theoretical discussion and extracted only what appears of immediate relevance and interest," he stated in the preface, dated 31 December 1813, to the first edition of the pamphlet. This accounts for the many references in the pamphlet to the Terror, the Jacobins, and Napoleon, as conqueror and usurper par excellence.

While I shall touch on a variety of points, the underlying theme I would like to explore in the following pages is that of modernity, for Constant insisted that there was a radical difference between the modern age and earlier ages, notably classical antiquity, which was still, in Constant's time, a point of reference and even a model for many thinkers and artists.

The theme itself is old enough. Earlier phases of the *Querelle des Anciens et des Modernes* in the sixteenth and seventeenth centuries had been centered on the idea of intellectual and scientific progress: as we Moderns stand on the shoulders of the Ancients, the argument of the Moderns ran, we see more and further. The order of nature itself, however, was unchanging; we simply understood it better. Likewise, as regards *human* nature, politics, and government, the common perception from the Renaissance to the end of the eighteenth century was of repetition: the same problems, the same situations, the same behaviors, the same arguments, it was held, recur in constantly changing guises, costumes or masks. Even the Moderns claimed only that the arts of civilization—more refined masks, costumes, codes of language and behavior—were a kind of cosmetic that had mitigated the harshness of earlier times without fundamentally altering nature.

Machiavelli's ambition to construct a secular "science" of politics rested on this view of history as repetition. Whoever studies "current and past affairs will recognize how the same desires and the same characters recur in all cities and among all peoples," he claimed, so that "whoever carefully studies past situations and events will find it easy, by virtue of the similarity of occurrences, to foresee and possibly forestall, in any state, those of the future." As the Spanish censor of a book of aphorisms drawn from Tacitus noted: "Nos ha de enseñar junto con ló que passó, lo que passerá en semejantes casos" ("Our task is to teach, along with what happened in the past, what will happen in the future in similar conditions").[6]

Despite lingering links with this neo-classical view of history as repetition and human nature as unchanging (we can observe it, for instance, in the taste for maxims and the absence of precise temporal and geographical definitions in *Adolphe*), Constant develops an idea already anticipated by Montesquieu, for whom the ancient republic and its principle of virtue, like some prelapsarian humanity, is irretrievably lost and impossible to recreate in the contemporary world: namely, that the modern world is truly different from the ancient world and that history is not simply a succession of different masks worn by essentially the same players, as Voltaire claimed, but is real and constitutive. Thus customs and institutions that served one age well are experienced as "abuses" when historical changes have made them no longer useful or effective. "Everything has had its function and usefulness in the movement of progress. What is abusive today was indispensable yesterday." Our own modernity, Constant notes reflectively, is subject to the same law of historical change: "Perhaps some of the principles that seem to us beyond dispute will meet with the same fate." The fact that a custom or institution was once useful in no way justifies attempting to resurrect it. "As long as it was useful it stood firm on its own. When it crumbles, it is because it has lost its usefulness."[7] In fact, the most dangerous and destructive of all policies consists in deliberately trying to turn back the clock. Along with the Scottish champions of "commerce" and of the 1707 Treaty of Union with England, and well before the Hegelians and the Marxists, Constant was already arguing that the policy-maker's task is to understand the movement of history—"l'esprit général" of his time, as Montesquieu expressed it—and adapt to it so as to make the best of the opportunities it affords at any given point. "Everything in the natural world runs its course. Men follow it, accelerate the pace, or slow it down, but they cannot escape it."[8] For Constant, human nature itself is historical. The progress of civilization, Constant declared, "has created for man new relations with his fellows and, as a result, a new nature."[9]

In light of these considerations, Constant rejected antiquity as a model for modern politics. To him there is little to be gained from weighing up theoretically the relative advantages and disadvantages of Sparta, the model of the Ancients, and Athens, the preferred model of the Moderns, or from *arguing* for this or that form of society in the manner of the Enlightenment philosophers. In practice, history limits the range of our options and the ancient republic is simply not one of them. It is not suited to modern life; and as historically inappropriate forms of government can only be imposed by violence, they create nothing but misery and in the long run cannot endure.

> There are things that are possible in one age, but that no longer remain so in another. This truth is often neglected, never without danger. It is a great evil when the men who hold in their hands the destiny of the world are mistaken about what is actually possible ... They read history and see what was done earlier, and do not stop to consider whether it can still be done now ... [S]ince they are at odds with the moods, the interests, the entire moral existence of their contemporaries, these forces react against them. And within a span of time all too long for their victims, but extremely short if we consider it historically, nothing is left of their enterprises but the crimes they have committed and the sufferings they have caused.[10]

Constant's critique is clearly directed at the Jacobins (though it has a strikingly topical resonance to those who today are confronted by another—religious—kind of fundamentalism). The principle underlying his critique is equally clear: the Jacobins' rejection of the limits set by centuries of aristocratic, provincial, and municipal privileges and liberties to the sovereign power, be it that of the monarch or that of his replacement, the sovereign state, their transgression of the modern boundary between the state and civil society, their failure, in short, to acknowledge the proper limits of state power in complex modern societies, betrays the *anachronism* of their program. You cannot revive the ancient Roman republic in the conditions of late eighteenth-century Europe, as Rousseau and Mably would have liked to do, Constant implies. Constant's criticism would apply equally to the medievalizing fantasies of Novalis (*Die Christenheit oder Europa*, 1799) or the self-contained community dreamed up by Fichte in *Der geschlossene Handelsstaat*—about which Constant had this to say in 1804:

> God bless them, with their Spartan ideals in the midst of our modern civilization, of material needs that have become part of our existence, of bills of exchange, etc. They

are madmen who, if ever they came to power, would begin Robespierre all over again, all with the best intentions in the world.[11]

Its anachronism is also the basis of Constant's critique of the Napoleonic regime. It is simply, he claims, unsuited to an age in which what people aspire to is no longer glory or the challenge and exaltation of combat, but individual comfort and wellbeing; no longer virtue, as Adam Ferguson put it regretfully in his *Essay on the History of Civil Society*, but that happiness, the pursuit of which was one of the rights enshrined in the American Declaration of Independence.

> I have sometimes wondered what one of these men who wish to repeat the deeds of Cambyses, Alexander or Attila would reply if his people spoke to him and told him: nature has given you a quick eye, boundless energy ... and an inexhaustible thirst for confronting and surmounting danger ... But why should we pay for these? ... Are we here only to build, with our dying bodies, your road to fame? You have a genius for fighting: what good is it to us? The leopard too, if it were transported to our populous cities, might complain of not finding the thick forests, the immense plains where it delighted in pursuing, seizing and devouring its prey, where its vigour was displayed in the speed and dash of the chase. Like the leopard, you belong to another climate, another land, another species from our own. Learn to be civilized, if you wish to reign in a civilized age. Learn peace, if you wish to rule over peaceful peoples ... Man from another world, stop despoiling this one.[12]

Napoleon, Constant observed in 1815, is a throwback to a more primitive stage of human history: "He is Attila, he is Genghis Khan."[13]

On the basis of his affirmation of the real importance of historical time and change, Constant offers in part I of *De l'Esprit de conquête et de l'usurpation* a critique of war and conquest as anachronistic, historically inappropriate ways of satisfying human desires; and in part II, a critique of usurpers, dictators, and the arbitrary seizure and exercise of power, along with a sustained reflection on the kind of government that is appropriate to modern times—that is, to a bourgeois, commercial society. Around these critiques, he develops his vision of politics and society for the nineteenth century.

A series of contrasts between ancient and modern life is generated by the argument that in modern times wealth no longer needs to be stolen from others by violence but can be acquired peacefully by commerce or created by industry; that an age of commerce has replaced the age of war.[14] First, ancient warfare is said to have developed greatness of spirit and heroism, in addition to enriching the victors. In contrast, modern warfare impoverishes all parties, the victors as well as the vanquished. Moreover, "the new way of fighting, the changes in weapons, [the use of] artillery have deprived military life of ... that pleasure of the will, of action, of the development of our physical and moral faculties, that made hand-to-hand fighting so attractive to the heroes of antiquity or the knights of the Middle Ages." Waged without "interest or passion," in an age "which values everything according to its utility and, as soon as one attempts to move out of this sphere, opposes its irony to every real or feigned enthusiasm," war must become a horrifyingly cynical and sadistic affair.[15] As too must love, if I may anticipate the lesson of both *Adolphe* and Constant's second short novel *Cécile* (written around 1810, but left unfinished, and not published until 1951).

A second contrast between the ancient and the modern world concerns political organization. Constant sets the ancient *polis* and the medieval city-republics over against the modern state. The former were small, autonomous, internally homogeneous communities, he claims, in which each (male) individual was entirely absorbed by his role and identity as a *citizen* and there was virtually no sphere of private life. "To the ancient Greek, or the Roman," Ferguson had asserted in his *Essay*, "the individual was nothing, and the public every thing. To the modern, the individual is every thing and the public nothing."[16] In the ancient world, differences were not between citizens, Constant explained, again following Ferguson, but between cities or *poleis*. The modern state, in contrast, is part of a commercial world in which differences of culture and ethnicity are being progressively ironed out by similar interests and desires and people are becoming more and more alike. Difference here no longer distinguishes and divides one state from another but has been internalized *within* individuals of all states. A man is no longer fully identifiable as a citizen (of this *polis* as opposed to that one), but is rather a private person, a bourgeois, an individual. Optimistically, Constant believes this development ought to make war between states anachronistic. (Understandably, after the wars of 1866, 1870, 1914, and 1939, Berlin did not share Constant's optimism on this score and did not evoke this aspect of his work.)

> Our world is, in this respect, the opposite of the ancient world. While in the past each nation formed an isolated family, the born enemy of other families, a great mass of human beings now exist who, despite the different names under which they live and their different forms of social organization, are essentially homogeneous in their nature. This mass is strong enough to have nothing to fear from hordes that are still barbarous. It is sufficiently civilized to find war a burden. Its uniform tendency is toward peace. To be sure, the warlike tradition, a heritage from distant ages, and above all the errors of governments, slow down the effects of this tendency, but every day it makes further progress.[17]

The fact that the ancient communities and *poleis* were unified around a shared myth or tradition, whereas modern societies are characterized by interest and rational calculation of advantage, results in a significant difference between the modern individual's attachment to the state and the ancient citizen's attachment to the *polis*. The patriotism of the Ancients was a kind of family loyalty; modern man's attachment to the state, according to Constant (himself a perfect cosmopolitan, as we observed earlier), is conditional on the advantages that accrue to him from it. To the Ancients, "fatherland embodied all that was dearest to a man. To lose one's country was to lose one's wife, children, friends, all affections, and nearly all communication and social enjoyment." But

> the age of that sort of patriotism is over; what we love now in our country, as in our liberty, is the property of whatever we possess, our security, the possibility of rest, activity, glory, a thousand sorts of happiness ... Individual existence today is less submerged in political existence; individuals can take their treasures far away; they can carry with them all the enjoyments of private life. Commerce has brought nations closer together and has given them virtually identical customs and habits; monarchs may still be enemies, but peoples are compatriots. Expatriation, which for the ancients was a punishment, is easy for the moderns; and far from being painful to them it is quite agreeable.[18]

(Again, with the nationalistic passions and excesses of the late nineteenth and early twentieth centuries still fresh in memory, Berlin was not inclined to take up this argument of Constant's. However, in the age of economic migrations, the "brain drain" from poorer to richer countries, and the "global economy," parts of Constant's argument may seem more compelling than they did half a century ago.)

Above all, Constant's distinction of ancient and modern led to the famous distinction between ancient and modern liberty or between "political" and "civil" liberty, a distinction with which he had to have become familiar during his years in Edinburgh, since it is central to the thought of Hume, Smith, Ferguson, and other leading figures of the Scottish Enlightenment, and which, in turn reflects the two strains, in Constant's thought, of Rousseau and Montesquieu.[19] This was the part of Constant's work that most strongly engaged Berlin, helping him to formulate the two concepts of "positive" and "negative" liberty which were the topic of the 1958 inaugural lecture on "Two Concepts of Liberty." I quote at length from the chapter of *De l'Esprit de conquête* in which the distinction is elaborated.

> [Ancient] liberty consisted in active participation in collective power rather than in the peaceful enjoyment of individual independence. And to ensure the former, it was necessary for the citizens to sacrifice a good deal of the latter. But it is absurd to ask for this sacrifice and impossible to exact it at the stage people have reached now.
>
> In the republics of antiquity, the extremely small scale of the territory meant that each citizen had, politically speaking, a great personal importance. The exercise of the rights of citizenship represented the occupation and, so to speak, the amusement of all. The whole people contributed to the making of the laws, pronounced judgments, decided on war and peace. The share of the individual in national sovereignty was by no means, as it is now, an abstract supposition ... It follows from this that the ancients were prepared, in order to conserve their political importance and their share in the administration of the state, to renounce their private independence and to permit institutions which maintain equality, prevent the increase of fortunes, proscribe distinctions, and obstruct the influence of wealth, talents, and even virtue. Clearly such institutions limit liberty and endanger individual security.
>
> Thus what we now call civil liberty was unknown to the majority of the ancient peoples ... The citizen had in a way made himself the slave of the nation of which he formed part. He submitted himself entirely to the decisions of the sovereign, of the legislator ... But the reason was that he was himself that legislator and that sovereign, and felt with pride all that his suffrage was worth in a nation small enough for each citizen to be a power.
>
> It is quite a different matter in modern states. Because their territory is much larger than that of the ancient republics, the mass of their inhabitants, whatever form of government they adopt, have no active part in it. They are called at most to exercise sovereignty through representation, that is to say in a fictitious manner...
>
> The immediate pleasure [of liberty] is [thus] less vivid among them [since] it does not include any of the enjoyments of power ... It would be impossible to exact from men as many sacrifices to win and maintain this kind of liberty. Moreover, these sacrifices would [now] be much more painful: the progress of civilization, the commercial tendency of the age, the communication among peoples, have infinitely multiplied and varied the means of individual happiness. To be happy, men need [now] only to be left in perfect independence in all that concerns their occupations, their undertakings, their sphere of activity, their fantasies.

The relation of liberty to pleasure and sacrifice has thus become the exact reverse of what it was in antiquity. "In the past, where there was liberty, people could endure hardship; now, wherever there is hardship, it is necessary to enslave people to get them to put up with it. The people most attached to liberty in modern times is also that which is most attached to its pleasures. It holds to its liberty above all because it is enlightened enough to see in it the guarantee of its pleasures."[20]

In part II, chapter 7 of *De l'Espirt de conquête* Constant warns of the danger of attempting to recreate ancient liberty in conditions which are no longer appropriate to it. The result, he says, will be an *inauthentic* community, which will be maintainable only by dictatorship and terror. So the attempt to recreate a historically inappropriate liberty will result in the destruction of liberty. Among Constant's contemporaries, no one could have mistaken the reference here to the Jacobin reign of terror.

In light of those reflections, Constant redefines the very terms of political thought. What matters is not so much the traditional distinction between the different forms of government (monarchy, aristocracy, democracy, etc.)—i.e. *who* exercises power—as the *manner* in which government, *any* government, exercises power—*how* power is exercised. "My aim in this work," he writes at the opening of part II of *De l'Esprit de conquête et de l'usurpation*, "is by no means that of undertaking the examination of the different forms of government. I wish to contrast a regular government with one that is not; I do not propose to compare regular governments among themselves." [21]

Constant's concern is the same as that expressed by Wilhelm von Humboldt in his *Limits of State Action* (written in the 1790s, but not published, except for some fragments, until 1851):

> In every attempt to frame or reorganize a political constitution, there are two main objects ... to be distinctly kept in view: first, to determine, for the nation in question, who shall govern and who shall be governed, and to arrange the actual working of the administration; and secondly, to prescribe the exact sphere to which the government, once constructed, should extend or confine its operations. The latter object, which more immediately affects the private life of the citizen and, more especially, determines the limits of his free, spontaneous activity, is, strictly speaking, the true, ultimate purpose; the former is only a necessary means for arriving at this end.[22]

Humboldt goes on to complain that far more attention has traditionally been paid to the former than to the latter, i.e. to the question of the *form* of government rather than to that of its scope and limits.

For Constant, then, as for Humboldt, the significant distinction is not between kinds of government but, first, between *legitimate* governments of whatever stripe (i.e. governments that can be said in one way or another to rest on the will of the people, whether by a long tradition of acceptance and consent or by constitutional enactment) and *illegitimate* governments (governments in which power has been usurped and is exercised without the consent or even against the will of the people); and, second, between governments that acknowledge legal limits to state power and governments that do not, i.e. governments that claim absolute power. For Constant subscribes fully to the modern distinction—of which he almost certainly heard much as a student in Edinburgh in the 1780s—between the varied sphere of civil society and the sphere of the state; and he holds that in the sphere of civil society—private life, culture, religion, economic activity, etc.—the individual has a right to freedom, and that no government, of any stripe, is entitled to interfere with that freedom. The sway of government should extend no further than the protection of each individual from external enemies and from other individuals who might seek to diminish his freedom.

> Two things are needed for a society to exist and enjoy happiness. One, it must be protected from internal disorder, and two, it must be protected from foreign invasion. Government's task is to suppress disorders and to repel invasions.[23]

In advocating strict limits on the power of government, Constant deliberately goes further than Montesquieu's separation of powers. He wants a more reliable defense of individual liberty than the separation of powers. "What matters to me is not that my personal rights cannot be violated by one source of power without the approval of another, but that my rights cannot be violated by any power whatsoever."[24] Or again: "According to Montesquieu, liberty is the right to do whatever the laws permit. No doubt there is no liberty when citizens cannot do what is not prohibited by law. But the laws might well prohibit so many things that there would be no liberty even under law."[25] And just before his death in 1829, Constant wrote:

> For forty years I have defended the same principle—freedom in all things: in religion, in philosophy, in literature, in industry, and in politics. ... The majority has the right to oblige the minority to respect public order, but everything which does not disturb public order, everything which is personal, such as our opinions, everything which, in giving expression to our opinions, does no harm to others, either by provoking physical violence or obstructing contrary opinions, everything which, in industry, does not prevent a rival industry from flourishing freely, all that belongs to the individual and cannot be legitimately surrendered to the power of the state.[26]

The essential thing for Constant, as for most early liberals like Humboldt or even Mill, one might want to conclude, is "negative liberty"—that liberty *from government*, derived from the jurisprudential, as distinct from the civic humanist tradition, and presented by most of the Scottish Enlightenment writers as appropriate to modern commercial societies, be they republics like the German city-states evoked by Adam Smith in his 1762–63 Glasgow University lectures on jurisprudence or the "civilised monarchies" admired by Hume.[27] "The axiom of popular sovereignty has been taken as a principle of liberty," Constant wrote. But in a modern society, "unless one has recourse to other principles to determine the extent of ... sovereignty, liberty could be lost, despite the principle of popular sovereignty, or even on account of it."[28] For

> when no limit is set to the power of the state, the leaders of the people in a popular government are not defenders of liberty but candidates for the exercise of tyranny ... The people that can do anything is as dangerous as—more dangerous than—any tyrant. It is not the small number of governors that constitutes tyranny or the large number of governors that guarantees liberty. Only the *degree* of state power, whatever the hands in which it is placed, determines whether a constitution is free or a government oppressive; and once a tyranny has been established, it is the more frightful as the tyrants are more numerous.[29]

So *any* form of government may claim absolute power and destroy liberty: democracy no less than monarchy and aristocracy. Equally, any form of government is compatible with limited government power. A liberal democracy would be "power placed in the hands of all, *but only as much power as is necessary to ensure the order and safety of the association."* A liberal aristocracy would correspondingly be one in which the same limited power is vested in a few; a liberal monarchy one in which limited power is vested in a single person. "The people can transfer its authority to a few or to a single individual, but *their* authority is as limited as that of the people which gave it to them."[30]

In sum, the emphasis is on the protection of the private sphere, private activities, private beliefs, private pleasures. This seemingly overriding concern with "negative liberty," inspired as it undoubtedly was by the experience of the Terror, occasionally led Constant to take a fairly benign view even of regimes that did not enjoy popular support, provided they did not interfere too much in the private sphere. (In the same way, Isaiah Berlin would argue in the 1958 inaugural lecture, delivered at the height of the Cold War and in the shadow of Stalinism, that negative liberty "is not incompatible with some kinds of autocracy, or at any rate with the absence of self-government.") In Constant's *Red Notebook* (a fragment of autobiographical narrative composed in 1811), the narrator recounts an episode from the 1780s, and comments on Bernese rule in the French-speaking *pays de Vaud*—Constant's birthplace—which became an independent canton only as a result of Napoleon's restructuring of Switzerland by the Act of Mediation (1803).

> The Bernese with whom I was travelling belonged to one of the aristocratic families of Berne. My father detested this government and had brought me up to do the same ... [He] spent his life declaiming against [it] and I used to repeat his declamations. We did not reflect that our very declamations proved their own falsehood, by the mere fact that we could utter them without inconvenience to ourselves. They were not, however, *always* unattended by inconvenience: by dint of accusing oligarchs, whose only faults were monopoly and insolence, of injustice and tyranny, my father finally caused them to treat him unjustly; which cost him his place, his fortune and a peaceful existence during the last twenty-five years of his life.
>
> Filled as I was with all my father's hatred of Bernese rule, I was no sooner in a post-chaise with this Bernese than I began to repeat all the well-known arguments against its policies, against the usurpation of the people's rights, against hereditary authority, etc. I did not fail to promise my travelling-companion that, if ever the opportunity offered, I would deliver the canton of Vaud from the oppression of his compatriots. Just such an opportunity presented itself eleven years later; but by this time I had before me the experience of France, where I had been a ... witness of what a revolution really means, as far as liberty is concerned; and I carefully refrained from any effort to revolutionize Switzerland.
>
> What strikes me, when I recall my conversation with this Bernese, is the small importance that was in those days attached to the expression of any sort of opinion, and the tolerance that characterized the period. If one nowadays expressed one quarter of such views, one would not be safe for half an hour.[31]

A few lines in the middle of this decidedly un-revolutionary passage ("They were not, however, always unattended by inconvenience ...") emit an important warning signal. An "illegitimate," "foreign" government that does not enjoy popular support but nevertheless allows for considerable personal liberty may in practice be preferable to some supposedly popular regimes. In the end, however, a government that is not answerable to the people provides neither security nor liberty, for it will act ruthlessly and without restraint the moment the freedoms it permitted out of indifference no longer seem harmless to it.

In fact, Constant acknowledges that something may be missing in "negative liberty" or "modern liberty"—and in modernity in general. This point can be illustrated by three passages from three very different works.

The first is from one of our two principal texts, *De l'Esprit de conquête et de l'usurpation*. Constant draws attention here to the isolation and *anomie* of the citizens of large modern states, even where negative freedom is enjoyed. Inspired no doubt in part by the strong particularist tradition of his native Switzerland and in part by the image of ancient Greece as a land of countless independent *poleis*, Constant anticipates Tocqueville's argument that there is a continuity between the more and more centralized state of the *ancien régime* French monarchy and the modern post-Revolutionary state in that both aim to eliminate the local identities and communities that stand in the way of their hegemony.

> In all those states where local life is destroyed, a little state is formed in their center. All interests are concentrated in the capital. There all ambitions make their way to exert themselves; the rest remain inert. Individuals, lost in an unnatural isolation, strangers in the place of their birth, without contact with the past, living only in a hasty present, cast like atoms upon an immense flat plain, detach themselves from a fatherland that they can nowhere see. Its entirety becomes a matter of indifference to them since their affection cannot come to rest on any of its parts ... One cannot help regretting those times when the earth was covered with numerous and vigorous peoples and mankind could stir and exert itself in every way in a sphere suited to its capacity.[32]

The second passage comes from *De la Religion*, a text on which Constant worked all his life and which he himself valued more than any of his other writings. It describes the somewhat bitter triumph of Enlightenment:

> Victorious in the battles he has fought, man looks on a world depopulated of protective powers, and is astonished at his victory. ... His imagination, idle now and solitary, turns upon itself. He finds himself alone on an earth which may swallow him up. On this earth the generations follow each other, transitory, fortuitous, isolated; they appear, they suffer, they die ... No voice of those that are no more is prolonged into the life of those still living, and the voice of the living generations must soon be engulfed by the same eternal silence. What shall man do, without memory, without hope, between the past by which he has been abandoned and a future from which he is excluded?[33]

The third passage is from a text of 1824, a commentary on an Italian work of 1794 entitled *Scienza della legislazione*:

> In the age of our excessive civilization, relations between fathers and children have become extremely difficult. Fathers live in the past. Their children's domain is the future. The present is nothing but ... the theater of a great combat in which some strive ceaselessly to hasten the collapse of what others would like to retain. Each day the torrent of affairs, pleasures, and ambitions separates the generation taking possession of life from the generations that life is abandoning.[34]

Modern life, these three passages seem to be saying, tends to destroy both the bonds of community and the bonds of history and tradition, to separate generations, isolate individuals, and decompose time into discrete instants. By eroding their sense of themselves as members or parts of a larger whole, it deprives people of an object for the passion, dedication, and enthusiasm that are the hallmarks of the human desire for self-transcendence, be it in the form of love of another individual, love of a larger community or love of God. Continuous self-reflection and the habit of skepticism also destroy spontaneity and conviction and cut the modern individual off from the wellsprings of energy and feeling in himself, from his own affective life.

> We have lost in imagination what we have gained in knowledge; as a result, we are even incapable of lasting emotion; the ancients were in the full youth of their moral life, we are in its maturity, perhaps in its old age; we are always dragging behind us some sort of afterthought, which is born of experience, and which defeats enthusiasm ... We are so afraid of being dupes, and above all of looking like dupes, that we are always watching ourselves even in our most violent emotions. The ancients had complete conviction in all matters; we have only a weak and fluctuating conviction about almost everything. We try to blind ourselves to this deficiency, but in vain.[35]

To be sure, there is no going back to the ages of community, unreflecting conviction, and spontaneity. "These times are no more and it is pointless to regret them."[36] However, Constant does appear to believe that something needs to be preserved of the *ancient* in order to sustain the *modern* and to secure the liberties modern individuals enjoy. Adam Smith himself acknowledged that "there are some inconveniences arising from a commercial spirit ... [:] the minds of men are contracted and rendered incapable of elevation, education is despised or at least neglected, and heroic spirit is almost utterly extinguished." Smith remarks that "To remedy these defects would be an object worthy of serious attention."[37]

So, while he regards the attempts of the French Jacobins to reinstate the ancient republic as misguided and dangerous, Constant also recognizes, as Ferguson in particular had done,[38] the human value of the old ways, of the old republics, even of war, in developing personal qualities of courage, independence, and dedication. He therefore protests his respect for the motives of those who had attempted, however misguidedly, to revive those qualities and the conditions that once sustained them. "Woe betide even today whoever does not feel a commitment, even while recognizing the errors of the friends of humanity, to the principles they have professed from age to age."[39] Though critical of Rousseau, Constant does not join the anti-Rousseauist bandwaggon. Instead, he emphasizes the limitation of interest alone as a motivation for defending freedom, and in the *Principes de politique* he criticizes Bentham's utilitarianism. "For men to unite together in face of their destiny, they need something more than mere self-interest; they need real beliefs."[40] When he wanted to truly insult Napoleon, he described him as "le calcul personnifié."

In other words, there is, after all, a need for something of the old "political liberty" in addition to modern "civil liberty." Otherwise, as Ferguson had repeatedly pointed out in his *Essay*, "civil liberty" itself might be lost while those who enjoy it are busy pursuing their private interests.[41] "While in this work we have considered only matters pertaining to civil liberty," Constant explains toward the end of his *Principes de politique*, "we have in no way intended to imply that political liberty is something superfluous. Those who would sacrifice political liberty in order to enjoy civil liberty in greater peace are no less absurd than those who would sacrifice civil liberty in the hope of ensuring and expanding political liberty. Provided the people is happy, it is sometimes said, it is not important that it be free politically ... But to declare political freedom useless is to declare that the edifice in which we live has no need of a foundation." In Stephen Holmes's pithy summary, "private independence can only be guaranteed by political responsibility."[42] Constant explains his anxiety in a prophetic passage of the Preface to *De la Religion*:

"Quand chacun est son propre centre, tous sont isolés. Quand tous sont isolés, il n'y a que de la poussière. Quand l'orage arrive, la poussière est de la fange." "When every one is his own center, all are isolated. When all are isolated, there is only dust. When the storm comes, the dust turns to mire." It is from anomic individuals that the "mass" arises.[43]

In his *Principes de politique* Constant repeatedly points out the dangers of a-politeia or political indifference. He warns against turning away, in the face of blatant abuses, in the hope that one will not be personally affected; he defends freedom of the press on the grounds that it permits and encourages a lively interest in public affairs, a spirit of criticism and a watchful concern for rights such as flourished formerly in a restricted way among the highly independent nobility of feudal times; he justifies love, religion, the pursuit of glory—"toutes les passions nobles, délicates et profondes"—as well as the joy we experience in "le dévouement," a joy that is "contraire à l'instinct habituel de notre égoisme."[44]

What is going on here, it seems to me, is not so much some Romantic critique of Enlightenment as a reaffirmation by Constant of his commitment to the ideals of Enlightened modernity and the freedoms won by the Revolution, along with an expression of concern about sustaining the qualities—the "virtue," as those who, like Ferguson, retained some fidelity to the old civic humanist tradition might have said—needed to hold on to these freedoms.[45]

One could argue that Constant's entire political career was devoted to defending the freedoms achieved by the Revolution against threats to them from the left and the right—and this argument has in fact been used to account for his apparent opportunism (agreeing to serve under Napoleon during the Hundred Days, for instance, only months after the publication of *De l'Esprit de conquête*!). It is also worth noting how much of the life of this man, who insisted that all of life should *not* be politicized—that the spheres of economic activity, artistic activity, religious belief, and private emotions are autonomous and should not be engulfed in politics—was in fact taken up with politics, and with political *action* as well as writing.

There is some difference of opinion among scholars about the relative place Constant ascribes to politics—as well as about his views on democracy and universal suffrage. This was no doubt inevitable, given Constant's explicitly declared focus less on *who governs* (i.e. whether a state is monarchical, aristocratic or democratic in traditional terms) than on *how government is carried out*. For the late George Armstrong Kelly, "Constant's portrait of liberty is not, all things considered, a summons to the individual to political participation, except in so far as he must do this to ensure his full exercise of rights in the private sphere. There is no surplus of exhilaration to be gained from a public role." Stephen Holmes, in contrast, holds that for Constant political liberty was "not merely a means to civil liberty" but "an integral part of civil liberty"—that, moreover, Constant looked forward to a time when "all citizens, without exception" would be "ennobled" by it.[46] Acknowledging that Constant presented arguments against universal suffrage—these were no more stringent, one might add, than Mill's—Holmes claims that such arguments were always strategic. In principle, for Constant, all citizens should participate in politics. To those who objected that the majority of people (in France) were incompetent to act as members of a jury, he responded that through participation in the jury system people *become* responsible jurors.[47]

In the same way, no doubt, participation in politics will itself make the people, at present judged incompetent to participate, progressively more competent to do so. In Constant's own words, "It has been objected that political liberty thrusts a nation into a condition of perpetual agitation. But it would not be difficult to demonstrate that if the acquiring of liberty intoxicates slaves, the enjoyment of it forms men worthy of possessing it."[48] Above all, only free men will care about the institutions that preserve freedom. "Citizens will take no interest in their institutions unless they are called to participate in them by voting."[49] So Constant is optimistic about the future of democracy: "In matters of government, the most absolute equality of rights ... must be and soon will be in all civilized countries, the prime condition for the existence of every government ... and all those who possess those rights will be authorized to co-operate in their defense, that is to say, to participate in making the laws that determine the action of government."[50]

In fact, political liberty ("positive liberty"), for Constant, seems to be considerably more than simply a means of defending and securing civil liberty ("negative liberty"). It both depends on those "passions nobles, délicates et profondes" (enthusiasm, dedication, the capacity for self-transcendence, etc.), which are eroded by self-interest, and at the same time stimulates and promotes them, enriching the individual, developing his talents and his personality, and saving him from the isolation, mediocrity, uniformity, and lack of "elevation" that Adam Smith himself allowed were the "disadvantages of a commercial spirit."[51] And the promotion and development of our humanity is ultimately Constant's ideal, as it was Humboldt's. "Gentlemen," Constant declared in his lecture on "Ancient and Modern Liberty" in 1819 in tones strikingly reminiscent of Ferguson's *Essay*, "I call to witness this better part of our nature, the noble restlessness that pursues and torments us, the eagerness to extend our understanding and develop our faculties. Our destiny does not call us to happiness alone, but to self-perfection, and political liberty is the most powerful and the most energetic means of self-perfection granted by heaven ... By submitting to all citizens, without exception, the care and assessment of their most sacred interests, [it] enlarges their spirit, ennobles their thought, and establishes among them a kind of intellectual equality which forms the glory and power of a people." Political liberty, "positive liberty," active participation in politics turns out to be what will save individuals from becoming the look-alike puppets that a highly developed civilization threatens to turn them into. "There are no more individuals," Constant once lamented to his younger friend, fellow-author, and fellow-liberal, Prosper de Barante, "but only battalions in uniform." Political liberty he believed, could save society from turning into another China, i.e. in the metaphoric language of the time, a lifeless, stagnant, uniform mass. [52]

III. Adolphe

As we inquire what common themes might be found in Constant's bitter love story—about a young man who engages casually in a love affair, tires of it, but cannot either break decisively with the woman he has detached from her former lover and protector or commit himself to her—and his political pamphlet on conquest and usurpation, we should take note that in the writer's own view, the public and the private, while separate, were linked. In a remark originally intended for the preface to the 2nd edition of *Adolphe*, he wrote: "It is not only in the ties of the heart that we can observe moral enfeeblement and an incapacity to develop durable feelings. Everything in nature is interconnected. Faithfulness in love is an energy similar to religious faith or the passion for freedom. Well, we have no energy now. We no longer know how to love, or believe, or will. Everyone doubts the truth of what he says, smiles at the passion he professes, and anticipates the waning of the emotions he feels."[53]

Common to all Constant's writing is an image of modern life as a wasteland, and of modern man as emancipated, alienated and isolated. We already quoted from two such passages in *De l'Esprit de conquête et de l'usurpation* and in *De la Religion*. Here now are the final pages of *Adolphe*, with their evocation of wintry sunshine (light without warmth), frozen grass (lifeless, insensate nature), loneliness, and desolation.

> It was one of those winter days when the sun seems to cast a dismal light over the greyish countryside, as though looking down in pity upon a world it has ceased to warm. Ellenore suggested we might go out. "It is very cold," I said.
> "Never mind. I should like to go for a walk with you." She took my arm and we went on for a long time without saying a word, she walking with difficulty and leaning heavily upon me. "Shall we stop for a moment?" "No," she said, "it is so pleasant to feel your support once again." We relapsed into silence. The sky was clear, but the trees were bare; there was not a breath of wind and no bird cleaved the still air. Everything was motionless, and the only sound to be heard was of the frozen grass being crunched beneath our feet. "How calm it all is!" said Ellenore. "Look how resigned nature is! Shouldn't our hearts learn resignation too?" She sat on a boulder, then dropped on to her knees and buried her head in her hands. I heard a few whispered words and realized she was praying...
> My grief was dismal and solitary. I knew I would not die with Ellenore, but would live on without her in the wilderness of this world, in which I had so often wanted to be an independent traveller. I had crushed the one who loved me, broken this heart which like a twin soul had been unfailingly devoted to mine in tireless affection, and already I was overcome by loneliness. Ellenore was still alive but already past sharing my confidences; I was already alone in the world and no longer living in that atmosphere of love with which she had surrounded me, and the very air I breathed seemed harsher, the faces of the men I met seemed more unconcerned.

With her death, Adolphe relates,

> I felt the last link snap and the awful reality come between her and me for ever. How irksome this liberty now was, that I had so desired to retrieve! ... Only recently ... I had felt restless and resentful that a benevolent eye was watching over all my movements and that another's happiness depended upon them. There was nobody to watch over my movements now, they interested nobody; there was none to dispute my comings and goings, no voice to call me back as I was going out. I was free, truly, for I was no longer loved. I was a stranger to the whole world.[54]

The lament over the dimming of enthusiasm and the capacity for commitment as a result of ever increasing rationality and Enlightenment is as essential to the fictional writing as to the political. A passage at the end of chapter 3 of the novel echoes the warning in *De l'Esprit de conquête* (referred to earlier) about the erosion of political conviction: "Woe to the man who in the first moments of a love affair does not believe that it will last for ever! Woe to him who even in the arms of the mistress who has just yielded to him maintains an awareness of trouble to come and foresees that he may later tear himself away."

A curiously matching observation in the *Principes de politique*, inspired by the French Revolution, concerns the political effects of modern reflectiveness and modern irony, of the modern incapacity to be wholeheartedly engaged in anything. "Whatever has been said about the inconsistency of the people in the ancient republics," Constant writes,

> nothing equals the mobility *we* have witnessed. If, during the outbreak of the best prepared upheaval, you watch carefully the obscure ranks of the blind and subjugated populace, you will observe that, even as it follows its leaders, the people casts a glance ahead toward the moment when these leaders will fall. And you will observe in its *artificial exaltation* [italics mine—L.G.] a strange combination of analysis and mockery. People seem to distrust their own convictions. They try to delude themselves by their acclamations and to reinvigorate themselves by jaunty raillery. The truth is that they foresee, so to speak, the moment when the glamour of it all will pass."[55]

Another similar observation, inspired in part perhaps by Schiller, concerns modern poets. They are "always haunted," Constant declares,

> by some sort of *arrière-pensée* that ... defeats enthusiasm. It seems that they fear to appear naive and gullible. Rather than surrendering themselves to an irresistible movement, they reflect on their own poetry along with their readers. The first condition for enthusiasm is not to observe oneself with too much wit and cunning. But modern individuals observe themselves even in the midst of their most sensuous and violent passions.[56]

Irony, unceasing self-observation, and an inability to be spontaneous or sure in his affective life stamp Constant's character Adolphe as a true child of Enlightenment and modernity. Like Constant himself, Adolphe grows up without a mother. He has only a father—and a mocking, self-mocking father at that, who represses emotion and cannot communicate affectively with his son. The only female presence in Adolphe's early life is "the aged woman whose remarkable and highly original mind had begun to influence my own" (a character usually assumed to have been inspired by Constant's friend and confidante Isabelle de Charrière), but by the time she brings her influence to bear on the hero, she has already been defeated, "disillusioned," and rendered "joyless" by an artificial, "civilized" society.[57] So, from the outset, isolation, not community or continuity, reason but not love defines the world of the modern anti-hero Adolphe—inasmuch as woman rather than man traditionally represents the totality and continuity of life as well as the capacity to devote oneself totally to another. Woman, in this sense, will be represented somewhat later by Michelet, an early admirer of Constant, as the *past* of man, as man *before* Enlightenment—*la mer (la mère)*, in Michelet's terms, before the too obviously phallic lighthouses Michelet admires so much have been constructed to illuminate and control it. And Ellenore's suffering and death in Constant's novel can also be read as the defeat of the "feminine" (of passion, love, religion, totality, spontaneity, nature), its inevitable victimization in the modern world.

If Adolphe frequently refers to the irresistible habit of self-analysis and self-consciousness that eats like a worm at his capacity for love, faith, and spontaneity,

Constant, the first-person narrator of the letters and *Journaux intimes*, describes himself in the same terms: "I have some excellent qualities: nobility of mind, generosity, loyalty. But I am not quite a real person. (*Je ne suis pas tout à fait un être réel.*) There are two people in me, one of whom observes the other."[58] Likewise in one of the remarkable letters to his friend, the historian and fellow-admirer of Mme. de Stael, Prosper de Barante: "One discovers that there is nothing real in the depths of the self" (*On s'aperçoit qu'il n'y a rien de réel au fond des âmes*). It is modern civilization itself and the very progress of reason that appear to turn men into mechanical creatures of artifice. "Sometimes I touch myself to check whether I am still alive," Constant confides to Barante. "I seem to live out of politeness, as I doff my hat in the street to people who greet me but whom I do not know."[59]

The irony of the protagonist is reflected in the form of Constant's novel. People and events are not presented objectively—"naively," Schiller might have said—but as reflected in the consciousness of the narrator who is also one of the principal characters of the action. The other characters, Ellenore in particular, are known to us only through him. Likewise, Adolphe is at one and the same time the prosecutor, the accused, and the defense in his own confessional story, constantly commenting on it and pre-empting the judgments of the reader. But the text itself is as self-observing and self-judging as its hero. It is framed, at the beginning, by two author's prefaces and by an editor's or publisher's note explaining, according to the conventions of eighteenth-century fiction, how Adolphe's manuscript was found, and at the end, by an exchange of letters between the "editor" and an individual who had supposedly known Adolphe and Ellenore, whom the "editor" had subsequently encountered by chance in Germany, and to whom he had sent the manuscript for authentification. These multiple textual framings allow the text to read itself and comment on itself, now this way, now that. There seems to be no objective truth of the text, nothing that has not already been reflected on, filtered through a consciousness—be it that of Adolphe, that of the "editor," that of the latter's "correspondent" in Germany, or that of the author himself in the prefaces.

In case we should be impatient with Adolphe, the text has already pre-empted our impatience: "I hate the vanity of a mind which thinks it excuses what it explains," the "editor" of the manuscript writes to the correspondent in Germany. "I hate the conceit which is concerned only with itself while narrating the evil it has done, which tries to arouse pity by self-description and which, soaring indestructible among the ruins, analyses itself when it should be repenting." In case we should be tempted to agree with the suggestion in one of the author's prefaces that social conventions are the cause of the failure of Adolphe's love affair, we are reminded in another place that "circumstances are quite unimportant; character is everything."[60] In case we should be skeptical of the argument from usefulness as a justification for publishing the story (according to the German correspondent, the story warns of the dangers of flouting social convention and of irregular liaisons, and exposes the seductions of the language and literature of love), the editor takes care to indicate in his answer that he is skeptical of such claims of usefulness: "Nobody in the world ever learns except at his own expense."[61] Finally, as if to pre-empt any serious judgment at all, we are told—this time by the voice of the author—that the whole work was simply the response to an artistic challenge: to write a story in which there are only two characters and nothing happens[62]—as Racine claimed he wrote *Bérénice*. What resulted should consequently be viewed as a pure product of French classical art: few characters, minimal action, no precise historical dates or places, only the most general descriptions, frequent use of maxims. The subject matter, from this perspective, is secondary; the artistry is all. So the reader who, losing his ironical perspective, takes the story too seriously and fails to perceive that it is a work of art—an illusion, a deception—will have allowed himself to be taken in, as Ellenore was taken in by Adolphe.

There are several accounts of a curious scene at Juliette de Récamier's, where Constant gave a reading of his novel in the spring of 1815—one of many in London and Paris in the years 1814, 1815, and 1816. According to the duc de Broglie, the son-in-law of Mme. de Stael,

> There were twelve to fifteen of us present. The reading had gone on for almost three hours. The author was tired. As he approached the denouement of the story, his emotion increased visibly, intensified by fatigue. By the end he could no longer contain it and burst into sobs. The entire audience, also deeply moved, joined in. Soon every one was weeping and groaning. Then, suddenly ... the heaving and sighing, which had become convulsive, turned into nervous, uncontrollable laughter.[63]

It is as though the audience had been brought up short by the realization that the intense feelings by which they had been moved were no more than the product of an unusually clever fiction, that everything was imaginary and nothing "real," that, sophisticated as they were, they had been well and truly taken in.

To ensure that the reader will remain in uncertainty about the significance he is to attribute to the work, the preface to the third edition performs a final pirouette. The author announces that he attaches almost no importance to "this little work" and would not have "bothered" to republish it, were it not that he had heard a pirated edition was being prepared in Belgium.[64]

With their exacerbated intelligence, reflection, and civilized self-consciousness, both Constant's text itself and its hero produce in the reader a sense of "uncertainty about everything," as Constant once put it himself.[65] It is as though civilized man is living off a dwindling natural capital. Constant has a beautiful image for this at the end of chapter 6 of *Adolphe*: "We were living, so to speak, on a sort of memory of the heart, strong enough to make the thought of separation painful, but too weak for us to find satisfaction in being together ... I would have liked to give Ellenore tokens of my love that would have made her happy, and indeed I sometimes went back to the language of love, but these emotions and this language resembled the pale and faded leaves which, like remains of funeral wreaths, grow listlessly on the branches of an uprooted tree."

The sense of the second-hand, the worn, the warmed-over is overwhelming in *Adolphe*. And insofar as its anti-heroic hero can be taken to represent modern, enlightened man, the reader may begin to suspect that everything in the modern world is derivative and secondary; that nothing is natural or original; that feelings do not come *before* the signs and words that supposedly express them, but are themselves *produced* by the manipulation of signs and words. The stage seems set for the desolate world of Flaubert.

To sum up and conclude: On the one hand, an elegiac sense of modern life as diminished, impoverished, alienated, and of modern man as a shadow, "not a real person"; on the other, repeated warnings of the futility and even danger of trying to recreate enthusiasm (patriotism, love, faith) that can no longer be spontaneous or authentic, and, on the whole, acceptance of that situation. Thus bourgeois marriage, in the end, Constant claims, is preferable to the disorders of passion, which, in any case, can no longer be authentic in modern circumstances. Wolmar, if you will, has triumphed over Saint-Preux. "Made more and more luke-warm by the ease with which it can be pursued and subject in real life to calculation, what remains of the passion of love no longer determines the entirety of a person's destiny, except in a few mostly unhappy and discouraging cases. Love has been put in its place, in France at least, by the younger generation itself. How many young men would sacrifice their convenience and their future in order to marry for love? Yet so far from being inclined to rebuke civilization for the abatement of a once disorderly passion, I am happy to admit that morals have improved because of it ... Habit and, above all, a common, shared interest sometimes produce an affection of minds" in the absence of passion.[66]

In an interesting passage of his superb book on Constant, Stephen Holmes takes up the question of Constant's intermittent world-weariness and "nihilism"—his loss of a sense of purpose or meaning of life. He refers to an anecdote, much appreciated by Constant, according to which the watchmaker-God of the eighteenth century died half way through his creation of the world leaving his work unfinished and humanity stranded. "We are like watches which have no dial," the story runs, as Constant recounted it to Isabelle de Charrière in 1790, "and whose wheels, endowed with intelligence, turn until they wear out, without knowing why and constantly telling themselves: I turn, therefore I must have a purpose." No purpose, however, is to be found.[67]

Man thus remains "un être double et énigmatique," and human nature, according to the author of *De la Religion*, includes a seemingly ineradicable "tendency to reach beyond ourselves toward ends that have nothing to do with rationally calculated utility or advantage and that transport us in the direction of an unknown, invisible centre, unrelated to our day-to-day lives and mundane interests."[68] This tendency is what sustains, against all reason, a residual capacity for faith, love, dedication, self-sacrifice, and a desire for fame and reputation. Even among the most skeptical denizens of a desacralized world this irrational tendency survives, Constant maintains. It may, however, be corrupted, if never entirely destroyed, by skepticism and utilitarianism, and may manifest itself in the most degraded and degrading forms. "We have proclaimed the empire of reason and the world is unhinged by madness. All our systems of philosophy are founded on calculation and appeal to our interest, yet our acts of waywardness have never been more shameful or our passions more unruly."[69] In a prophetic passage of one of his letters to Prosper de Barante, Constant writes his version of Goya's Sleep of Reason. "I have seen men who believe in nothing rush into magic. I have seen men who are weary of their incredulity and incapable of putting anything in its place except ecstasies, unbridled enthusiasms, and excesses that are the more incurable for having sprung from reasoning and being methodically deranged."[70]

Stephen Holmes argues plausibly that Constant's liberalism was in part a response to the challenge of this dual nature of man—an attempt to cope with the surrender of a meaningful and purposive cosmic order. "Constant strove to fashion a humane, stable, and self-regulating polity without ontological or theological foundations," he writes. "Liberal freedom, including self-government, was conceived as a morally responsible reaction to the sudden disappearance of nature's purposes."[71] Likewise, I would add, love of liberty, patriotism, and dedication to the public weal appear to have been seen by Constant as appropriate channels in which to guide essential human energies that civilized life had anaesthetized, in his view, but could never completely deaden, and that might, if repressed or thwarted, find new and monstrous applications.

NOTES

* My contribution to the Tel Aviv seminar was developed from a segment of an undergraduate course on "Writers and Politics in France 1750–1950," which I had been teaching in the Romance Languages Department at Princeton University for a couple of decades. The course focused on a number of French writers whose work embraces both literary and political writing (Montesquieu, Rousseau, Constant, Gobineau, Renan, Montherlant, Sartre) or explicitly combines the literary and the political (Hugo and Michelet). The aim of the course was to investigate the political dimension of literary texts and the literary dimension of political writing and so to challenge the anti-rhetorical definition of "literature" that accompanied Romanticism and was later reinforced by academic specialization. At the same time, the class on Constant was also intended to point toward one of the great themes of nineteenth-century French literature, among liberally inclined as well as conservatively inclined writers (Stendhal, Mérimée, Flaubert), namely the association of post-Enlightenment modernity with inauthenticity. My concern here is Constant's vision of political liberty (as distinct from civil liberty) as an antidote to the smoothing out of differences and the stifling of spontaneity allegedly produced by modern manners and modern civilization.

Notes

1. See Conor Cruise O'Brien, *The Great Melody: A Thematic Biography and Commented Anthology of Edmund Burke* (London: Sinclair-Stevenson, 1992), Appendix ("An Exchange with Sir Isaiah Berlin"), pp. 605–18, on p. 615. I am indebted to Professor Brian Cowan of the Department of History, Yale University, for bringing this exchange to my attention.
2. José Ortega y Gasset, "Socialización de Hombre," in *Gesammelte Werke* (Stuttgart: Deutsche Verlags Anstalt, 1952–56), 4 vols., vol. 1, p. 537.
3. Harold Nicolson, *Benjamin Constant*, (London: Constable, 1949), Dennis Wood, *Benjamin Constant: A Biography*, (London: Routledge, 1993). In addition, John Cruickshank, *Benjamin Constant*, (New York: Twayne, 1974) and Tzvetan Todorov, *Benjamin Constant. La passion démocratique*, (Paris: Hachette, 1997) offer highly readable general accounts of Constant's life and work. The introductions to Ephraim Harpaz's many editions of articles and pamphlets by Constant, including the popular French edition of the *Esprit de conquête* in the Garnier-Flammarion series (Paris, 1986), provide excellent summary accounts of his political thought. Finally, special mention needs to be made of two penetrating and comprehensive scholarly studies of Constant's political philosophy—Stephen Holmes's already classic *Benjamin Constant and the Making of Modern Liberalism* (New Haven: Yale University Press, 1984) and the

late George A. Kelly's *The Humane Comedy: Constant, Tocqueville, and French Liberalism* (Cambridge: Cambridge University Press, 1992).

4. In his classic study of a century ago, Gustave Rudler held that the two chief influences on Constant were "l'une, celle de la France; l'autre celle de l'Ecosse." France "fournit à Benjamin ... ses idées philosophiques et religieuses; l'Ecosse entre au moins pour moitié..dans la formation de ses idées politiques." (*La Jeunesse de Benjamin Constant* [Paris: A. Colin, 1909], p. 184) More recently, a leading authority on Constant's political writings has again underlined the influence of Scottish thought on Constant, and in particular "the overwhelming presence of the *Wealth of Nations* in the background of Constant's political reflection." (Biancamaria Fontana, "Commerce and Civilisation in the Writings of Benjamin Constant," *Annales Benjamin Constant*, 5 [1985], pp. 3–15, at p. 4) Likewise Lothar Gall, *Benjamin Constant: seine politische Ideenwelt und der deutsche Vormärz* (Wiesbaden: F. Steiner, 1963), pp. 2–3: "Die in unserem Zusammenhang wichtigsten Impulse aber empfing er nicht so sehr in Frankreich als während seines Studiums an der Universität Edinburg." According to Constant's friend and sometime rival for the favors of Germaine de Stael, the historian Prosper de Barante, the influence of Germany on Constant was also deep and enduring: "il eut toute sa vie quelque chose de l'étudiant allemand, rêveur, ... préférant la solitude studieuse, distraite par les plaisirs sensuels ou les émotions du jeu, à la vie du monde et la société des salons." (Quoted by Rudler, p. 161)

5. Benjamin Constant, *Adolphe & The Red Notebook*, with an introduction by Harold Nicolson (London: Hamish Hamilton, 1948), p, ix.

6. N. Machiavelli, *Discorsi sopra la prima deca di Tito Livio*, ed. Giorgio Inglese (Milan: Rizzoli, 1984), I, 39, p. 145; Antonio de Covarrubias in his censor's report on Baltasar Acamos de Barrientos, *Aforismos de Tacite* (1614), quoted by Else-Lilly Etter, *Tacitus in der Geistesgeschichte des 16. und 17. Jahrhunderts* (Basel: Helbing & Lichtenhahn, 1966), p. 109, note 91. (All translations by L.G. unless otherwise indicated.)

7. "Dans le mouvement progressif, tout a servi, et ... les abus d'aujourd'hui étaient les besoins d'hier. Peut-être le même sort est-il réservé à quelques-uns des principes qui nous paraissent incontestables." As for customs and institutions, "tant qu'ils sont utiles, ils se conservent d'eux-mêmes. Quand ils s'écroulent, c'est que leur utilité a cessé." Constant, "De la perfectibilité de l'esprit humain," *Oeuvres completes*, ed. P. Delbouille et al., (Tübingen: M. Niemeyer, 1998), vol. III, I (*Ecrits littéraires 1800–1813*), pp. 442, 443.

8. "Tout dans la nature a sa marche. Les hommes la suivent, l'accélèrent ou la retardent, mais ne peuvent s'en écarter." (Ibid,. p. 443) Likewise to Ferguson, "nations stumble upon establishments, which are indeed the result of human action, but not the execution of any human design." (*An Essay on the History of Civil Society*, ed. Duncan Forbes [Edinburgh: Edinburgh University Press, 1966], part III, section ii, p. 122)

9. "The age of commerce has given man a new nature." *Commentaire sur l'ouvrage de Filangieri, Science de la Législation*, 2 vols. 1822–24. Both passages cited by Holmes, *Benjamin Constant and the Making of Modern Liberalism* p. 188.

10. *De l'Esprit de conquête et de l'usurpation*, foreword to 4th ed. Quoted from the English translation, "The Spirit of Conquest and Usurpation," in Constant, *Political Writings*, trans. and ed. by Biancamaria Fontana (Cambridge: Cambridge University Press, 1988), pp. 48–49. Hereafter SC (with occasional slight modifications of the translated text). Constant clearly has Montesquieu's *"esprit général"* in mind.
11. Benjamin Constant, *Journaux intimes*, ed. Alfred Roulin and Charles Roth (Paris: Gallimard, 1952), p. 91. The same entry (for 27 May, 1804) contains a similar comment on August Wilhelm Schlegel (like Constant, a member of Mme. de Stael's circle at Coppet): "Schlegel is one of those people who, never having had anything to do with real life, believes that everything can be accomplished by ordinances and laws, never dreaming of the struggle that vexatious laws provoke between citizens and the authorities or of the ensuing necessity for the laws to become progressively more rigorous, so that in the end they embrace all the individuals in a country."
12. SC, I, 15, p. 82. See also Constant's *Principes de politique (version de 1806–1810)*, ed. Etienne Hofmann (Paris: Hachette, 1997), VI, 5, p. 135.
13. Constant, *Journal des Débats*, 19 March 1815.
14. SC, I, 2, p. 53. For a modern confirmation of the crucial importance of war in the economy of the Roman Empire, see the recent study by Aldo Schiavone, *Ancient Rome and the Modern West*, trans. Margery J. Schneider (Cambridge, Mass.: Harvard University Press, 2000).
15. SC, I, 2, p. 51; I, 3, p. 55. See also I, 4, pp. 56–57 and I, 15, p. 81.
16. Ferguson, *Essay on the History of Civil Society*, part I, section viii, ed. cit., p. 56. Likewise, part III, section vi, p. 158: in the ancient republics, such as Sparta (much admired by Ferguson, to the dismay of Hume and Smith), "the citizen was made to consider himself as the property of his country, not as the owner of a private estate."
17. SC, I, 2, pp. 52–53.
18. SC, II, 18, p. 141 and p. 141n. Constant here echoes the concluding paragraphs of Ferguson's *Essay on the History of Civil Society*, part I, section iii, p. 19. Needless to say, the antithesis of the "sanguine affection which every Greek bore to his country" or "the devoted patriotism of an early Roman," compared by Ferguson to the affection binding the members of a family, and modern "valuing society on account of its mere external conveniences" (i.e. the antithesis of "virtue" and "commerce," as described by John Pocock in his *The Machiavellian Moment: Florentine Political Thought and the Atlantic Republican Tradition* [Princeton, N.J: Princeton University Press, 1975]), corresponds to a number of similar antitheses aimed at discerning the identity of the modern that can be found in a variety of other writers and fields. They are seemingly an essential structuring device of a good deal of thinking about history, society, and culture: Schiller's categories of naive and sentimental poetry (and their twentieth-century counterpart, Lukacs' epic and novel); Walter Scott's *gules* (scarlet in heraldry) and *sable* (black), evoked in the introduction to *Kenilworth* to set off the old forms of conflict—war, courage, heroism—from the newer forms in which blackrobed lawyers fight court battles; Stendhal's version of this in *The Red and the Black;* Tönnies's *Gemein-*

schaft and *Gesellschaft*; Max Weber's *bezauberte* and *entzauberte Welt*. In their various ways, all these match Constant's distinction between *"impulsion sauvage"* or *"enthousiasme,"* on the one hand, and *"calcul civilisé"* and *"ironie,"* on the other (*SC*, I, 2, p. 53 and I, 3, p. 55).

19. On "political" and "civil" liberty in the Scottish Enlightenment, see Duncan Forbes, *Hume's Philosophical Politics* (Cambridge, U.K: Cambridge University Press, 1975), pp. 155–66. The distinction was also important to Constant's friend and compatriot, the Genevan Simonde de Sismondi, who was for a time a follower of Smith, and who may have been the first to use the term "liberté négative" to describe "modern" or "civil" liberty. (Jean-Charles L. Simonde de Sismondi, *Histoire des républiques italiennes du moyen âge* [Paris, 1840; 1st ed. 1809–18], 19 vols., vol. 10, ch. 8, p. 340) According to Sismondi, liberty in this sense was unknown to the ancient republics, the Italian city-republics of the High Middle Ages, the German free cities or the Swiss cantons. "Until the seventeenth century the liberty of the citizen was always understood as participation in the sovereignty of his country, and it is only the example of the British constitution which taught us to consider liberty as a protection of repose, happiness, and domestic independence." Sismondi defines "civil liberty" as "that passive faculty, claimed by the moderns, that guarantees against the abuse of power in whatever hands it is lodged," while the term "political liberty" should be reserved for an active faculty, "participation ... in the power exercised, the association of free men in sovereignty." Such "political liberty," Sismondi points out, whether restricted to a particular caste, as in Venice, or shared by all citizens, as in Florence, was entirely compatible with a form of government which "according to our current principles, could be considered tyrannical," since it "set no limit to the extent of the power that could be exercised in the name of the nation." (pp. 330–32) Ultimately, the goal of ancient liberty, "like that of ancient philosophy, is virtue." In contrast, "the end of modern liberty, like that of modern philosophy, is happiness." (p. 363)

20. *SC*, II, 6, pp. 102–104, 105. See Todorov's summary of the argument, in his *Benjamin Constant: La passion démocratique*, p. 40: "The most eloquent distinction is that between the liberty of individuals as described, i.e. modern civil liberty, freedom from interference by the state in all areas where one's activity does not threaten others, and a quite different form of social action, which consists of participating in the political life of one's country, but which can also be identified in a different sense of the term by the word 'liberty.' In order to designate this new opposition, Constant speaks sometimes of civil liberty and political liberty, or of negative liberty and positive liberty, or, again, as in a lecture he gave at the Athénée Royal in 1819, of the liberty of the Moderns and the liberty of the Ancients." On political liberty as a means of ensuring civil liberty—the true goal—see n. 46 below.

21. *SC*, II, 1, p. 85.

22. Wilhelm von Humboldt, *The Limits of State Action*, ed. J. W. Burrow (Cambridge, UK: Cambridge University Press, 1969; rprt. The Liberty Fund, Indianapolis, 1993), p. 3. Though Constant does not mention Humboldt, he must have known him through Madame de Stael, to whom Humboldt taught German (J. Christopher Herold, *Mistress to an Age: A Life of Madame de Stael* [Indianapolis: Bobbs Merrill, 1958], p. 268). Humboldt was also closely con-

nected with Madame de Stael's circle at Coppet, as, inevitably, was Constant. She thought well of him: "Il est difficile de rencontrer nulle part un homme dont l'entretien et les écrits supposent plus de connaissances et d'idées." (cit. by Carlo Pellegrini, "Corinne et son aspect politique," in *Mme de Stael et l'Europe* [Paris, 1958], p. 257) In *De l'Allemagne* (ch. xii), he is mentioned as the author of "the most philosophical and stimulating comments" on Goethe's *Hermann und Dorothea* (Paris, 1958), 5 vols., 2:170–71.
23. Constant, *Principes de politique* (1997 ed.), II, 5, p. 59.
24. Constant, *Principes de politique*, II, 3, p. 56.
25. Constant, *Principes de politique*, I, 3, p. 5.
26. Benjamin Constant, *Œuvres*, ed. Alfred Roulin (Paris: Bibliothèque de la Pléiade, 1957), p. 801.
27. Report of 1762–63, in Adam Smith, *Lectures on Jurisprudence*, ed. R.L. Meek, D.D. Raphael, and P.G. Stein (Indianapolis: Liberty Fund, 1982), The Glasgow edition of the Works and Correspondence of Adam Smith, vol. V, p. 289. On the jurisprudential and civic traditions, see John Robertson, *The Scottish Enlightenment and the Militia Issue* (Edinburgh: Edinburgh University Press, 1985) pp. 48–50 (on William Seton and the supporters of Union with England) and 72–73 (on Hume).
28. Constant, *Principes de politique*, I, 3, p. 35.
29. Constant, *Principes de politique*, I, 6, pp. 47, 44 (in order of citation).
30. Constant, *Principes de politique*, p. 46 (italics added).
31. Constant, *Adolphe & The Red Notebook*, pp.148–49. Cf. A remark of Gibbon, perhaps the most distinguished resident of Lausanne in the 1780s, in which the historian suggests to his friend Catherine de Sévery that at Lausanne, "la tranquillité du gouvernement, dont vous ne sentez pas assez le prix ... vaut mieux peut-être que notre orageuse liberté" (*Letters of Edward Gibbon*, ed. G. E. Norton, 3 vols. [London: Cassell, 1956], vol, 3, p. 71 [letter of September 1787]).
32. *SC*, I, 13, pp. 76, 78.
33. Benjamin Constant, *De la Religion*, preface and notes by Pierre Deguise (Lausanne: Bibliothèque romande, 1971), pp. 65–66; also in *Œuvres* (Paris, 1957), p. 1426.
34. Benjamin Constant, *Commentaire sur Filangieri*, vol. 2, p. 82, quoted by Holmes, *Benjamin Constant and the Making of Modern Liberalism*, p. 187.
35. *SC*, II, 6, pp. 104–105. (Translation slightly emended)
36. *SC*, I, 13, p. 78.
37. Adam Smith, *Lectures on Jurisprudence*, report of 1766, pp. 539–41; also *The Wealth of Nations*, chapter on "Education of Youth," (New York: Modern Library Edition, 1937), pp. 732–40.
38. Ferguson, *Essay*, part II, sec. I, ed. cit., pp. 74–81. Cf. Smith, *Lectures on Jurisprudence* (report of 1766), pp. 540–44.
39. *SC*, II, 7, p. 106.
40. *SC*, I, 4, p. 58. On the critique of Bentham's utilitarianism, see Constant, *Principes de politique*, II, 7, pp. 61–64.
41. "If to any people it be the avowed object of policy, in all its internal refinements, to secure the person and the property of the subject, without any regard to his political character, the constitution indeed may be free, but its members may likewise become unworthy of the freedom they possess, and

unfit to preserve it. The effects of such a constitution may be to immerse all orders of men in their separate pursuits of pleasure, which they may now enjoy with little disturbance; or of gain, which they may preserve without any attention to the commonwealth. If this be the end of political struggles, the design, when executed, in securing to the individual his estate, and the means of subsistence, may put an end to the exercise of those very virtues that were required in conducting its execution." (Ferguson, *Essay on the History of Civil Society*, part V, sec. iii, ed. cit., pp. 221–222). Similarly, Dugald Stewart, Ferguson's successor in the Chair of Moral Philosophy at Edinburgh, maintained that "the only effective bulwark against the encroachments of tyranny is to be found in the political privileges secured by the constitution to the governed," that, in other words, it is necessary for the people to possess political liberty in order to place their civil liberties beyond the danger of violation. (See Duncan Forbes, *Hume's Philosophical Politics*, pp. 166–167). Ferguson kept coming back to the difference between the "order of free men," which does not exclude a considerable degree of dissent and agitation, and the "tranquillity," which may allow individuals to go about their private business, but is ultimately not incompatible with "despotism." "Our notion of order in civil society is frequently false ... we consider commotion and action as contrary to its nature. ... The good order of stones in a wall, is their being properly fixed in the places for which they are hewn; were they to stir the building must fall: but the order of men in society, is their being placed where they are properly qualified to act. The first is a fabric made of dead and inanimate parts, the second is made of living and active members. When we seek in society for the order of mere ... tranquillity, we forget the nature of our subject, and find the order of slaves, not that of free men." (*Essay on the History of Civil Society*, part VI, section v, pp. 268–69, footnote)

42. Constant, *Principes de politique*, XVII, 3, p. 388; Holmes, *Benjamin Constant and the Making of Modern Liberalism*, p. 41.
43. Constant, *De la Religion*, Preface, p. 23.
44. Constant, *Principes de politique*, V, 3, p. 92 and VIII, 1, p. 141.
45. The "excesses" of the Revolution did not shake Constant's faith in its ultimate rightness. "You seem not to be a Democrat," he wrote to Mme de Charrière in 1790. "However much I agree with you that what we are witnessing is fundamentally knavery and fury, I still prefer the knavery and fury that overthrow fortified castles and destroy titles and similar follies ... to the knavery and fury" that are deployed in defence of "wretched monstrosities" and "barbarous stupidity." "As between scoundrels and scoundrels I am for the Mirabeaus and Barnaves rather than the Sartines and Breteuils" (Letter of 10 December, 1790, in Isabelle de Charrière, *Œuvres complètes*, ed. Jean-Daniel Candaux, C.P. Courtenay, et al. [Amsterdam: Oorschot, 1979–84], 10 vols., vol. 3, pp. 250–251)
46. Kelly, *The Humane Comedy: Constant, Tocqueville, and French Liberalism*, p. 44; Holmes, *Benjamin Constant and the Making of Modern Liberalism*, p. 43. The passage quoted is from "De la liberté des anciens comparée à celle des modernes" in Constant, *Cours de politique constitutionnelle*, ed. Edouard Laboulaye (Paris: 1872, rprt. Geneva,: Slatkine, 1982), 2 vols., vol. 2, p. 559. Holmes' Constant would appear to be closer to the still quite "republican" Ferguson,

Kelly's to Dugald Stewart, for whom, according to Duncan Forbes, "happiness is the only object of legislation which is of intrinsic value, and what is called political liberty is only one of the means of obtaining that end" (*Hume's Philosohical Politics*, p. 167). Sismondi describes this position in his *Histoire des Républiques italiennes*: "On a cherché à donner [à la liberté civile] pour garantie les droits politiques des citoyens. Ils ont dès lors été considerés, non plus comme étant eux-mêmes la cause de la liberté, mais seulement une de ses sauvegardes" (vol. 10, p. 340). But, like Constant, Sismondi retains great respect for the inspiring and elevating power of "republican liberty." Though the latter is by no means identifiable, like civil liberty, with "happiness," "elle fait sur les hommes l'effet que les poëtes attribuaient au nectar des dieux; une fois qu'un mortel en a goûté, il dédaigne toute nourriture humaine; mais aussi il trouve en lui-même de nouvelles forces et une nouvelle vertu; sa nature est changée, et, s'asseyant à leur table, il sent qu'il s'égale aux immortels." (p. 350)

47. Constant, *Cours de politique constitutionnelle*, ed. Laboulaye, vol. 1, pp. 235, 238.
48. Constant, *Principes de politique*, XVII, 3, p. 392.
49. Constant, *Les "Principes de politique" de Benjamin Constant*, ed. Etienne Hofmann (Geneva: Droz, 1980), XV, 5 (additions), p. 397: "Les citoyens ne s'intéressent à leurs institutions que lorsqu'ils sont appelés à y concourir par leurs suffrages. Or cet intérêt est indispensable pour former un esprit public, cette puissance sans laquelle nulle liberté n'est durable ... Sans l'élection populaire, les citoyens d'un pays n'ont jamais ce sentiment de leur importance, qui leur présente la gloire et la liberté de leur pays comme la portion la plus précieuse de leur patrimoine individuel. L'on a, je le sais, [conçu parmi nous] dans ces derniers temps beaucoup de préventions contre les élections populaires, Néanmoins, jusqu'à nos jours, toutes les expériences déposaient en leur faveur."
50. *Mélanges de littérature et de politique* (1829), in Constant, *De la liberté des modernes. Ecrits politiques*, ed. Marcel Gauchet (Paris: Livre de poche, 1980), pp. 517–612, at pp. 520–21.
51. Smith, *Lectures on Jurisprudence*, p. 541.
52. Passage from lecture on ancient and modern liberty in *Cours de politique constitutionnelle*, ed. Laboulaye, vol. 2, p. 559. Passage on individuals and battalions in "Lettres de Benjamin Constant à Prosper de Barante," ed. Baron de Barante, *Revue des Deux Mondes*, vol. 34, 1906, pp. 241–72, 528–67, letter of 25 February 1808, p. 250. References to China ("La Chine! La Chine! Nous y tendons, nous y marchons à grands pas") ibid., p. 251; also letter of 21 October 1808, p. 268 ("La France est une Chine européenne"), and letter of 1810, p. 537. Cf. the famous passage on China in John Stuart Mill, *On Liberty*, Ch. 3 (Everyman's Library ed., pp. 128–31). Ferguson on happiness in *Essay on the History of Civil Society*, part I, sec. viii, ed. cit.: "The most animating occasions of human life, are calls to danger and hardship, not invitations to safety and ease: and man himself, in his excellence is not ... destined merely to enjoy what the elements bring to his use; but ... to follow the exercises of his nature, in preference to what are called its enjoyments" (p. 45). "That mysterious thing called *Happiness* ... is not the succession of mere animal pleasures ... which can fill up only a few moments in the duration of a life" and "on too

frequent a repetition, ... turn to satiety and disgust." Nor is it "that state of repose, or that imaginary freedom from care, which at a distance is so frequent an object of desire, but with its approach brings ... tedium." Happiness arises, Ferguson claims, "more from the pursuit, than from the attainment of any end whatever; and in every new situation to which we arrive, ... it depends more on the degree to which our minds are properly employed, than it does on the circumstances in which we are destined to act, on the materials which are placed in our hands, or the tools with which we are furnished."

53. Quoted in *Adolphe*, ed. Gustave Rudler (Manchester: Manchester University Press, 1919), pp. xii-xiii. The terms "now" and "no longer" imply comparison with an earlier, pre-modern culture. Such a comparison had already been spelled out, as far as personal life is concerned, in a passage of the *Principes de politique* (p. 368) that also clearly anticipates the exacerbated yet somehow nerveless sensibility of the modern hero of *Adolphe*: "Nothing in nature is completely separate from anything else. Literature always bears the mark of the general character of an age. Less worn down by civilization, the Ancients had greater vivacity of expression. Their bellicose way of life filled them with love of action, firm confidence in their own strength, fearlessness before death, and indifference to pain; whence greater dedication, energy, nobility of spirit. We Moderns, wearied by experience, have a sadder and for that reason more delicate sensibility; we are more susceptible to emotions and more often moved. The egoism that accompanies that capacity for feeling may corrupt it, but cannot eliminate it. To resist the power that suffering has over us, we have to avoid the sight of it. The Ancients, in contrast, faced up to it without fear and bore it without pity."

54. Constant, *Adolphe*, trans. Leonard W. Tancock (Harmondsworth: Penguin Classics, 1964), pp. 116, 117-118, 120-21. All quotations are from this translation, with occasional slight modifications.

55. Constant, *Principes de politique* XVI, 7, p. 372. Cf. *SC*, II, 4, p. 100: "If one could scrutinize the obscure ranks of a people apparently subject to the usurper who is oppressing them, one would see them as by some confused instinct fixing their eyes in advance on the moment when this usurper should fall. Lacking much faith in their own convictions, they seem to be trying at one and the same time to stupefy themselves with acclamations, relieve themselves by raillery, and anticipate the moment when the glory will be past."

56. Les *"Principes de politique" de Benjamin Constant* (1980 ed.), p. 430.

57. Constant, *Adolphe*, chapter 1.

58. Constant, *Journaux intimes*, ed. Alfred Roulin and Charles Roth (Paris, 1952), p. 76 (11 April 1804). The hero of the strongly autobiographical novel *Cécile*, the manuscript of which was rediscovered in the late1940s and first published in the early 1950s, also shares with Adolphe the same suggestibility, the same incapacity to stick for long with any feeling or engagement.

59. "Lettres de Benjamin Constant à Prosper de Barante," ed. Baron de Barante, p. 534 (letter of 8 August 1810); p. 562 (letter of 23 Sepember 1812): "Je me tâte quelquefois pour savoir si je vis encore. J'ai l'air de vivre par politesse, comme j'ôte mon chapeau dans la rue aux gens qui me saluent et que je ne connais pas."

60. Constant, *Adolphe* p. 125.
61. See the prefaces to the 2nd and 3rd editions at the beginnng and the letter from the correspondent in Germany at the end of the novel.
62. Constant, *Adolphe* (Penguin Classics edition), Preface to 3rd ed., p. 30.
63. Quoted in Paul Delbouille, *Genèse, structure et destin d'Adolphe* (Paris: Edition les Belles Lettres, 1971), p. 388. Constant himself noted in his journal for 19 April 1815: "Lu mon roman. Fou rire" (p. 387).
64. Constant, *Adolphe*, preface to 3rd ed., p. 30.
65. See Holmes, *Benjamin Constant and the Making of Modern Liberalism*, p.161.
66. Constant, "Réflexions sur la tragédie" (1829), *Œuvres*, ed. Roulin, pp. 939–40.
67. See Holmes, *Benjamin Constant and the Making of Modern Liberalism*, p. 163. The story of the watchmaker is from a letter to Mme. de Charrière of 4 June, 1790, first cited by Gustave Rudler in his *La Jeunesse de Benjamin Constant 1767–1794*, pp. 376–77: "Je sens plus que jamais le néant de tout, combien tout promet et rien ne tient, combien nos forces sont au-dessus de notre destination, et combien cette disproportion doit nous rendre malheureux ... Un Piémontais, homme d'esprit dont j'ai fait la connaissance à La Haye, un chevalier de Revel, envoyée de Sardaigne ... prétend que Dieu, c'est-à-dire l'auteur de nous et de nos alentours, est mort avant d'avoir fini son ouvrage; qu'il avait les plus beaux et vastes projets du monde et les plus grands moyens; qu'il avait déjà mis en oeuvre plusieurs des moyens, comme on élève des échafauds pour bâtir, et qu'au milieu de son travail il est mort; que tout à present se trouve fait dans un but qui n'existe plus, et que nous en particulier, nous sentons destinés à quelque chose dont nous ne nous faisons aucune idée; nous sommes comme des montres où il n'y aurait point de cadran, et dont les rouages, doués d'intelligence, tourneraient jusqu'à ce qu'ils fussent usés, sans savoir pourquoi et se disant toujours: Puisque je tourne, j'ai donc un but. Cette idée me paraît la plus profonde et la plus spirituelle que j'ai ouie." ("I feel more and more the nothingness of everything, how much is promised and how little fulfilled, how much higher we are able to think than our actual destination, and how unhappy that disproportion is bound to make us ... A witty Piedmontese whom I got to know at The Hague, the envoy of Sardinia, a chevalier Revel, argues that God—that is to say the author of us and of the environment we live in—died before finishing his work; that he had the most beautiful and the grandest plans as well as the greatest means of executing them; that he had already begun to use some of those means, like scaffolding that is put up in order to raise a building, and that in the midst of his work, he died; that everything presently existing was thus made for a purpose that is no more, and that we, in particular, feel we were destined for something of which we have no idea; we are like watches which have no dial and whose wheels, endowed with intelligence, turn until they wear out, without knowing why and constantly telling themselves: I turn, therefore I must have a purpose. This conceit seems to me the wittiest and most profound extravagance I have ever heard.")
68. Constant, *De la Religion*, in *Œuvres*, ed. Alfred Roulet, p. 1414. Cf. p. 1413: "The sight of a virtuous action, a glorious sacrifice, an act of courage in the face of danger, a suffering individual being assisted and consoled, superiority to the impulses of vice, devotion to the unfortunate, resistance to tyranny—all those

things awaken and nourish in the soul of man the mysterious disposition [to rise above all individual and particular thoughts]."
69. Constant, *De la religion*, p. 1425. Cf. the description on pp. 1423–24 of the disorders and excesses of the Romans at a time of widespread incredulity and religious skepticism.
70. Letter of 2 December 1811, in "Lettres de Benjamin Constant à Prosper de Barante," p. 549.
71. Holmes, *Benjamin Constant and the Making of Modern Liberalism*, p. 163.

10 | Berlin's Marx: Enlightenment, Counter-Enlightenment, and the Historical Construction of Cultural Identities

John E. Toews

Isaiah Berlin accepted an invitation from H. A. L. Fisher to write the volume on Karl Marx for the Home University Library in 1933. He was twenty-four years old. The manuscript was completed five years later, in the summer of 1938, and after radical editorial cuts which reduced it to one half of its original size, it was published as *Karl Marx: His Life and Environment* in 1939. A new edition with only minor corrections appeared in 1948 and further editions with more significant revisions and additions were published in 1963 and 1978. Michael Ignatieff has claimed that the five years of extensive preparatory reading for this volume, not only of Marx's texts but also of the texts that constituted Marx's intellectual heritage and environment, provided Berlin with "the intellectual capital on which he was to depend for the rest of his life."[1] The distinctive, breathless prose style and the signature Berlin ability to combine perceptive reconstruction of personal identity with the historical and critical exegesis of ideas, to examine conceptual systems as individualized re-makings of inherited worlds of meaning, were also developed in this book, or at least transposed from talk to the written word. In writing the Marx book Berlin discovered the history of ideas as the appropriate genre for examining his philosophical concerns and articulating his philosophical positions, for doing philosophy in a different key. It was a genre that allowed for a more richly textured, nuanced, ambivalent, and open-ended analysis than the Oxford philosophy in which he had been trained, and that was especially suited to illuminate the historically shifting conceptual and categorial frameworks, the sets of fundamental assumptions within which individual thinkers in different epochs and cultures attempted to address and resolve the basic existential questions of who we are, how we should organize our experience into meaningful lives, how we should live together, and where we are going.[2]

For all of these reasons it seems legitimate to view *Karl Marx* as both a point of origin and a continuous center of Berlin's later talks and essays. The most important and influential of these later works can be seen as amplifications, revisions, and clarifications of themes first presented or at least suggested in this youthful work. Lengthy essays on both Marx's historical precursors, the shapers of his intellectual inheritance, and on his historical contemporaries whose alternative choices highlighted the historical particularity of Marx's own constructions, persistently returned to the problem of defining and redefining the distinctive and troubling historicism that Berlin found at the center of both Marx's inheritance and the Marxian legacy.

The Marx book, however, was a peculiarly negative origin and center for Berlin's own contributions to intellectual history. He wrote about Marx in order to examine and clarify his distrust of, and critical opposition to, Marx's particular transformation of the conceptual frameworks provided by his intellectual environment and, by extension, to the various theoretical and practical Marxisms so predominant in his own environment during the 1930s. Most strikingly he used the historical examination of Marx to turn Marx on his head, by asserting that Marx's own attempt to refute the power of ideas in history was in turn refuted by the ways in which his ideas permanently altered "the ways in which men think and act,"[3] and by showing how his claims about the impersonal historical necessity that defined the meaning of all individual human identities emerged from Marx's own personal and particular struggle to achieve a viable historical identity.

The distinction between Enlightenment and Counter-Enlightenment as opposing historical patterns of assumptions about "the way men think and act," a distinction that became so crucial to Berlin's own intellectual project, emerged within the critical context of his *Auseinandersetzung* with Marx. Marx provided an avenue for probing the problematic implications, the distinctive dangers, especially as they related to the questions of human freedom and human solidarity, in both cultural stances, and particularly for analyzing the ambiguities of the Counter-Enlightenment historicization of the truths, meanings, and values that defined the nature of human existence.

The term "Counter-Enlightenment" was not yet a part of Berlin's vocabulary in the 1930s. In the chapter of his Marx book devoted to Marx's dual intellectual inheritance, Berlin juxtaposed the "semi-empirical rationalism" or "scientific empiricism" of the English and French Enlightenment against the "romantic philosophy" of post-Kantians like Fichte and Schelling in Germany, and especially against what he called the "metaphysical Historicism" of Herder and Hegel.[4] The title of this chapter—"The Philosophy of the Spirit"—clearly enunciated Berlin's view at this time that Hegelian philosophy was the most influential proponent of the German historicist opposition to the Enlightenment and the epitome of the "counter-attack" against the dominant universalist traditions in Western culture.

Although Berlin was not yet ready in 1939 to characterize the assumptions of the Enlightenment in the succinct, somewhat formulaic set of propositions which became such a familiar part of his later work, the substantial content of that characterization was clearly present in this initial assessment. As an "independent system" of thought propagated by Voltaire and the Encyclopedists, and grounded in a merger of the positions of seventeenth-century rationalists (the subsumption of all existential particularity under a timeless, "transcendent" or formal pattern of universal rational truth) and their empiricist critics (who transformed this transcendent pattern of universal truth into an immanent truth based on the empirical examination of man as an object in a natural and historical order governed by the laws determining all natural beings), the Enlightenment was based, first of all, on a conception of man as a part of nature that was assumed to have universal validity across all temporal and cultural boundaries. The essential and integral core of human characteristics, of passions, interests, and purposes, was deemed knowable like all objects in nature, and by the scientific methods that had proved so successful in grasping the laws of the natural world. Every legitimate question about man and the world (that is, every question which did not transcend the boundaries of immanent earthly or natural existence) had "one true answer" which could be "infallibly discovered" through empirical observation and rational analysis, and all such answers were perceived as ultimately in harmony with each other. Human behavior, both personal and collective, could be fully understood within the system of laws that defined the mechanical order of all natural existence. Human purposes and intentions, the pursuit of values like security, happiness, equality, solidarity, and freedom, could be known by the same methods as physical objects and events and were inherently compatible with each other and realizable within the terrestrial realm. Man was not inherently flawed or somehow misplaced within the world of nature and thus in need of transcendent redemption.

As was true with every object in nature, the possibilities of satisfaction and fulfillment among humankind were commensurate with its desires and potentialities. Disparities between human potential and human actualization or conflicts between different values (as exemplified in cultural differences) were due to practices based on ignorance or willful deception. The historical and cultural differences which separated human beings from each other were ultimately evanescent. Rational knowledge of the world given to man in sense experience could and would demonstrate the unity or harmony among all values inherently grounded in human nature and the identity between the achievement of those values and the empirical behavior that followed the inherent impulses or laws of that nature without misguided interference. Berlin discerned one major paradox in the set of assumptions that characterized the Enlightenment construction of the world. On the one hand, it tended toward a scientific positivism in which all human actions were determined by the laws governing man as an object within the natural world. On the other hand, it assumed that through the discovery of those laws, human beings could freely choose to liberate themselves from the artificial chains of unnatural authority, prejudice, and inequality, from the irrationality of conflict and of frustrated desire. Rational knowledge of the laws of nature could form the ground for criticism and judgment of that which had been produced in the empirical world by unreason and justify policies that would correct error and reform a social world constructed according to error. Human beings as the agents of rational knowledge were seen as capable of a freedom in relation to the actual existing world of historical institutions and relations which seemed to be denied them as the objects of rational knowledge.[5]

The "Counter-Enlightenment" that Berlin presented in terms of Marx's Hegelian inheritance in 1939 was focused on the historicization of the Enlightenment's immanent rational perfectibilianism. The historicism articulated by the array of late eighteenth- and early nineteenth-century, mostly German, thinkers, was first of all a metaphysical position. In Berlin's terms this meant that it assumed that the empirical world was an epiphenomenal expression of an underlying reality which was not accessible to sense experience. Hegel did not of course jettison the assumptions of universality in human values or full rational knowledge of the total system of beings. But he conceived these organizing principles in ways that opened up radical new possibilities for grasping human experience in differentiated space and progressive time. The human essence was no longer conceived as an unalterable object in nature but as the constantly changing embodied representative of a suprahuman agency or purpose which was conceived on the analogy of an individual personal character, a purposefully acting subject or self that developed through stages of teleologically directed growth. The meaning and identity of the empirically accessible objects of rational knowledge, of individual persons and different cultures, as well as of objects and events in the world of nature, were not construed in terms of generalized empirical traits or in mechanical relations of cause and effect between unalterable units in which such traits were inherent, but as unique, individualized expressions of forms of common life, or cultural organizations of experience, that represented stages in the development of the metaphysical subjective agency. Rational understanding of empirical existences involved construing those existences in relation to the purposes of the "personality," the idea or spirit, the "cultural impulse," that was expressed or communicated through them: "Hegel had asserted that the thoughts and acts of men who belong to the same period of a given culture are determined by the working in them of an identical spirit which manifests itself in all the phenomena of the period."[6] Human nature in this schema was culturally and historically particularized. Not only what men perceived or were able to know, but what men were, their identities as human beings, differed at each stage of cultural development: they were produced within the internal relations of specific and particular forms of common life.[7]

In this earliest formulation of the idea of the Counter-Enlightenment Berlin's focus seemed to be on the assumption of a contextual ("organic") determinism in both a cross-sectional and a progressive temporal sense. All cultural expressions within a particular historical epoch were connected to each other not through relations of cause and effect but as diversified expressions or forms of the same characteristic purpose or agency. Individuals were defined by the organizing frame of the cultural epoch in which they were situated. The horizons of human knowledge and human values were tied to time and place. At the same time, however, the claim to organic development within a unified and knowable pattern seemed to take away the sting of this intimation of a human nature defined by inherent historical diversity and pluralism. The "universal" meaning of an individual existence was accessible retroactively, as an understanding of the way that any and every particular historical epoch was assimilated into the unity of an overall purpose or teleology which moved in a necessary, law-governed, developmental pattern from one epoch to another and one culture to another. There was little analysis of any actual Hegelian text or particular claim in these passages: It was Romantic and Idealist Historicism in general rather than Hegel in particular that seemed to be the object of Berlin's descriptions. The analysis of "spirit" or the "cultural impulse" as creative, self-transforming subjectivity, the redefining of reason and freedom in terms of self-determination and self-mastery, for example, seemed noticeably absent from Berlin's descriptions.

What Berlin discerned in Hegel was the general principle that cultural differences, differences in human value and meaning, were not the result of defects in rational understanding and practices based on that understanding but the consequence of an historically necessary development. The individual could not escape the historical/cultural contexts "by which every man is made to be what he is, which are the man, are what he is; to wish to escape from this is to wish to lose one's proper nature, a self-contradictory demand, which could be made only by one who does not understand what he is demanding, one whose idea of personal liberty is childishly subjective."[8] Freedom and rationality within the assumptions of metaphysical historicism consisted primarily in the self-conscious integration of one's own values and purposes into the cultural totality and historical epoch to which one belonged, through a knowledge (rational assimilation) of the historical necessity of one's own nature. All other behavior was not only futile but inherently irrational. The conflict between values embodied in different cultures and epochs could not be resolved by removing artificially constructed resistances to the unity of mankind but by understanding the differences as stages in a necessary evolution of mankind toward the perfected maturity of complete understanding. Like the *philosophes*, Hegel was a perfectibilian and a rationalist, but by connecting reason and perfectibility to the necessity of cultural and temporal difference rather than the universality of nature, he derogated the contingent individual choiceof values and action based on such choices to the realm of irrelevant subjective opinion and futile, pointless (historically irrelevant) practice.

Berlin's description and analysis of Marx's theoretical positions in 1939 focused on the 1840s and particularly on the formation of the theory of historical materialism first articulated in 1845–1846. Historical materialism in Berlin's interpretation evolved as a critical merger of the Hegelian form of historicist Counter-Enlightenment with Enlightenment traditions that Marx had inherited from his father and which had apparently "inoculated" him against the most obviously idealist elements in metaphysical historicism and thus also prepared him to join the critical attack on Hegel's doctrine of the Spirit led by Feuerbach in the early 1840s. In contrast to Hegel's historical phenomenology with its assumption of a suprapersonal spirit that embodied itself in the empirical particulars of historical existence, Marx asserted, in good Enlightenment fashion, that only the concrete, "real objects in space and time" and their "observable empirical relations to each other"[9] were legitimate objects of rational knowledge and that all explanations of historical processes must "be supported by the evidence of scientific observation." The edifice of rational knowledge of the whole must be built "solely in accordance with the results of this empirical method of investigation."[10] Marx also maintained the critical Enlightenment stance toward all of those symbolic aspects of culture which purported to provide insight into a reality of underlying or transcendent value-laden purpose and that evaded naturalistic explanation, and thus distorted human knowledge of the immanent realities of historical existence. All such phenomena were explained in terms of their instrumental use within the sphere of secular, worldly relations.

However, Berlin was most interested in the ways in which the fundamental patterns of the Hegelian Counter-Enlightenment sustained themselves within Marx's apparent scientific empiricism and in his insistence on reductive naturalistic explanations of cultural phenomena. The core of Hegelian Counter-Enlightenment within historical materialism was the belief (a metaphysical assumption, Berlin called it) that the history of mankind proceeded according to necessary laws that determined the formation of epochal sociocultural systems or forms of common life and the progressive transitional conflicts between them. Historical materialism historicized human existence in two senses, according to the Hegelian pattern. First, human existence was historical in the sense that individual existence was always embedded in and defined by the particular contextual relations of epochal systems, different ways of organizing experience and defining "what man is." Although such systems were now defined as systems of social organization based on modes of production, that is, in terms of differing historical modes of the relations between man and nature rather than as cultural expressions of divergent relations between human identity and the developmental logic of absolute spirit, they remained particular, self-contained worlds which contained their own categories of interpretation and understanding. The values of one historical epoch could not be applied to another because they were grounded in the developmentally distinct forms of social practice which defined all systems of value and meaning. Like Hegel, Marx rejected the Enlightenment belief that a unified system of rational truths transcended historical differentiation and could be used to judge individual actions, thoughts, and purposes in any culture or historical epoch. The ideal of a brotherhood of man grounded in a common nature rationally known was shattered. Secondly, human existence was historical in the sense that the relations between such organizations of existence were historically determined by impersonal forces beyond individual control. Not individual acts based on contextually framed choices among alternative values, but general laws governing the historical transformation of social systems were the motive force of historical development. Human existence was subject to a necessary dialectical law in which the evolving contradictions within social systems articulated in the conflict of classes eventually produced cataclysmic transformations that replaced one system of class hegemony by another. Individual human agents were reduced to representatives of objective forces, instances of historical laws that operated with the inexorability of laws of nature.[11]

The combination of the idea of historical necessity, conceived in structural terms with the idea of the conflict of incommensurable social worlds, produced the peculiar ethical implications of Marxian theory. No standards of right and wrong, or truth and error existed outside of the social systems in which individuals were inserted by their relations to historical modes of production. Human actions and human thoughts were shaped by the determinants of their concrete, material situation within each system. Individuals had no access to universal truths or values outside their historically determined situation. There were no natural rights but only historical rights: "the only real rights are those conferred by history, the right to act the part which is historically imposed on one's class."[12] There were no universal terms for truth or value that cross the boundaries of social systems of class rule. Dialogue, compromise, or accommodation between the historically distinct and unique organizations of human reality were inherently impossible. Moreover, the distinction between empirical determination of behavior and the purposeful pursuit of meaning or value was demolished: "Judgments of fact cannot be sharply distinguished from those of value; all of one's judgments are conditioned by practical activity in a given social milieu." For an ethical judgment to claim objective validity, according to Marx, it would have to refer "to empirical phenomena and be verifiable by reference to them." The only meaning left to judgments of good or bad, right or wrong, was whether or not something "accords or discords with the historical process."[13] Individual human freedom was identified with "knowledge of the laws of necessity":

> If you know in which direction the world process is working, you can either identify yourself with it or not; if you do not, if you fight it, you thereby compass your own certain destruction, being necessarily defeated by the forward advance of history; to choose to do so deliberately is to behave irrationally. Only a rational being is truly free to choose between alternatives; where one of these leads to irresistible destruction, he cannot choose it freely, because to say that an act is free, as Marx employs the term, is to deny that it is contrary to reason.[14]

However much Berlin may have insisted on the brilliance of Marx's insights into the social transformations of his age, on the concentrated theoretical power of his conceptualizations, and on the intensity of his search for empirical verification, or marveled at his pervasive influence on social theory and social practice in the century that followed the creation of historical materialism, it was quite obvious in 1939 that the Marxist form of Counter-Enlightenment Historicism was seen more as a danger than an inspiration. The war years provided little reason for Berlin to change his views. The 1948 edition left the portrait of Marx as the rigid historical determinist of all individual identity, as a kind of positivist Hegelian, firmly in place. During the 1950s, however, Berlin increasingly devoted his energies to a historical clarification of the issues raised by his Marx book and thus to a self-clarification of his own views of the relationship between historical identity and freedom. Those of Marx's contemporaries who criticized or eventually rejected the Hegelian-Marxian paradigm, particularly Herzen and Hess, drew his special attention. At the same time he began to examine the great variety of Counter-Enlightenment critiques of rational systems of truth and universal human values, both among eighteenth-century thinkers like Vico and Herder (for whom the recognition of historical and cultural difference was not assimilated into a linear teleological pattern), and among the non-Hegelian historicists of the Romantic movement.[15]

In the well-known essay "Historical Inevitability," first published in 1954, Berlin distinguished more clearly than he had in 1939 between scientific-empirical and teleological models of historical necessity. Both patterns reduced individual actions and choice of values to determinations of the inexorable lawful movement of suprapersonal entities, but in different ways. The Hegelian teleological model, whose origins he now saw as reaching back to the "beginnings of human thought,"[16] was perceived as more fundamental for an interpretation of Marx's position than the naturalistic mechanistic empiricism of Enlightenment social science. In fact during the mid-1950s Berlin began a process of differentiating Marx's position from the Enlightenment scientism so influential in the late nineteenth-century orthodox Marxism propagated by Engels and Plekhanov.[17] Teleological determinism was grounded upon the Judeo-Christian model of narrative meaning rather than the classical and Enlightenment model of a cosmic mechanism. Individual life stories were inserted as functions and purposes within a meta-narrative structure, their identity was defined by their role in the preconceived patterns imposed by the history of peoples, cultures, states, religious communities, nationalities, classes, etc. Such meta-stories provided the meaning of all individual stories. Individual identities were scripted by the story-teller. This was not to say that Berlin suddenly abandoned completely his previous conceptions of Marx's commitment to scientific empiricism, but the emphasis had shifted to Marx as the narrator of a salvational story, more interested in the meanings that provided individual historical existences with identity than the construction of a unified systematic, objective, causal order among the empirical realities of the evolution of mankind's social existence. "Teleology is not a theory, or a hypothesis," he insisted in 1954, "but a category or framework in terms of which everything is, or should be conceived and described."[18] Berlin's relatively positive evaluation of Marx's empiricism, which in the terms of the 1939 and 1948 editions had kept Marx from becoming as schematic and dogmatic a Marxist as his followers, began to fade. What Marx lacked was not so much a commitment to providing empirical evidence for his descriptions of social formations and their transformations but a sense of "reality,"[19] that is, a sympathetic understanding of the indeterminacy of historical processes marked by diverging and converging stories constructed from alternative scripts (historically constructed traditions and cultural formations) by individuals making value-choices within the temporal and cultural parameters of historical worlds that had no discernible single meaning. The emergence of this "new" Marx alongside the old was undoubtedly influenced by the emergence of a new generation of Marxist scholars (some of them Berlin's own students) interested in the Hegelian humanism of the early Marx, as well as by the historical events of the late 1950s in Hungary, Poland, Russia, and the Suez that shaped the interests and outlook of this new generation. It was also deeply marked by Berlin's growing interest in Romantic notions of human existence as the creative activity of self and world construction, and of "positive" human freedom as the subjective agent's self-sufficiency and self-determination.[20] But it did not lead Berlin to a more sympathetic reading of Marxian theory. Rather, it clarified and amplified his reasons for viewing Marx as the most formidable opponent of his own (increasingly defined and refined) positions on the inherently historical nature of human existence. It was not so much the emancipatory hopefulness of the New Left as the "totalitarian" threats of the Cold War that shaped Berlin's views of Marx in the late 1950s.

The shifts in Berlin's position during the 1950s were articulated in the extensive additions to the chapter on "Historical Materialism" in the third edition of *Karl Marx*, published in 1963. The analyses of Marxian theory from the 1939 and 1948 editions were not deleted from this new edition. Instead Berlin simply inserted two new sections within the old chapter, virtually doubling its length.

The first insertion reconceptualized Marx's theory of history as teleological narrative which translated Hegel's phenomenology of the spirit into "semi-empirical terms." Marx, like Hegel, constructed history as the story of human beings' struggle to "realize their full human potentialities" as free self-determining beings by becoming masters of themselves and of the natural world of which they were a part. This struggle was construed not as the struggle of thinking activity or "spirit" to come to self-conscious transparency through the medium of individual human beings constructing objective ethical and symbolic worlds, but as the struggle of human material subjectivity, creative labor, to construct a world in its own image through the medium of historical systems of production. In both cases, however, the goal of the story was the "harmonious realization of all human powers in accordance with the principles of reason,"[21] a goal that involved both freedom, defined as self-determination or self-mastery, and unity, defined as the uncoerced integration of the individual into the universal community of humanity through the victory of that form of self-creation and self-determination represented by the class that incorporated the essential human activity of material self-determination, the industrial proletariat. It was creative labor (a translation of the Romantic doctrine of the self-transforming and self-making subject into material and social terms) that now appeared as the center of the Marxian story. Labor transformed the identity of human beings as it transformed the natural world. As the core of social practice, labor externalized human creative potentials in the objective world of its products. The division of labor, the formation of classes, and the process of class conflict arose as instruments of this deeper struggle of man to produce himself in the world and recognize himself in his product as a free and social being. It was the "constant self-transformation which is at the heart of all work and creation, which rendered absurd the very notion of fixed timeless principles, unalterable universal goals and an eternal human predicament."[22] The only permanent factor in this process was the dynamic transformative activity of laboring man himself. "Work in the cosmic vision of Marx," Berlin claimed, "is what cosmic love had been for Dante—that which makes men and their relationships what they are, given the relatively invariant factors of the external world into which they are born."[23] For Marx, therefore, the empirical phenomenal reality of individual historical existences found its core meaning in the teleology of man's creative powers as a laboring being constantly transforming himself and the world in the struggle to be both free and at home in the world of nature and society.

In the second inserted passage Berlin reinterpreted the Marxian conception of freedom in terms of the laws of the dialectic as a self-determining process, that is, as a process inherent to the subject of labor.[24] The dialectic was now construed as a story of alienation and its overcoming. As human beings externalized themselves in their products they produced historically specific economic, social, political, and cultural structures, generalized organizations of their collective existence that first articulated and then hindered the process of self-transformation. That which had been created as an instrument to actualize human purposes became an objective hindrance to further development: it took on the character of a self-imposed prison. Dialectics was not simply the objective law, modeled on the laws pertaining in the world of natural forces, of the tension and confrontation between opposing forms of social organization, as it had been described in 1939 and 1948, but an internal process of self-production, self-criticism, and self-transformation. Alienation, Berlin now insisted, was for Marx "the heart of history itself."[25] Classes were objectifications of mankind's struggle at a particular moment that "artificially prevented [human beings] from living as their natures demand."[26] Romantic and historicist conceptions of the self-transforming character of human nature were thus ultimately subordinated to universalist teleological conceptions in which all human values were integrated within a perfect social form. Historical difference once again proved evanescent as individuals finally achieved their essential identity as "members of a unified society, capable of understanding the reasons for doing what they do, and of enjoying the fruits of their own united, free and rational activity."[27] Human identity was not simply determined by the individual's place in particular systems of production and social organization. There was also a deeper universal determination, in which man's own inherent purposes, that which his nature "craves,"[28] defined who he was and what he did.

Yet Berlin was skeptical of the "freedom" that defined human history in this teleological story of the human struggle for self-fulfillment as self-determination. The struggle itself was defined as determined by inexorable laws that controlled the purposes humans pursued in their creative activity; individuals were still seen as actors in a single plot. They were not "mechanically" determined (that perception was a part of the alienated objectification of human practice in bourgeois scientific conceptions), but determined by meanings and goals over which, as particular individuals, they had no control. Freedom had only one form, recognition of the collective story of Promethean labor as one's own essential story. Freedom was identified with full self-conscious participation in a collective social practice of self-mastery and world-mastery. To reject one's role in this story was to fall out of the historical narrative altogether, to be less than human, to forfeit one's essential human identity.

Berlin apparently did not feel the need self-consciously to integrate his new more Romantic and teleological Marx into his older, more Enlightenment-oriented analysis, because he did not see the Enlightenment Marx and the Counter-Enlightenment Marx as in fundamental contradiction.[29] A lengthy essay published in 1964, "Marxism and the International in the Nineteenth Century,"[30] clearly revealed why he did not feel that his earlier assessments needed to be revised. Recognition that Marx was not the crude scientific materialist and sociological determinist that he was occasionally portrayed to be in the later interpretations of Engels and Plekhanov unveiled, not a prophetic conception of human emancipation, but a "terrifying vision" of spiritual despotism. As rational perfectibilians, Marx and Hegel were now situated in a tradition of Western thinking that could be traced back to Plato and included members of the pre-Romantic and Romantic Counter-Enlightenment like Rousseau and Fichte. What differentiated Hegel and especially Marx within this tradition was the combination of a belief in universal rational values, in one knowable answer to all questions of meaning and value, with a commitment to evolutionary historical determinism. The doctrine of the unity of theory and practice articulated in the Marxian concept of man as creative labor identified both truth and value as inherent products of social practice. However, this notion of the historical diversity of standards of knowledge and ethics was tied to the teleological assumption that identified a particular group with the goal of complete knowledge and full human self-realization (the harmonious actualization of all human values).

Conceived within the framework of a self-determining, collective Romantic subject, of a kind of collective artist who found his freedom in the creation of a world that articulated his total self-sufficiency and self-mastery, the incommensurability and plurality of organized systems of existence were tied to a belief in the ultimate universality of one of those systems, in the absolute validity of one particular group-construction of meaning and truth. This claim marked an absolute break with the past. "The identification of truth and authority with the activity, theoretical or practical, of an identifiable group of human beings had hitherto never been maintained by secular thinkers."[31] Marx's theory split mankind into two worlds, those who possessed the universal simply in being what they were, and those who were left behind and hindered the realization of the universal simply because of what they were. Since knowledge and value were bound to group practice, no communication or accommodation between these different worlds was possible. By tying the Romantic conception of man as the maker of his own self and maker of his world to the historical evolution of modes of social organization, Marx had produced a theory of "historically inevitable hatred" that completely undermined all humane, democratic values. Even in the religious wars of the Middle Ages, conversion had been imagined as a possibility. Like National Socialist doctrines of racial determination (which Berlin actually described as a translation of Marxism into racial terms[32]), Marxist historicism justified the massacre of those not among the elect; it was an "unparalleled moral and spiritual catastrophe." "The Marxist truth is a terrible new weapon, for its truth entails there are sections of mankind which are literally expendable." This "terrifying vision," although not self-consciously recognized and articulated in Marx's texts, Berlin claimed, was not just a construction of Marx's enemies or disciples, but a legitimate explication of the implications of Marx's original theory. The moral recoil from Marxism was not based on a mis-recognition or exaggeration but on "Marxism itself," on the "real Marx."[33] Stalin's Gulags were the legitimate product of the theory of freedom as self-determination and mastery contained with the Marxian texts of the 1840s.

Isaiah Berlin's Marx thus became an epitome of all the negative ethical and political implications of the discourses of both Enlightenment and Counter-Enlightenment. But Berlin's analysis of the Marxian project also clarified what might be salvaged from these traditions for the present and future. Although Berlin rejected the mono-causality that transformed Marxian and Hegelian historicism into a teleological system, he did not reject their critique of Enlightenment universalism on the basis of an historicist and self-transformative conception of human existence. Human identities were inherently historical in two senses. First, they were always constructed within the particularity of diverse forms of common life, of cultures, traditions, ethnicities, social organizations. The diversity in these forms was inherent and unreconcilable, not subordinated to a single teleological determinant. It was not labor or spirit but individual freedom of choice that undergirded the historical, pluralist nature of human existence. The objectification of value choices in common forms of life could be empirically examined and understood—it was clearly possible to understand human values through appropriate interpretive and empathetic methods for reconstructing communicative cultural systems—but the value-choices embedded in such historical cultures or discourses remained unpredictable and inherently diverse. Individuals were situated in such cultural forms, but never completely determined by them. Individual processes of self-identification always involved some element of rationally unpredictable choice in assimilating or transforming inherited cultural forms. And it was precisely the difference sustained by humanity's inherent ability to choose the values they would live by that also sustained Enlightenment conceptions of universal standards and the brotherhood of mankind. The process of self-fashioning that created the incommensurable differences between human beings and between human communities became itself the common element that sustained rational communication and ethical standards across cultural difference. Difference became the sign of identity. Our common humanity was articulated precisely in the struggle to create self-identity and sustain it within communal systems of mutual recognition. Identities were shaped, but not ultimately determined, by historically objective cultural traditions and social forms. Freedom, equality, solidarity, justice, etc., could be reconstituted (although never fully harmonized or integrated) as objective and universal values through both our knowledge of others as contextually shaped self-makers of their own identities and stories, and our recognition of them as identity-constructors and story-makers like us.

In 1968, five years after the revisions of his Marx biography, Berlin applied the insights he had drawn from his struggle with Marx to an analysis of Marx's own struggle for identity. In the essay "Benjamin Disraeli, Karl Marx and the Search for Identity," Marx was approached not so much from the point of view of the ways in which his theory was shaped by his dual inheritance in the Enlightenment and Counter-Enlightenment traditions, but from the perspective of why Marx chose to shape and transform those inherited value-frameworks in particular ways as he constructed his own set of values. Here Berlin saw Marx's development in terms of a number of negative choices based on his own insecurities as a culturally homeless exile, on his craving for recognition and for compensation for the humiliating wounds perpetrated on his group of historical origin, the first generation of emancipated Jews in central Europe.[34] Unlike Moses Hess, Marx could not accept the values that framed the common life which was his traditional inheritance, and this gravely distorted his social perceptions:

> Those who are born in the social security of a settled society, and remain full members of it, and look upon it as their natural home, tend to have a stronger sense of social reality; to see public life in a reasonably just perspective, without the need to escape into political fantasy or romantic invention.[35]

Instead of recognizing the cultural pluralism of the historical reality into which his situation had thrown him, and building his mature self on the firm ground of the identity (however attenuated and conflicted) that had been given to him within the cultural community of his birth, Marx chose to create a new, completely invented self that could secure self-mastery only in fantasy, that disavowed rather than built on the identities he had inherited. To destroy within himself the doubts about the importance of his own Jewish origins, Marx built a theory that made ethnicity, religion, and nationality evanescent phenomena. The intensity and exclusivity of Marx's remaking of the intellectual inheritances of Enlightenment and Counter-Enlightenment into a meta-narrative of heroic group self-determination reduced and assimilated all historical difference and the freedom of choice on which difference was grounded. However, to be empirical or "objective" required a sense of human reality as a reality that embodied the activity of human beings as culturally contextualized but not fully determined agents of their own values and identities. Marx's theory, in Berlin's view, was thus ultimately an unempirical and subjective explanation of human existence that disavowed the objective reality of diverse cultural forms and the ability of individuals to act as free agents in transforming both themselves and those forms, a theory of the type whose function was "not primarily to describe or analyze reality, but rather more to comfort, strengthen resolution, compensate for defeat and weakness, generate a fighting spirit, principally in the authors of the doctrines themselves."[36] Marxian theory was a historically situated construction of a world that reproduced and sustained a particular kind of choice of personal and sociocultural identity. Berlin's construction of Marx, we might suggest, suffered from similar characteristics, though guided by different values. Berlin's *Marx* was in many ways a vehicle for the construction of his own moral positions and historical identity and should be read, perhaps, as much for the story it tells about Isaiah Berlin as the story it tells about Karl Marx.

Notes

1. Michael Ignatieff, *Isaiah Berlin: A Life* (New York: Henry Holt, 1998), p. 71. See also p. 70: "To write about Marx was to join the swim of the major ideological current of his age and to take the measure of the challenge that it represented to his own inchoate liberal allegiances."
2. "The Purpose of Philosophy" (1962), *Concepts and Categories: Philosophical Essays*, edited by Henry Hardy and with an introduction by Bernard Williams (London: Hogarth, 1978), p. 9: "Its (philosophy's) subject matter is to a large degree not items of experience, but the ways in which they are viewed, the permanent or semi-permanent categories in which experience is conceived and classified."
3. Isaiah Berlin, *Karl Marx: His Life and Environment* (London: T. Butterworth, 1939), p. 249.
4. Berlin, *Marx* (1939), pp. 41, 42, 49.
5. Berlin, *Marx* (1939), pp. 40ff, but especially pp. 43–4. In his introduction to a selection of Enlightenment texts published in 1956 (*The Age of Enlightenment: The Eighteenth Century Philosophers*, Oxford: Oxford University Press, 1956, pp. 11–29), Berlin characterized the Enlightenment in terms of the reduction of philosophical questions (meta-questions about the conditions of statements about meaning and value) to formal and empirical (i.e., unphilosophical) "scientific" questions, which produced the illusion that all questions could eventually find single answers.
6. Berlin, *Marx* (1939), p. 77
7. Berlin, *Marx* (1939), p. 54: "Hegel transferred the concept of the personal character of the individual which gradually unfolds itself throughout a man's life to the case of entire cultures and nations, he referred to it variously as the Idea or Spirit, distinguished stages in its evolution and pronounced it to be the motive, dynamic factor in the development of specific peoples and civilizations and so of the sentient world as a whole."
8. Berlin, *Marx* (1939), p. 60.
9. Berlin, *Marx* (1939), p. 79.
10. Berlin, *Marx* (1939), p. 87.
11. Berlin, *Marx* (1939), pp. 117–34.
12. Berlin, *Marx* (1939), p. 133.
13. Berlin, *Marx* (1939), p. 134.
14. Berlin, *Marx* (1939), p. 136.
15. In "The Romantic Revolution: A Crisis in the History of Thought" (1960), printed in Isaiah Berlin, *The Sense of Reality: Studies in Ideas and their History*, edited by Henry Hardy and introduced by Patrick Gardiner (London: Chatto and Windus, 1996), pp. 172–3, Berlin distinguished "The German historical school" which included Herder and Savigny as well as Edmund Burke, from Romanticists proper because they maintained the ideal of the ultimate convergence of historical and cultural difference in some vast harmonious unity.

16. Berlin, "Historical Inevitability" (1954) in Berlin, *Four Essays on Liberty* (Oxford: Oxford University Press, 1969), p. 51.
17. Berlin, "Historical Inevitability," p. 79.
18. Berlin, "Historical Inevitability," p. 53.
19. Berlin, "The Sense of Reality" (1953), printed in Berlin, *The Sense of Reality*, pp. 1–39.
20. Berlin, "Two Concepts of Liberty" (1958), in Berlin, *Four Essays on Liberty*, p. 131: "The desire to be governed by myself, or at any rate to participate in the process by which my life is controlled may be as deep a wish as that of a free area for action, and perhaps historically older." In 1958 Berlin claimed that this idea of "positive freedom" "rules over half our world."
21. Berlin, *Karl Marx: His Life and Environment*, 3rd ed., (New York: Oxford University Press, 1963) p. 130. The new passages are inserted on pp. 127–34.
22. Berlin, *Marx* (1963), p. 130.
23. Berlin, *Marx* (1963), p. 131.
24. Berlin, *Marx* (1963), pp. 136–43.
25. Berlin, *Marx* (1963), p. 137.
26. Berlin, *Marx* (1963), p. 139.
27. Berlin, *Marx* (1963), p. 139.
28. Berlin, *Marx* (1963), p. 143.
29. In "Two Concepts of Liberty" (1958), Berlin stated: "Herder, Hegel and Marx substituted their own vitalistic models of social life for the older, mechanical ones, but believed, no less than their opponents, that to understand the world is to be free. They merely differed from them in stressing the part played by change and growth in what made human beings human" (p. 142).
30. Printed in *The Sense of Reality*, pp. 116–67.
31. Berlin, "Marxism and the International in the Nineteenth Century," p. 120.
32. Berlin, "Marxism and the International in the Nineteenth Century," p. 139: "When this separation into the elect and the evil who cannot help themselves was translated into racial terms, it led, in our century, to an enormous massacre—a moral and spiritual catastrophe unparalleled in human history."
33. Berlin, "Marxism and the International in the Nineteenth Century," pp. 139, 141.
34. Berlin, "Benjamin Disraeli, Karl Marx and the Search for Identity," *Against the Current: Essays in the History of Ideas*, edited by Henry Hardy, Introduced by Roger Hausheer (New York: Penguin Books, 1982), p. 259, where Marx's craving for recognition is analyzed as "an effort to escape from the weakness and humiliation of the depressed or wounded social group by identifying oneself with some other group or movement that is free from the defects of one's original condition: consisting in an attempt to acquire a new personality, and that which goes with it, a new set of clothing, a new set of values, habits, new armour which does not press upon the old wounds, on the old scars left by the chains one wore as a slave."
35. Berlin, "Benjamin Disraeli, Karl Marx, and The Search for Identity," p. 258
36. Berlin, "Benjamin Disraeli, Karl Marx, and The Search for Identity," p. 286.

11 | Isaiah Berlin, Alexander Herzen, and Russia's Elusive Counter-Enlightenment

Michael Confino

The Enlightenment and the Counter-Enlightenment were complex phenomena which left their mark on eighteenth- and nineteenth-century European thought and culture. They become even more intricate subjects of study when linked to the context of intellectual life in Russia at the time. On the surface, it might seem that there is little scope for such a topic, given the major differences between Western Europe and Russia and given the latter's seeming lack of concepts and ideas normally associated with these two great constellations of European thought.

I. Russian peculiarities?

Why such an impression? With regard to Western Europe, scholars, whatever their approaches and interpretations, are, more or less, in agreement on the *terminus a quo* of the Enlightenment and on the main tenets of its beliefs and theories. There is, to say the least, a common ground, a shared understanding of the essentials, regardless of the not negligible differences of opinion as to, for instance, whether the Enlightenment was "a movement," as Isaiah Berlin assumed, or an assemblage of a wide range of ideas lumped together and called for convenience's sake "Enlightenment." Similarly, most scholars assume that the Counter-Enlightenment was a counter-ideology, or a counter-movement; in either case they succeed in outlining its basic ideas within certain agreed-upon temporal and theoretical limits. Finally, this conceptual unity would prevail (although it might be seriously shaken) if one considers, as I do, that the term "Counter-Enlightenment" is essentially a convenient and elegant metaphor signifying a loosely connected, and sometimes even opposed, set of thinkers and ideas; or, on the contrary, if one believes that this is a powerful paradigm which imposes order and hierarchy on the intricate taxonomy of the eighteenth- and nineteenth-century Western world of ideas and ideologies.[1]

But when we turn to the Russian scene, the answers to these preliminary questions suggest that there is no sufficient basis for an examination of the "Enlightenment/Counter-Enlightenment" problematic in view of what we know about the parameters of intellectual life in Russia, and the course of its history of ideas. This is not to say, of course, that Russia is and has always been *sui generis*. That attractive but worn-out notion has been disproved by extensive historical research and empirical evidence. By definition, *sui generis* entities—being discrete, unique, and unrepeated—are not comparable to any other, yet we know that in all areas of historical development and scholarly enquiry Russia stands the test of comparability with the other European countries. In this regard Berlin's writings on Russia brilliantly demonstrate time and again that it is not *sui generis*, but rather belongs to Europe, and participated in, and responded to, the events, the currents of ideas, and "the spirit of the times," that reigned in Europe at any given moment. In his view Russia was not "a world apart" (as Michael Ignatieff interprets Berlin's opinion),[2] nor a different species vis-à-vis the other European countries. On the contrary, Russia shared a basic unity and commonality with other European countries and, at the same time, like them, had its own national and religious peculiarities and differences.

On this subject, there is nowadays a puzzling revival of the metaphysical stereotype of the "Russian soul"—*l'âme russe* of old—now often referred to with trendy terms such as the "Russian cultural heritage," the "Russian mentality," or the "burden of history." It is the "Russian soul" that supposedly explains why "Russia is so different." It is the root cause of why, for instance, Russia cannot have a market economy, a democratic régime, or a civil society. "Russian culture," like "culture" *tout court*, is one of many concepts that are increasingly used and badly misused, which explain too much and nothing at all. They should be treated with caution, for they are often used in lieu of specious notions like "race," "genes," "national character," and the like: such usage marks a cultural U-turn which, paradoxically, is leading back to such utterly discredited and reactionary pseudo-explanations.

"*L'âme russe et ses mystères*": in a kind of parody of eternal return, *fin-de-siècle* fashions are repeating themselves after a hundred-year interval, this time with no Ballets Russes or Rasputins around to serve as alibis. But even if some aspects of the present state of Russia's economy and society are more reminiscent of Al Capone's times than of John Maynard Keynes' theory, it is not the Russians, after all, who invented the Mafia system (although they borrowed the word) or jungle capitalism (i.e., capitalism without a human face). True, Russia's economic development—whether inspired by Harvard business management wizards or not—reminds one at times of the raw, early capitalism described by Karl Marx and bolstered now by the current globalization. But there is nothing peculiarly Russian in this; other countries have trodden this path before, and as an explanatory hypothesis the "Russian soul" cliché is less than adequate.

II. An Eighteenth-century Russian Enlightenment?

In the eighteenth century Russia was not "a world apart," but it was indeed different; and if the same can be said of the Enlightenment in Russia the reason was not its *sui generis* quality or the unfathomable "Russian soul." In short, no matter how one defines the Enlightenment, no such phenomenon appeared in Russia.[3] To be sure, in the eighteenth century there were a handful of enlightened people, among them Catherine II, Nikolai Novikov, Alexander Radishchev, Alexander Betskoi, and some others, but there was no "movement" in the sense that Berlin used this term. Logically, then, one might be inclined to say: no Enlightenment, hence no Counter-Enlightenment. Yet this is not necessarily the case. Indeed, there is one possibility that explains how this could not have been so, and that a Russian Counter-Enlightenment could have existed, namely, that it developed as a reaction to the Enlightenment in Western Europe. This is neither an idle hypothesis nor counterfactual fancy: in Russia, as elsewhere, exogeneous events and ideas have often generated indigenous movements, schools of thought and ideologies. Thus, it is not impossible that there might have been a Russian Counter-Enlightenment without a Russian Enlightenment.

The late Alexander Gerschenkron, a good friend and admirer of Isaiah Berlin, would perhaps have attributed such a development to the "advantages (or disadvantages) of backwardness," a concept he magisterially elaborated.[4] But in the eighteenth century this did not occur. At that time, Russian educated society's interest in the ideas of the *philosophes* created lively conversations and a certain demand for foreign books and publications (thus generating a flow of import dues for Catherine's customs); but in practical terms, in "real life," this interest came to naught and led nowhere. The main reason for the impracticality of the Enlightenment in Russia was the widespread conviction that its otherwise lofty and admirable ideas were not applicable in that country (at least—as the cliché goes—not "for the time being"), and that they had no practical role in the "cursed Russian reality" epitomized by autocracy and serfdom. This point is well illustrated in Berlin's description of Herzen's father:

> Shrewd, honourable, and neither unfeeling nor unjust, a 'difficult' character like old Prince Bolkonsky in Tolstoy's *War and Peace*, Ivan Yakovlev emerges from his son's recollections a self-lacerating, grim, shut-in, half frozen human being, who terrorised his household with his whims and his sarcasm. He kept all doors and windows locked, the blinds permanently drawn, and, apart from a few old friends and his own brothers, saw virtually nobody. In later years his son described him as the product of the 'encounter of two such incompatible things as the [western] eighteenth century and Russian life'—a collision of cultures that had destroyed a good many among the more sensitive members of the Russian gentry in the reigns of Catherine II and her successors.[5]

In addition, the *philosophes*' advocacy of "enlightened despotism" had in Russia a rather paradoxical effect, condoning despotism, which was very palpable anyway, and postponing enlightenment to some distant future. Additional circumstances which seemed to endorse this state of affairs included, for instance, Diderot's visit to St. Petersburg and his long (and well publicized) conversations with Catherine II; the latter's assiduous correspondance with Voltaire, whose letters to her are a model of obsequiousness; and Catherine's public "confession" to having "plagiarized shamelessly" (*j'ai pillé sans vergogne*) Montesquieu's *Esprit des lois* in writing her new Code of Laws, the *Nakaz* of 1767 (which in any case was never put into practice).[6] These and other public relations moves were quite successful; Catherine had a flair for public relations management and for make-believe (whether the *philosophes* really believed her or not is an open question, but they behaved "as if"), and her success in this respect greatly mitigated in Russia the radical, humanistic, and revolutionary elements of the Enlightenment.

After 1789 Catherine—together with most of Russian educated society—repudiated the French Revolution, that "monstrous child of perverse and subversive teachings," but while she energetically encouraged the kings of Prussia and Austria to wipe out the "Jacobin pest" in Paris, she herself took advantage of the fact that their armies were positioned against France, in order to swallow up large chunks of Polish territory, pretending that she was routing Jacobinism in ... Warsaw (!), thus orchestrating the Second and Third Partitions of Poland and diverting Prussia's and Austria's attention from the battle against France to the spoils in Poland. Russia's expansion was more important than fighting French revolutionaries. Thus, *Finis Poloniae* and the eradication of Polish independence became a fact of life for 125 years, and Jacobinism (to a certain extent because of Catherine's strategy) was to haunt Europe for the next two hundred years, until François Furet announced to everybody's relief: "*la Révolution Française est terminée*," and Mikhail Gorbachev brought about one more tangible proof of it.

III. The Decembrists

The following stage of intellectual development came in the early nineteenth century and represented a strengthening of the reaction against what was perceived as the result of Enlightenment ideas: the Revolution's excesses, the execution of Louis XVI, the abolition of the monarchy, the persecution of the nobility, and finally the rise of "Buonaparte." The court historian Nikolai Karamzin was the epitome of this change of mood: once a sympathizer of the Parisian *sans culottes*, he became a kind of Russian Chateaubriand, *le talent en moins*. The opposition to these developments was moral (because of the Jacobin Terror), social (because educated society in Russia was almost exclusively of noble rank and had a sense of solidarity with the French aristocracy), and finally, political and nationalistic (because of the strong anti-French sentiments born during the wars against Napoleon). In a way, this intellectual and psychological phenomenon was a sort of bastard Counter-Enlightenment, but one that obviously bears no relation to that discussed in this volume.

A qualitatively new political and ideological development occurred with the formation of the Decembrists' secret societies from 1814 onward up until their unsuccesful rebellion against Nicholas I in December 1825, when he ascended the throne with the death of Alexander I. Strictly speaking, however, the Decembrists were not disciples of the *philosophes*. They disagreed with many of their conceptions and theories, and rejected the political and ideological path that led to Napoleon's rise to power and "despotic regime."

Several Western scholars and specialists in Soviet historiography have argued that most of the Decembrists were followers of the Encyclopedists, and that they were influenced by the revolutionary movement in France and in other countries. The Decembrists did indeed acquire some enlightened ideas from their foreign tutors (mainly Frenchmen) and from foreign books, but the authors who caught their attention were Adam Smith, Condorcet, Benjamin Constant, Beccaria, Benjamin Franklin, Jean-Baptiste Say, Jeremy Bentham, Byron—not exactly proponents of the Jacobin type of catechism.[7]

Like other young Russian noblemen the Decembrists had travelled abroad and studied in foreign universities where they were exposed to the latest Western European intellectual fashions. But their universities of choice—Leipzig,

Heidelberg, Göttingen, Strassburg, Berlin, and Königsberg—were not hotbeds of radical thought. It is typical that in Pushkin's *Eugene Onegin* the protagonist Lensky returns to his estate after a course of studies at Göttingen and, inspired by the enlightened ideas acquired there, decides to alleviate the burden of his serfs—not to free them, as one might expect, but to treat them less harshly and more humanely.

Much more influential than these studies abroad (which were in a sense part of the customary "grand tour"), were the Russian Army's campaigns abroad. Many Decembrists had served as officers during the Napoleonic wars, and the military campaigns across Europe during these long and tense years brought them to Austerlitz, Friedland, the Berezina, Leipzig, and to the heart of Paris, where they made camp on the Champ de Mars (the wide park that extends today from the Ecole Militaire to the Eiffel Tower). Victorious, they then returned all the way home through Europe. That long march brought these army officers in contact with foreign peoples and wider strata of society, quite different from their closed nobiliary milieu in Russia and in Göttingen. It upset many of their notions and led them to discover new ways of life, of behavior, and of managing public affairs. At the same time, the ethos of war, the ordeals of battle, and hatred of the enemy, Napoleon, created a strong national, even nationalistic, attitude. At the end of it all, the Decembrists returned home as "national liberals," for lack of a better term. It is this existential mindset that characterizes them collectively, and not some vague links to the Enlightenment.

In the Decembrists' intellectual formation and mentality the existential dimension was of much more consequence than were abstract ideas and philosophical theories. Their "grand tour" in Europe as Russian soldiers was different from that usually undertaken by young noblemen as part of the traditional *éducation sentimentale*. At the end of the journey their return home was ecstatic. Here is how Pushkin, who had several close friends among them, describes their homecoming, in the "Snowstorm":

> Meanwhile the war had been gloriously ended. Our regiments were returning from abroad. The people were running to meet them. The bands were playing songs of victory: 'Vive Henri Quatre,' Tyrolean waltzes, airs from 'Joconda' ... The soldiers talked gaily among themselves, continually mingling German and French words in their conversation. A never-to-be-forgotten time.

Russian soldiers and officers had seen in Europe more civility, more justice, more freedom. This is what many of them hoped that Russia would adopt after these glorious wars. When this did not transpire, their hopes turned to disappointment, then to frustration and anger, and finally to the uprising against the regime on 14 December 1825. But their rebellion was first and foremost an existential one, a rebellion of men of action, not of thinkers. Certainly, it had philosophical undertones (everything had "philosophical undertones" in that *début de siècle*) and some disparate enlightened ideas, but essentially it was more psychological than ideological. The Decembrists were rebels, as Albert Camus conceived this notion, not revolutionaries. They thought of reforms, and they wanted change. As one of them wrote in 1826 from his jail to Nicholas I:

> After the end of the Napoleonic wars we were all hoping that the Emperor would give his attention to questions of home government. We were impatiently expecting

a constitution and a reform of the law courts. What have we seen? Twelve years have passed and nothing has been changed except the colour of our uniforms.

They then attempted change through insurrection. They failed, but their legacy endured.

The Decembrists were not, as some historians think, a "proto-intelligentsia," heralding the immanent rise of the famed and turbulent Russian intelligentsia.[8] They were army officers, not intellectuals; they were not *intelligenty*, nor were they *hommes de lettres*, with the exception of the poet Ryleev and the generous dreamer Küchelbecker. The remaining more than one hundred men sentenced by Nicholas's (unreformed) courts—five of whom were hanged and the rest exiled to Siberia—were primarily soldiers, although some of them were well-educated and well-versed in philosophy, history and literature. Nevertheless, they were professional soldiers, not intellectuals, not "pupils of the Enlightenment." If so, what makes them relevant to the search of the Enlightenment and of the Counter-Enlightenment in Russia?

IV. The next stage: Herzen and friends

In his memoirs, *My Past and Thoughts,* a young Alexander Herzen writes that his political awakening dated from the events surrounding the Decembrists' uprising and its aftermath, which left a deep imprint on him and on his lifelong friend Nikolai Ogarev.[9] This holds true for other eminent people of Herzen's generation, and leads to the third intellectual development relevant to the search for a Russian Enlightenment and Counter-Enlightenment.

It takes place in the 1830s and 1840s, which include the well known "remarkable decade,"[10] when there appeared on center stage Alexander Herzen, Ivan Turgenev, Vissarion Belinsky, Mikhail Bakunin, Nikolai Stankevich, Ogarev, Timofei Granovsky, as well as the influential and not less original group, the Slavophiles. In fact, in spite of the impression that one gets from history books, the Slavophiles (who should not be confused with the Panslavists) included an array of powerful personalities and scholars of philosophy, ethnography, history, and theology: Aleksei Khomiakov, the brothers Ivan and Konstantin Aksakov, Ivan Kireevsky, Iurii Samarin, Alexander Koshelev, and others.[11]

Logically, the most likely participants in a Counter-Enlightenment movement in Russia should have been the Slavophiles: bred by German Romanticism, they were an ensemble of organicists, conservatives, evolutionists, and explicitly rejected the rationalism and universalism of the eighteenth-century Enlightenment. But what may seem logically sound turns out to be historically wrong, for in spite of these similarities, the Slavophiles did not espouse the main ideas usually attributed to the Counter-Enlightenment, and were even strongly opposed to the core of its *Weltanschauung*. They were not representatives of a Russian Counter-Enlightenment, and in fact they represented no one but themselves, for, as Walicki aptly pointed out, "Slavophile doctrine ... is particularly intractable to classifications by ... traditional intellectual taxonomy"[12]

This being the case, one must ask whether there were other possible representatives of Counter-Enlightenment in Russia? Is Herzen, as some scholars imply, the missing Russian candidate for a Counter-Enlightenment thinker? One commentator on Berlin's conception of Counter-Enlightenment writes:

Berlin's intellectual heroes are those thinkers who formulated a pluralist *Weltanschauung* from within the Enlightenment movement and against it: Giambattista Vico, Johann Gottfried Herder, Johann Georg Hamman or Alexander Herzen ... In spite of the considerable differences between them, these thinkers and others, whom Berlin defines as belonging to the "Counter-Enlightenment," were united in the assumption that the sciences of man are different in their essence from the natural sciences, for the object of their enquiry—man—is not one more atom acting according to fixed physical attributes of its nature and the material needs that ensue from them, but also, and above all, acting out of spiritual yearnings and cultural traditions.[13]

This interesting interpretation invites two remarks. First, Berlin's assumption that the sciences of man are different from the natural sciences, although basically correct, seems insufficient as a basis for defining the Counter-Enlightenment or for that matter, any other coherent set of ideas bound by more than a few general propositions. Secondly, I would hesitate to include Herzen in this company of thinkers, for he did not belong to the Enlightenment, and therefore could not have been against it "from within." Before explaining this proposition, let me add that Isaiah Berlin, so it seems, never defined Herzen as "belonging to the Counter-Enlightenment," and I have found only one instance in Berlin's writings where Herzen is mentioned in the company of Vico and Herder. It appears in the essay "The Pursuit of the Ideal," and it reads as follows:

> If the old perennial belief in the possibility of realising ultimate harmony is a fallacy, and the positions of the thinkers I have appealed to—Machiavelli, Vico, Herder, Herzen—are valid, then, if we allow that Great Goods can collide, that some of them cannot live together, even though others can—in short, that one cannot have everything, in principle as well as in practice—and if human creativity may depend upon a variety of mutually exclusive choices: then, as Chernyshevsky and Lenin once asked, "What is to be done?" How do we choose between possibilities? What and how much must we sacrifice to what? There is, it seems to me, no clear reply.[14]

What can we learn from this quotation, its context and, for that matter, from the whole corpus of Berlin's writings on Russia and on Herzen? I believe that Herzen—whom Isaiah Berlin admired and with whom he identified more than any other thinker he wrote about—stood high in Berlin's esteem on account of four major positions which Herzen gradually adhered to: the notion of individual liberty; the refusal to sacrifice the present for the future; the rejection of great magnificent abstractions, and a skepticism about the meaning and value of abstract ideas as such[15]; and, finally, Herzen's sense of reality.[16] I will examine below their role in defining Herzen's place on the ideological spectrum of the age, after a few remarks on the historical and intellectual background of the formation of ideas in Herzen's time.

In terms of both temperament and theoretical works, Herzen was a thinker who came close to the kind of radical pluralism which Isaiah Berlin has expounded—explicitly or implicitly—in most of his writings. As with all the members of the Moscow Circles, and the Slavophiles too, the chief philosophical source of Herzen's intellectual formation was Hegel. His theories were debated at length both in private meetings, and in public, for instance at Mme. Elagina's *salon littéraire*, the headquarters of the Slavophiles. Among the many episodes recounted by Herzen's friends was the story of how hard Bakunin toiled in translating and annotating Hegel's texts for Belinsky who did not read German. Incidentally, his *critique de texte* is perhaps one of the reasons for Bakunin's mastery of Hegel's ideas, and on that account Marx is said to have thought that the only redeeming quality of Bakunin (whom he deeply hated) was that he was one of the few people in the nineteenth century who really understood Hegel. (Notwithstanding the compliment, Bakunin's hatred of Marx remained a constant fixture in his *Weltanschauung*; unfortunately it also engendered—by a sort of chain reaction—a persistent and deplorable anti-Germanism and anti-Semitism.)

In spite of having such a gifted teacher, Belinsky (unlike Herzen) got Hegel's dialectics muddled and at a certain point he conceived the (erroneous) idea that everything ideal is real, and that everything real is ideal. This confusion led to his notorious—but short-lived—"crisis of conscience" (in 1840–1842), since Hegel's tenet, as he interpreted it, meant that all the miseries, oppression, "political orgies" (as he put it later in a letter to Bakunin) and corruption of Nicholas I's autocratic political regime and the serfdom of the peasantry were a "rational and ideal reality."[17] For Herzen this was dangerous nonsense, and he had some harsh words both for Bakunin and Belinsky. The latter, after painful soul-searching, recanted, announced his "reconciliation with reality," distanced himself from Hegel's theories—which he now called "the German book"—and ceased spinning "the German web." Thereafter, his attention was increasingly drawn to revolutionary thought, and he embarked, like Herzen, on a study of Proudhon, Fourier, Saint-Simon, and Louis Blanc.

However, Herzen himself was at no time an orthodox Hegelian, neither of the serious (Marx and Bakunin) brand, nor of Belinsky's tragicomic variety. As, with all the ideas he came across in the course of his life, he transformed Hegel's doctrines into something peculiarly his own, mixing them with other (different and often contradictory) views to form his particular *Weltanschauung* blend. As Isaiah Berlin aptly remarked: Herzen took from thinkers such as Hegel, George Sand, Fourier, Proudhon, and the others just "what he needed, and poured it into the vehement torrent of his own experience."[18] In any case, adds Berlin, when Herzen eventually wrote his memoirs, "almost all traces of Hegelian influence [were] gone."[19]

The important point in Berlin's analysis is that out of the philosophical Tower of Babel of his time Herzen "took what he needed, and poured it into the … torrent of his own experience." Life experience was thus paramount in the formation of Herzen's ideas, for they were always intimately connected to existential issues. The centrality of existential factors in the formation of Herzen's ideas explains also, to a certain extent, the changes and fluctuations of his views over time and from one period to the next in connection with his personal and political life-experiences. There is a concrete example of this point in Berlin's explanation of Herzen's attitude toward the Russian peasant commune (formulated in Herzen's open letter to Jules Michelet, and usually attributed to the influence of Herder, to the Romantic *Zeitgeist*, or to Counter-Enlightenment tenets):

> …[While in exile, Herzen] lived the life of an affluent, well-born man of letters, a member of the Russian, and more specifically Moscow, gentry, uprooted from his native soil, unable to achieve a settled existence or even the semblance of inward or outward peace, a life filled with occasional moments of hope and even exultation, followed by long periods of misery, corrosive self-criticism and most of all overwhelming, omnivorous, bitter nostalgia. It may be this, as much as objective reasons,

that caused him to idealise the Russian peasant, and to dream that the answer to the central 'social' question of his time—that of growing inequality, exploitation, dehumanisation of both the oppressor and the oppressed—lay in the preservation of the Russian peasant commune. He perceived in it the seeds of the development of a non-industrial, semi-anarchist socialism.[20]

In other words, in the formation of this major aspect of Herzen's worldview—the peasant commune—which earned him the title of "father of Russian socialism," that is, "populism," which Isaiah Berlin described so brilliantly in his introduction to Franco Venturi's *Il populismo russo*,[21] the role played by personal circumstances was much greater than any supposed influence of Herder and Romanticism.

This close connection between Herzen's life and ideas is what makes him so original and different, and renders his "particular blend of *Weltanschauung*" so intractable for classification purposes. He was not *sui generis*, but he was unique; he was not individualistic, but he had an anarchistic streak, which led him to say that he felt good only when he found himself in a minority of one—another expression of the feature of uniqueness. For this reason Herzen's *Weltanschauung* cannot be classified as either an offshoot of the Enlightenment or as a representative of the Counter-Enlightenment. *À la limite* it was both and neither. Given this paradox Berlin was right in saying that "Herzen is neither consistent nor systematic."[22] Sir Isaiah did not mean it as a reproach, and he may have seen in it a trait common to Herzen and himself, a point to which I will return below.

The question of whether Herzen belonged to the Enlightenment or to the Counter-Enlightenment bears some similarity to another vexed issue, namely, was Berlin himself a fox or a hedgehog? Whoever succeeds in answering the one may also hold a clue with regard to the other. Indeed, one has the impression that very often in writing about Herzen Berlin is speaking about himself, or at least indicating how he would like to be perceived by others:

> [H]e was a brilliant and irrepressible talker ... always in an overwhelming flow of ideas and images; the waste, from the point of view of posterity ... is probably immense: he had no Boswell and no Eckermann to record his conversation, nor was he a man who would have suffered such a relationship. His prose is essentially a form of talk, with the vices and virtues of talk: eloquent, spontaneous, liable to the heightened tones and exaggerations of the born story-teller, unable to resist long digressions which themselves carry him into a network of intersecting tributaries of memory or speculation, but always returning to the main stream of the story or the argument; but above all, his prose has the vitality of spoken words.[23]

The above citation is not a description of Sir Isaiah, as those who knew him might immediately assume, but rather an excerpt from his portrait of Herzen. Similar passages abound in Berlin's writings, and I wonder if in some of them Sir Isaiah was providing food for the thought that he, perhaps unconsciously, was depicting himself.

V. Three stages in the formation of Herzen's worldview

As I have already noted, it is no easy task to give a rigorous definition of Herzen's *Weltanschauung*, which shifted more than once in his lifetime. Following Berlin, we may say that there were *grosso modo* three main stages in the evolution of Herzen's ideas and worldview.[24] At the beginning—in the Moscow circle and during the years of the "marvellous decade"—he had an ideal vision of human life, and ignored the chasm which divided it from the present, whether the Russia of Nicholas I, or the corrupt constitutionalism in the West. At that time he glorified enlightened radicalism and condemned its opponents in Russia—and especially the tendency to blind conservatism, Slavophile nostalgia, and the cautious gradualism of his friends, the westernizers Granovsky and Turgenev, as well as Hegelian appeals to patience and rational conformity to the inescapable rhythms of history, which seemed to him designed to ensure the triumph of the new bourgeois class.

The second stage began around 1847, when Herzen left Russia for Western Europe, and at first tended toward a more critical outlook. All genuine change, he began to think, is necessarily slow; the power of tradition is very great; men are less malleable than had been believed in the eighteenth century, nor do they truly seek liberty, only security and contentment; Communism is but tsarism in different garb, the replacement of one yoke by another. At this stage (notwithstanding his faith in the Russian peasant commune as the prototype of the future society), he no longer felt certain that the gap between the enlightened élite and the masses could be bridged (a view which becomes an obsession in later Russian thought under the label *"intelligentsia i narod,"* the intelligentsia and the people), since the awakened people may, for unalterable psychological and sociological reasons, despise and reject the gifts of a civilization which will never have enough meaning for them. (In this regard Herzen's fears were shared even by such radical populists as Chernyshevsky and Mikhailovsky.) Later on, he spoke of something even more disquieting, a haunting sense of the ever widening and unbridgeable gulf between the human values of the relatively free and civilized élites (to which he knew himself to belong) and the actual needs, desires and tastes of the vast voiceless masses of mankind.[25]

Finally, in the third stage, Herzen asked himself: If these doubts were justified, is radical transformation either practicable or desirable? From this followed his growing sense of obstacles that might be insurmountable, limits that may be impassable, leading him to empiricism, skepticism, and a latent pessimism and despair in the mid-1860s. The most eloquent document which conveys this way of thought are his open letters *To an Old Comrade*, addressed to Bakunin, who proclaimed that the act of destruction is also an act of creation. In these letters, written in 1869, one year before his death, Herzen expressed his admiration for Peter the Great and the Jacobins because they dared to do something instead of nothing. Yet he says also that Petrogradism, the behavior of Attila, and the policy of the Committee of Public Safety in 1793—in a word, any method which presupposes the feasibility of simple and radical solutions—in the end always leads to oppression, bloodshed, and collapse.

But this three-stage intellectual development presented by Berlin invites some remarks and qualifications. Firstly, it indicates (again) how difficult it is to associate Herzen with the Enlightenment or Counter-Enlightenment, and in any case begs the question of when and to what extent he shared his or that idea attributed to one of these two movements. Secondly, this three-stage development, even if it provides some order for Herzen's intellectual evolution, does not explain the numerous contradictions, inconsistencies, and paradoxes which, in my view, existed in Herzen's thought at each and every given moment. Thirdly, it illustrates

Berlin's deep insights, which are reflected on two levels: his capacity to present at times a very complex and intricate picture of Herzen's personality and thought, and at other times to do the opposite, namely, single out one subject (for instance, Herzen's views on "liberty"), and, by a tour de force of extreme reductionism, present the core of Herzen's stand in complete isolation from important aspects of his whole mindset, thereby ignoring these contradictions.

VI. Conclusion

By way of conclusion to these brief remarks on such complex and elusive topics and personalities one should perhaps recall the four main elements in Herzen's thought and mindset which help explain the tortuous path of his intellectual development, and which Berlin described time and again, stressing that Herzen was "neither consistent nor systematic," and therefore—like the Slavophiles, in Walicki's words—"intractable to classification by traditional intellectual taxonomy." Hence his equal distance from Enlightenment and Counter-Enlightenment alike, a position reinforced by each of these four elements.

The first element was Herzen's opposition to all kind of abstractions. Although he believed in reason, scientific methods, individual action, and empirically discovered truths, he tended to suspect that faith in general formulas, and prescription in human affairs were an attempt, sometimes catastrophic, to escape from the uncertainty and unpredictable variety of life.

Like Isaiah Berlin and Ivan Turgenev, Herzen believed that human problems are too complex to demand simple solutions or to receive ready-made answers from abstract principles and recipes. On the contrary, he held that in principle there could be no simple or final answer to any genuine human problem and that if a question was serious, the answer could not be clear and neat. Above all, answers could never consist of some symmetrical set of conclusions, drawn by deductive means from a collection of self-evident axioms. Central to Herzen's thought was the notion that the basic problems are perhaps not resoluble at all.[26]

The second idea concerned the absolute value of life. Although Herzen believed in human progress, he rejected the view that a generation, a social group, or an indidividual should be sacrifised today for the sake of progress and happiness tomorrow. His skepticism about the meaning of abstract ideals as such was in tune with the value he began to attach to the concrete, short-term, immediate goals of living individuals—specific freedoms, reward for the day's work, immediate acts of justice. In Berlin's words,

> He believed that the ultimate goal of life was life itself; that the day and the hour were ends in themselves, not a means to another day or another experience. He believed that remote ends were a dream, that faith in them was a fatal illusion; that to sacrifice the present or the immediate and foreseeable future to these distant ends must always lead to cruel and futile forms of human sacrifice.[27]

This meant that Herzen disagreed fundamentally with revolutionary doctrines which required the sacrifice of one or more generations for the hypothetical benefit of humankind in the future. He distrusted those who asked for sacrifices now and promised *des lendemains qui chantent*, a singing tomorrow, for he knew that almost always the day after tomorrow is a day of mourning.[28]

The third element consists in Herzen's idea of liberty, a topic to which Berlin reverts time and again and which also is closely linked to Herzen's life experience:

> [Herzen's] moods alternate sharply [writes Berlin]. Sometimes he believes in a great, cleansing, revolutionary storm, even were it to take the form of a barbarian invasion likely to destroy all the values that he himself holds dear. At other times he reproaches his old friend Bakunin ... for wanting to make the revolution too soon; for not understanding that dwellings for free men cannot be constructed out of the stones of a prison.... History has her own tempo. Patience and gradualism—not the haste and violence of a Peter the Great—can alone bring about a permanent transformation. At such moments he wonders whether the future belongs to the free, anarchistic peasant, or to the bold and ruthless planner [whether capitalist or communist]. Then again he returns to his early moods of disillusionment and wonders whether men in general really desire freedom; perhaps only a few do so in each generation, while most human beings only want good government, no matter at whose hands; and he echoes de Maistre's bitter epigram about Rousseau: "Monsieur Rousseau has asked why it is that men who are born free are nevetheless everywhere in chains; it is as if one were to ask why sheep, who are born carnivorous, nevertheless everywhere nibble grass." Herzen develops this theme. Men desire freedom no more than fish desire to fly. The fact that a few flying fish exist does not demonstrate that fish in general were created to fly, or are not fundamentally quite content to stay below the surface of the water, forever away from the sun and the light. Then he returns to his earlier optimism and the thought that somewhere—in Russia—there lives the unbroken human being, the peasant with his faculties intact, untainted by the corruption and sophistication of the West.[29]

The "West" in this case means also the insidious and constant growth of the middle classes and of the petit bourgeois character of society, whose main feature is what Vladimir Nabokov made known in the West as *poshlost'*, philistinism, vulgarity, kitsch, and nouveau-riche arrogance and bad taste. The petit bourgeois, writes Herzen, "has two talents, prudence and punctuality. The life of the middle class is full of petty defects and petty virtues; it is self-restrained, often niggardly, and shuns what is extreme, what is superfluous ... a life self-satisfied with its narrow mediocrity [and] vulgarity."[30] The middle classes and the petit bourgeois are neither fighters for liberty nor its guarantors.

Neither fighters for liberty nor bearers of culture, the middle classes and the petit bourgeois, are in Herzen's aristocratic eyes the scourge and the curse of the new world. In a memorable passage, reminiscent of our age, he summarizes this new face of the West:

> All trade, especially in England, is based now on quantity and cheapness, and not at all on quality, as old-fashioned Russians imagine when they reverently buy Tula pen-knives with an English trademark on them. Everything has a wholesale, ready-made, conventional character, everything is within the reach of almost every one, but does not allow of aesthetic distinction or personal taste. Everywhere the hundred-thousand-headed hydra [the petit bourgeoisie] lies in wait close at hand round a corner, ready to listen to everything, to look at everything indiscriminately, to be dressed in anything, to be fed on anything—this is the all-powerful crowd of 'conglomerated mediocrity' (to use Stuart Mill's expression) which purchases everything, and so dominates everything. The crowd is without ignorance, but also without culture.

The zenith of the crowd's cultural creation is the *café chantant*, "an amphibious product, half way between the beer-cellar and the boulevard theatre."[31]

The fourth key element of Herzen's thought is his sense of reality. His initial Rousseau-inspired faith in the innate goodness of man becomes less and less secure as he grows older, both because of the tragedies in his family life,[32] and as a result of his acute sense of reality:

> His sense of reality [writes Isaiah Berlin] is too strong. For all his efforts, and the efforts of his socialist friends, he cannot deceive himself entirely. He oscillates between pessimism and optimism, scepticism, and suspicion of his own scepticism, and is kept morally alive only by his hatred of all injustice, all arbitrariness, all mediocrity as such—in particular by his inability to compromise in any degree with either the brutality of reactionaries or the hypocrisy of bourgeois liberals. He is preserved by this, buoyed up by his belief that such evils will destroy themselves, and by his love for his children and his devoted friends, and his unquenchable delight in the variety of life and the comedy of human character.[33]

At least twice in his writings Berlin underlines Herzen's "sense of reality," a quality which he finds so commendable that he confers on it the status of a philosophical notion, and proposes it as the criterion which should guide people faced with conflicting values and irreconcilable goals. In the above quotation Berlin emphasizes Herzen's strong sense of reality; in another one he writes: "Herzen's sense of reality ... is unique in his own [age], and perhaps in any age."[34] Given the importance that Berlin attributed to the sense of reality in individual decisions and in the life of society, one can fully understand the high praise contained in this one short sentence on Herzen.

Armed with his sense of reality in a period of turmoil, revolution, and reaction, but neither a disciple of the Enlightenment, nor a proponent of the Counter-Enlightenment (notions that were of little substance in the Russian setting), Alexander Herzen anticipated Berlin's central idea that there are conflicts with regard to values and goals that are irreconcilable, and that in states and society there should be structures and processes that allow these conflicting interests to coexist in peace. Herzen did not express this idea in these words, but of all his contemporaries—and compared to later thinkers—he was the one closest to the spirit and content of this quintessential vision of Isaiah Berlin.

Notes

1. Isaiah Berlin, "The Counter-Enlightenment" and "Vico and the Ideal of the Enlightenment," in *Against the Current. Essays in the History of Ideas*. ed. Henry Hardy, with an introduction by Roger Hausheer (New York: Viking, 1980).
2. Michael Ignatieff, *Isaiah Berlin. A Life* (New York: Henry Holt, 1998).
3. With the exception of Soviet historiography (which held that there was a full-fledged Western-style progressive Enlightenment in Russia), most historians tend to qualify in various degrees the existence and/or character of the "Russian Enlightenment" (using in many cases this expression as a metaphor rather than as a well-defined concept). See Marc Raeff, "The Enlightenment in Russia and Russian Thought in the Enlightenment," in *The Eighteenth Century in Russia*, ed. J. G. Garrard (Oxford: Clarendon Press, 1973), pp. 25–47; James F. Brennan, *Enlightened Despotism in Russia: The Reign of Elisabeth, 1741–1762*

(New York: P. Lang, 1987); D. Griffiths, "Catherine II: The Republican Empress," *Jahrbücher für Geschichte Osteuropas* 21 (1973), pp. 323–34; Gary Marker, "The Age of Enlightenment, 1740–1801," in *Russia. A History*, ed. G. L. Freeze (Oxford and New York: Oxford University Press, 1997), pp. 114–42. And see also the books on Catherine II by Isabel de Madariaga and by John T. Alexander indicated in note 6 below.

4. See Alexander Gerschenkron, *Economic Backwardness in Historical Perspective* (Cambridge, Mass.: Harvard University Press, 1962).

5. Isaiah Berlin, "Herzen and His Memoirs," in *Against the Current*, p. 191; emphasis added.

6. Grandly entitled "The Great Instruction" (*Bol'shoi nakaz*), it consisted of 22 chapters and 655 articles; 294 of them were pillaged from Montesquieu (most of them misrepresented); others plagiarized from Beccaria, Jacob Bielfeld, Johann Justi, and Diderot's *Encyclopédie*; Voltaire proclaimed it "the finest monument of the age," while Diderot wrote on it a rather acerbic commentary. See Isabel de Madariaga, *Russia in the Age of Catherine the Great* (New Haven and London: Yale University Press, 1981), pp. 151–63; John T. Alexander, *Catherine the Great. Life and Legend* (New York and Oxford: Oxford University Press, 1989), pp. 100–102, writes that the Great Instruction "signified [Catherine's] first bid for the title of philosopher-sovereign."

7. For a sample of views on the Decembrist movement, see Anatole G. Mazour, *The First Russian Revolution—the Decembrist Movement: Its Origins, Development and Significance* (Stanford: Stanford University Press, 1962); Hans Lemberg, *Die nationale Gedankenwelt der Dekabristen* (Köln-Graz: Böhlau, 1963); George Luciani, *La Société des Slaves Unis, 1823–1825* (Bordeaux: Université de Bordeaux, 1963); Marc Raeff, ed., *The Decembrist Movement* (Englewood Cliffs: Prentice-Hall, 1966) (documents); Glynn Barratt, *Voices in Exile. The Decembrist Memoirs* (Montreal and London: McGill-Queen's University Press, 1974). The Soviet orthodox version was: Militsa V. Nechkina, *Dvizhenie Dekabristov* [The Decembrist Movement], 2 volumes (Moscow, 1955); see J. Gooding, "The Decembrists in the Soviet Union," *Soviet Studies* 40 (1988), pp. 196–209. For a post-Soviet and critical re-evaluation, see Nathan Eidelman, *14 dekabrja 1825 i ego istolkovateli* [The 14th December 1825 and Its Interpreters] (Moscow, 1994); Valerii Senderov, "Razoblachenie mifa. Dekabrizm v svete sovremennykh diskussii" [Unmasking a myth. Decembrism in the light of contemporary discussions], *Russkaia mysl* [Paris], 12–18 October 1995, p. 3.

8. Leonard Schapiro, for instance, defined the Decembrists as "intellectuals in uniform": "The Pre-Revolutionary Intelligentsia and the Legal Order," in Richard Pipes, ed., *The Russian Intelligentsia* (New York: Columbia University Press, 1961), p. 461.

9. Several events greatly affected Herzen's family. First came the shock at the news that General Nikolai Miloradovich, an old regiment comrade of Herzen's father, was killed on the Senate Square during the insurrection. Then, during the following months, Herzen's family shared the anguish and sorrow of the Moscow nobility upon the arrest of sons of respected families. Among them were the brothers Obolensky, relatives of Herzen's aunt, Princess Khovanskaia. For more details, see Martin Malia, *Alexander Herzen And the Birth of Russian Socialism, 1812–1855* (Cambridge, Mass.: Harvard

University Press, 1961), p. 31–2. This book remains the best one on the early years of Herzen's life.
10. "A Remarkable Decade" (1838–1848): originally the title of an essay by the literary critic Pavel Annenkov (*Zamechatelnoe desiatiletie, 1838–1848*) published in 1880; it contains his reminiscences of the intellectual movement in those years and of its participants whom Annenkov knew well. Berlin borrowed this title for four essays which appeared in serial form in *Encounter* in 1955–1956 (then entitled "A Marvellous Decade"), and are now included in Berlin, *Russian Thinkers*, ed. Henry Hardy and Aileen Kelly with an introduction by Kelly (New York: Viking, 1978); "The Birth of the Russian Intelligentsia"; "German Romanticism in Petersburg and Moscow"; "Visarion Belinsky"; and "Alexander Herzen"; on p. 114–5 Sir Isaiah explains why he chose this title.
11. A good book on the subject is Andrzej Walicki's *The Slavophile Controversy. History of a Conservative Utopia in Nineteenth-Century Russian Thought* (Oxford: Clarendon Press, 1975).
12. Walicki, *The Slavophile Controversy*, p. 3.
13. Joseph Mali, review of the Hebrew translation of Isaiah Berlin, *The Crooked Timber of Humanity*, trans. A. Ophir (Tel Aviv: Am Oved, 1995), in *Yediot Aharonot*, 31.3.1995 (in Hebrew); emphasis added.
14. Isaiah Berlin, "The Pursuit of the Ideal," in *The Crooked Timber of Humanity. Chapters in the History of Ideas*, ed. Henry Hardy (New York: Viking, 1992), p. 17.
15. Berlin, "Herzen and His Memoirs," p. 196.
16. Berlin, "Herzen and His Memoirs", p. 207.
17. For more details on this episode, see E. Lampert, *Studies in Rebellion* (London: Routledge and Kegan Paul, 1957), p. 67–81.
18. Berlin, "Herzen and His Memoirs," p. 198.
19. Berlin, "Herzen and His Memoirs," p. 206.
20. Berlin, "Herzen and His Memoirs", p. 205–6; for Herzen's open letter to Michelet, written originally in French and published in 1852, see "Le peuple russe et le socialisme (Lettre à Jules Michelet)," in A. Herzen, *Textes philosophiques choisis* (Moscow, 1948), p. 501–39; English version: *The Russian People and Socialism*, trans. R. Wollheim, with an introduction by Isaiah Berlin (London: Weidenfeld and Nicolson, 1956).
21. Franco Venturi, *Il populismo russo*, 2 volumes (Turin; J. Einaudi, 1952); English translation: *Roots of Revolution. A History of the Populist and Socialist Movements in Nineteenth-Century Russia*, trans. F. Haskell (London: Weidenfeld and Nicolson, 1960). See also Malia, *Alexander Herzen and the Birth of Russian Socialism* quoted above.
22. Berlin, "Herzen and His Memoirs," p. 206.
23. Berlin, "Herzen and His Memoirs," p. 188.
24. I will add below some qualifications to this analysis of Berlin.
25. Berlin, "Herzen and His Memoirs," p. 196.
26. Isaiah Berlin, "Alexander Herzen," in *Russian Thinkers*, pp. 202, 205.
27. Berlin, "Alexander Herzen," p. 194–5.
28. "*Des lendemains qui chantent*" was a major slogan of the French Communist Party's propaganda in the 1950s and 1960s. The irony of the message, then and now, will not be lost to the astute reader.

29. Berlin, "Herzen and His Memoirs," p. 206–7; see also Berlin, "Herzen and Bakunin on Individual Liberty," in *Russian Thinkers*, p. 82–113.
30. [A.I. Herzen], *My Past and Thoughts. The Memoirs of Alexander Herzen*, trans. Constance Garnett, revised by Humphrey Higgens, with an introduction by Isaiah Berlin, vol. 4 (New York: Knopf, 1968), p. 10 (an essay written on June 10, 1862 in the Isle of Wight).
31. Herzen, *My Past and Thoughts*, p. 15–16. Similar indictments of the petty bourgeoisie can be found in Herzen's *Letters from the Avenue Marigny* (1847) and *Letters from Via del Corso* (1847–1848), writings known from 1854 on as *Letters from France and Italy*.
32. Herzen's memoirs form arresting testimony to the many misfortunes that struck him and his family. See also Edward Hallet Carr, *The Romantic Exiles. A Nineteenth-Century Portrait Gallery* (London: V. Gollancz, 1933), a portrait painted with more irony than empathy, and without the benefit of most source material published even before the 1930s; following editions of the book were not updated in the light of the abundant documentary evidence available since its first edition. See also Michael Confino, *Daughter of a Revolutionary. Natalie Herzen and the Bakunin-Nechaev Circle* (London: Alcove Press, 1974), which includes also the diary of "Tata," found and published for the first time by the author in 1969 in Michael Confino, "Un document inédit: Le Journal de Natalie Herzen, 1869–1870," *Cahiers du monde russe et soviétique* X (1) (1969), pp. 52–149 (Russian original with a French translation and an introduction).
33. Berlin, "Herzen and His Memoirs," p. 207; emphasis added.
34. Berlin, "Alexander Herzen," p. 207.

Index of Names

Aarsleff, Hans – 16–17, 20
Adorno, Theodor – 9, 46
Akhmatova, Anna – 21
Aksakov, Ivan – 182
Aksakov, Konstantin – 182
Alembert, Jean d' – 5, 6, 7, 21
Alexander I, Emperor of Russia – 180
Allamand, abbé d'– 93
Anderson, Perry – 14, 23–24
Annunzio, Gabriele d' – 117, 123
Aristotle – 37, 59, 61
Arnauld, Antoine – 66
Arnim, Karl Joachim – 42
Arnold, Gottfried – 111
Attila – 138
Augustine, St. – 6–7, 11, 57, 80, 96, 126
Austin, John L. – 20, 35
Ayer, Alfred – 35

Bacon, Francis – 2, 4, 5
Baker, Keith – 93
Bakunin, Mikhail – 123, 182, 184, 186, 188
Balzac, Honoré de – 34
Barante, Prosper de – 147, 150, 152
Barrett, William – 13
Barrès, Maurice – 123
Barruel, Augustin – 96
Barth, Karl – 2
Baumgarten, Alexander Gottlieb – 23
Bayle, Pierre – 20, 22, 66, 80, 83–84, 134
Beccaria, Cesare – 5, 76, 180
Beck, Christian August – 108
Becker, Carl – 18–19, 23
Beethoven, Ludwig van – 22
Begin, Menachem – 22
Belinsky, Vissarion – 182, 183–184
Belloc, Hilaire – 123
Bellow, Saul – 15–16
Benjamin, Walter – 2
Bentham, Jeremy – 5, 133, 145, 180
Bergson, Henri – 38
Berlin, Isaiah –
  on the Counter-Enlightenment: v, 4, 13–16, 41- 48, 62–67, 73–75, 91–93, 99, 105–115, 164–175, 177–189; on the Enlightenment: 18–25, 33–48, 64–65, 73–74, 79–80, 91–93, 164–175, 177–189; and Fascist ideology: ix-x, 14–17, 43–44, 52, 61, 71, 74, 92, 117–128, 173; on the human sciences: 15, 19, 36–48, 54–60; intellectual career of: vii-x, 13–25, 35–36, 51–53, 73–74, 92, 133–134, 163–175, 178, 182–185, 187–189; and Jewish identity: vii, 21–25, 34–35, 124; on theory and history of Liberalism: viii–ix, 14–15, 23–25, 45, 106–115, 118, 139; on liberty: 14, 17–18, 34, 43, 133–134, 140, 143; and Marxism: 24, 34–38, 163–175; on monism: 17, 37–38, 40–42, 60–61, 91–92, 127; on nationalism: vi, 21–22, 43–45, 60–61, 120, 125–126, 173–175; on pluralism: viii–x, 15–18, 35, 40–42, 44–45, 61–67, 118; and Russian intellectual tradition – ix, 21, 33, 177–189; on Romanticism and its legacy – 15–16, 18, 42–47, 105–115, 119, 123–124, 134, 164–166, 169–175, 184–185; and Zionism: viii, 21–24
Betskoi, Alexander – 178
Biester, Johann Erich – 110
Blanc, Louis – 184
Boehme, Jakob – 111
Bollnow, Otto Friedrich – 39
Bonald, Louis de – 3, 92, 122
Bosch, Hieronymus – 92
Bossuet, Jacques Bénigne – 19, 122–123
Boswell, James – 185
Bradley, Owen – 120, 125, 127
Brandes, Ernst – 109
Brecht, Berthold – 23, 24
Broglie, duc de – 151
Buffon, comte de – 6
Burke, Edmund – 64, 97, 121–123, 133
Burke, Peter – 51, 59
Burney, Charles – 19
Byron, Lord – 180

Calvin, John – 113
Cambacérès, abbé de – 94
Cambyses – 138
Camus, Albert – 181
Carlyle, Thomas – 43, 123
Carmichael, Gershom – 83, 84
Cassirer, Ernst – 23, 75
Catherine II, Empress of Russia – 178–180
Charrrière, Isabelle de – 149, 152
Chartier, Roger – 77, 98
Chateaubriand, vicomte de – 180
Chaudon, Louis Mayeul – 93
Chernyshevsky, Nikolai – 186
Churchill, Winston – 24

Index of Names

Cioran, Emile M. – 124, 126–127
Clément, Jean-Marie Bernard – 97
Cobbett, William – 123
Cole, G.D.H. – viii
Collingwood, Robin G. – 41, 54, 55
Collins, Anthony – 95
Comte, Auguste – 35, 38
Condorcet, marquis de – 7, 18, 21, 35, 75, 180
Constant, Benjamin – vii, xi, 7, 14, 45, 133–153, 180
Constantine, Emperor of Rome – 7
Cortes, Donoso – 3
Crillon, abbé de – 96
Croce, Benedetto – 10, 51, 52, 53, 57

Dante Alighieri – 171
Darcel, Jean-Louis – 126–127
Darnton, Robert – 74, 77, 93
Deroulede, Paul – 123
Derrida, Jacques – 20
Descartes, René – 2, 4, 5, 38, 54, 60
Diderot, Denis – 5, 19, 21, 34, 62, 93, 179
Dilthey, Wilhelm – 38, 41, 53, 47
Doria, Paolo Mattia – 83
Dostoyevsky, Fyodor – 21
Drumont, Edouard – 123
Dunn, John – 59

Eberhard, Johann August – 108
Eckermann, Johan Peter – 185
Edelmann, Christian – 111
Einstein, Albert – 23
Engel, Johann Jacob – 110
Engels, Friedrich – 169, 172
Epicurus – 80, 83, 84, 92
Epstein, Klaus – 99
Erasmus, Desiderius – 134
Eusebius, Bishop of Caesarea – 6, 7
Eysenck, Hans – 24

Ferguson, Adam – 20, 85, 135, 138, 139, 140, 145, 146, 147
Feuerbach, Ludwig – 167
Fichte, Johann Gottlieb – 42–43, 118, 137, 164, 172
Filangieri, Gaetano – 85
Fischer, H. A. L. – 163
Flaubert, Gustave – 151
Fletcher, Andrew – 83
Fleury, Jean-Omer – 93
Fontenelle, Bernard de – 19, 134
Foucault, Michel – 64
Fourier, Charles – 5, 123, 184
Franck, Sebastian – 111
Francke, August – 111
Franklin, Benjamin – 180
Freud, Sigmund – 17, 92
Friedrich II, King of Prussia – 107–112
Frost, Robert – 22
Furet, François – 180

Galanti, Giuseppe Maria – 85
Galiani, Ferdinando – 76
Galileo Galilei – 2, 4, 37, 56

Galipeau, Claude – 134
Gardiner, Patrick – 16
Gassendi, Pierre – 80
Gauchat, Gabriel abbé – 93–94
Gay, Peter – 74
Gedike, Friedrich – 110
Gellner, Ernest – 14
Genghis Khan – 138
Genovesi, Antonio – 84–85
Gentile, Giovanni – 52
Gentz, Friedrich – 105
Gérard, abbé – 96
Gerschenkron, Alexander 179
Gerstenberg, Heinrich Wilhelm – 41
Giannone, Pietro – 62, 79
Gibbon, Edward – 64
Goethe, Johann Wolfgang – 22, 41, 135
Goodman, Dena – 77
Gombrich, Ernst – 24
Gorbachev, Mikhail – 180
Goya, Francisco – 152
Gramsci, Antonio – 52
Granovsky, Timofei – 182, 186
Gray, John – 18, 20
Gropius, Walter – 23
Grotius, Hugo – 61
Grumbrecht, Hans-Dietrich – 98
Guizot, François – 133

Habermas, Jürgen – 46, 77
Hamann, Johann Georg – vii, ix, xi, 2, 14, 15, 20, 23, 41–42, 44, 51, 61, 62, 64, 92, 99, 106–114, 118, 133, 183
Hamsun, Knut – 117
Hardy, Henry – 14, 15, 17
Hayek, Friedrich von – 24
Hayer, J-N-H – 93
Hegel, Georg Wilhelm Friedrich – 4, 7–10, 13, 16, 38, 53, 92, 121, 164–170, 172–173, 183–184, 186
Heidegger, Martin – 2, 20, 38, 39
Heine, Heinrich – 22
Helvétius, Claude Adrien – 5, 18, 37
Herder, Johann Gottfried – vii, ix, xi, 2, 14, 15, 17, 20, 38, 42, 43, 61, 62, 64, 92, 99, 106–114, 164, 169, 183–185
Herrero, Javier – 99
Herzen, Alexander – 21, 45, 134, 169, 179, 182–189
Hess, Moses – x, 23, 169, 174
Hirschman, Albert – 75
Hitler, Adolf – 45, 117
Hobbes, Thomas – 3, 4, 61, 83, 127
Hoffman, E.T.A – 42–43
Hofman, Amos – 94
Holbach, baron d' – 5, 18, 20, 37
Holmes, Stephen – 145, 146, 152
Homer – 63
Horkheimer, Max – 9, 46
Humboldt, Wilhelm von – 134, 141, 142, 147
Hume, David – 5, 6, 7, 14, 20, 55, 59, 64–65, 78, 84–85, 140, 142
Husserl, Edmund – 38
Hutcheson, Francis – 5, 84

INDEX OF NAMES

Ignatieff, Michael – 21, 163, 178
Israel, Jonathan – 79

Jacobi, Friedrich Heinrich – xi, 14, 39, 92, 106–115
Jahanbegloo, Ramin – 18, 23
Joseph II, Emperor of Austria – 108, 109
Joyce, James – 52–53
Justi, Johann Heinrich – 108

Kandinsky Wassily – 23
Kant, Immanuel – 2, 5, 6, 10–11, 13, 16, 38, 47, 59, 75, 77, 80–81, 91, 98, 111–112
Karamzin, Nikolai – 180
Keats, John – 34
Kelley, Donald – 57
Kelly, George Armstrong – 146
Keynes, John Maynard – 178
Khomiakov, Aleksei – 182
Kierkegaard, Søren – 2
Kireevsky, Ivan – 182
Klein, Ernst Ferdinand – 108
Klein, Melanie – 24
Kleist, Heinrich von – 42
Klinger, Friedrich Maximilian – 41
Kosellek, Reinhart – 9
Koshelev, Alexander – 182
Kraus, Christian Jacob – 111
Küchelbecker, Wilhelm – 182

Labriola, Antonio – 52
Lafargue, Paul – 52
Lafayette, Madame de – 134
Lamennais, Félicité Robert de – 3
La Mettrie, Julien de – 5, 20
Lamourette, Antoine Adrien – 96–97
Laski, Harold – 18
Lawrence, D.H. – 117, 123
Lebrun, Richard – 127
Leibniz, Gottfried Wilhelm – 23
Leibowitz, Yeshayahu – 22
Leisewitz, Johann Anton – 41
Lenz, Jakob Michael Reinhold – 41
Lessing, Gotthold Ephraim – 2, 5, 62, 109, 111
Liger, abbé – 97
Lilla, Mark – 63
Locke, John – 5, 13, 22, 64, 95
Löwith, Karl – 57
Louis XVI, King of France – 180
Lukács, Georg – 24
Luther, Martin – 11, 111, 113

Mably, Gabriel Bonnot – 98, 137
Machiavelli, Niccolò – 4, 40, 52, 55, 62, 126, 136, 183
MacIntyre, Alasdair – 13, 106
Maistre, Joseph Marie de – ix, xi, 14, 15, 16, 44, 52, 61, 74, 92, 117–128, 133, 188
Malebranche, Nicholas – 80
Malinowski, Bronislaw – 24
Malle, Louis – 25
Mandeville, Bernard – 80, 83–84
Mann, Thomas – 23, 24

Marx, Karl – xi, 17, 22, 35–6, 38, 43, 45, 53, 163–175, 178, 184
Maurras, Charles – 117, 123
Meinecke, Friedrich – 38, 41, 47
Melon, Jean-François – 84
Mendelssohn, Felix – 22
Mendelssohn, Moses – 5, 6, 7, 13, 22, 91, 109
Merleau-Ponty, Maurice – 38
Michelet, Jules – 52–53, 149, 184
Mikhailovsky, Nikolai – 186
Mill, James – 133
Mill, John Stuart – viii, 14, 45, 142, 146, 188
Millar, John – 85
Möser, Justus – 92, 105, 109, 133
Momigliano, Arnaldo – 16, 17, 62
Monod, Albert – 100
Montaigne, Michel de – 134
Montesquieu, baron de – 5, 6, 19, 20, 75, 125, 136, 137, 140, 142, 179
Mornet, Daniel – 77

Nabokov, Vladimir – 188
Namier, Lewis – 21, 24
Napoleon Bonaparte – 134–136, 138, 143, 145–146, 180, 181
Newton, Isaac – 2, 4, 37, 48, 54, 59, 65, 95
Nicholas I, Emperor of Russia – 180, 181, 182
Nicolai, Friedrich – 110
Nicolson, Harold – 135
Nietzsche, Friedrich – 2, 10–11, 17, 33, 52, 117, 123
Novalis – 7, 9, 137
Novikov, Nikolai – 178

O'Brien, Connor Cruise – 133
Ockham, William of – 113
Ogarev, Nikolai – 182
Ortega y Gasset, José – 134

Pagano, Francesco Mario – 85
Palmer, Robert – 100
Palmieri, Giuseppe – 84
Pareto, Vilfredo – 52, 117, 123
Pascal, Blaise – 11, 59, 80
Paul, St. – 11
Peter I, Emperor of Russia – 186, 188
Phillipson, Nicholas – 76
Pico della Mirandola – 62
Plato – 37, 61, 172
Plekhanov, Georgi – 169, 172
Pocock, John – 24–25, 57, 59, 64, 76, 93
Pompa, Leon – 56
Pope, Alexander – 17
Popper, Karl – 24
Porter, Roy – 76–77
Prévost, abbé – 19
Proudhon, Pierre Joseph – 123, 184
Purchas, Samuel – 19
Pushkin, Aleksander – 181

Racine, Jean – 150
Radishchev, Alexander – 178
Rasputin – 178
Raynal, abbé – 19, 98

Index of Names

Récamier, Juliette de – 151
Rehberg, August Wilhelm – 105, 109
Reichhardt, Rolf – 98
Reinhold, Karl Leonhard – 13
Richard, Charles-Louis – 97–98
Rickert, Heinrich – 47
Rigoley de Juvigny, J-A – 98
Robertson, William – 85
Robespierre, Maximilien – 138
Roche, Daniel – 77
Roosevelt, Franklin – 24
Rorty, Richard – 18–19, 106
Rousseau, Jean Jacques – 2, 10, 15, 16, 19, 21, 34, 52, 79, 80, 98, 101, 137, 140, 145, 172, 188, 189
Ryleev, Kondratii – 182
Ryle, Gilbert – 60

Sack, James – 99
Sade, Marquis de – 5
Saint-Simon, Henri de – 5, 184
Salvemini, Gaetano – 51–52
Samarin, Iurii – 182
Sand, George – 184
Sartre, Jean-Paul – 38
Say, Jean-Baptiste – 180
Scheler, Max – 41
Schelling, Friedrich Wilhelm – 47, 53, 164
Schiller, Friedrich – 42, 150
Schlegel, Friedrich – 47
Schleich, Thomas – 98
Schleiermacher, Friedrich – 47
Schmidt, Jochen – 92
Schmitt, Carl – 2
Schopenhauer, Arthur – 17
Schwenkfeld, Caspar – 111
Scouten, Arthur – 16–17
Séguier, Antoine-Louis – 93–94
Shaftesbury, Earl of – 5, 84
Shakespeare, William – 34
Simmel, Georg – 41
Skinner, Quentin – 14, 25, 59, 93
Smith, Adam – 5, 84–85, 135, 140, 142, 145, 147, 180
Socrates – 10, 11
Sonnenfels, Josef von – 108
Sorel, Georges – 51, 52, 61, 117, 123
Soret, Jean – 93
Spener, Philipp Jakob – 111

Spinoza, Benedict – 22, 66, 79, 83
Stael, Madame de – 133, 135, 151
Stalin, Josef – 45, 173
Stankevich, Nikolai – 182
Steuart, James – 84
Strauss, Leo – 16–17
Suarez, Francisco – 122
Svarez, Carl Gottlieb – 108
Swift, Jonathan – 19, 62

Tacitus – 136
Tagliacozzo, Giorgio – 52
Talmon, Jacob – 18
Taylor, Charles – 64
Tertullian – 11, 113
Thomas Aquinas, St. – 10–11, 57, 122, 123
Tieck, Ludwig – 42–43
Tillich, Paul – 23
Tindal, Matthew – 95
Tocqueville, Alexis de – 3, 7, 144
Toland, John – 79
Tolstoy, Leo – 16, 21, 120, 179
Troeltsch, Ernst – 38, 41, 47
Turgenev, Ivan – 21, 182, 186, 187
Turgot, Robert Jacques – 7

Venturi, Franco – 76, 185
Vico, Giambattista – vii, ix, 2, 14, 15–17, 38, 40–42, 44, 47, 51–67, 80, 83–85, 92, 169, 183
Voltaire – 2, 5, 7, 18, 19, 21, 22, 55, 64, 75, 93, 98, 101, 124, 136, 164, 179

Walicki, Andrzej – 182, 187
Walker, Alexander – 134
Walsh, William – 16, 17
Walter, Bruno – 23
Weber, Max – 41, 53, 124
Weigel, Valentin – 111
Weizmann, Chaim – x, 24
White, Hayden – 16
Wieland, Christoph Martin – 5, 13
Windelband, Wilhelm – 38, 41, 47
Wittgenstein, Ludwig – 24
Wolff, Christian – 23, 59
Wood, Dennis – 135

Young, Brian – 76

Zagorin, Perez – 56

www.ingramcontent.com/pod-product-compliance
Lightning Source LLC
Chambersburg PA
CBHW021828300426
44114CB00009BA/371